T0339425

China's New Retail Economy

Retail is the essential link between production and consumption. The dynamics of a nation's economy cannot be fully understood without a good understanding of its retail sector. This book is written to achieve three broad objectives. First, it provides a comprehensive assessment of the changes in consumption patterns in China, the current size of the Chinese consumer market, and the regional variations. Second, it presents an interpretation of the changes in the country's regulatory system and the corresponding policy initiatives, including the new state spatial strategies devised after its admission to the WTO. Third, it delivers a systematic analysis of the transformation of China's retail sector. This includes the entry and expansion of foreign retailers, the development of indigenous retail chains as a national strategy to modernize China's retail industry, and the changing retailer-supplier relations. This book is a useful reference not only for university students and faculty researchers, but also for international retailers and commercial real estate developers who contemplate business and investment opportunities in China.

Shuguang Wang is Professor of Geography at Ryerson University in Canada.

Routledge Advances in Geography

China's New Retail Economy

A Geographic Perspective

Shuguang Wang

Routledge
Taylor & Francis Group
New York London

First published 2014
by Routledge
711 Third Avenue, New York, NY 10017

and by Routledge
2 Park Square, Milton Park, Abingdon, Oxon OX14 4RN

First issued in paperback 2017

*Routledge is an imprint of the Taylor & Francis Group,
an informa business*

Library of Congress Cataloging-in-Publication Data
Wang, Shuguang, 1956–
    China's new retail economy : a geographic perspective / Shuguang
Wang.
        pages cm. — (Routledge advances in geography ; 11)
    Includes bibliographical references and index.
    1. Retail trade—China.   2. Consumption (Economics)—China.
3. Business enterprises, Foreign—China.   I. Title.
    HF5429.6.C5W36 2014
    381'.10951—dc23
    2013032050

ISBN 13: 978-1-138-30849-7 (pbk)
ISBN 13: 978-0-415-63623-0 (hbk)

Typeset in Sabon
by IBT Global.

This book is dedicated to Feng and Jia.

Contents

Figures

Tables

Foreword

Dr. Wang has made a significant contribution to our understanding of one of the greatest consumer revolutions in history. Long before it became fashionable, Dr. Wang, through personal observation and detailed empirical work, documented the evolution of the contemporary Chinese retail system. Over the last two decades, he has witnessed and measured the emergence of the Chinese consumer society that has altered the flow of goods and capital in the global economy. This transformation has been led, in large part, by the emergence of, and response of retailers to, the large Chinese middle class. This demographic segment now is larger than the total population of the United States. Further, it is estimated that this group will continue to explode and soon will approach the total population of Europe.

The book uses a geo-spatial approach to examine the growth and characteristics of the Chinese retail economy from a variety of perspectives. The book can be divided into two parts. The first focuses on a detailed empirical examination of the fundamental agents of change that have been responsible for shaping Chinese retailing. Initially, the geography of demand is discussed. Here various fundamental indicators of the burgeoning Chinese market are presented such as the growth of market income, changing consumption patterns, and regional variations in demand. This is followed by a discussion of the regulatory environment that has controlled and shaped China's retail transformation. This chapter is fundamental to any understanding of retailing in post-reform China. The fourth chapter concludes the first section of the book with an interpretation of the nature of the various retail structures and formats that now characterize the Chinese distributive system.

The second part of the book provides insights into four major shifts that have fundamentally changed the distribution and supply of retail goods in modern China. First, the experiences, entry strategies, successes and failures of various international retail chains are discussed. The following two chapters evaluate both the national strategy that was implemented in 2004 to support the competitive position of 20 domestic chains and the particular strength of the two dominant Chinese retail chains in the consumer electronics sector. Finally, the book provides insights and raises fundamental questions regarding the growth of shopping centres in China and the strength of the luxury retail market in China.

Wang's work fills a missing void in our understanding of the retail economy in China. It is timely, relevant and improves our understanding of the transformation of one of world's major economies. Anyone with an interest in the current and future growth of Chinese market should find this book invaluable.

Ken Jones
Professor Emeritus
Ryerson University
Toronto, Canada

Preface

Retailing is the essential link between production and consumption. The dynamics of a nation's economy cannot be fully understood without a good understanding of its retail sector. Despite this importance, there has been a lack of attention to the transformation of China's retail sector in the large body of literature concerning economic reform and regional development in China. For one example, among Routledge's Contemporary China Series of publications and its series of Studies on China in Transition (over 60 titles in total), no book deals with China's burgeoning retail economy, leaving a gap to be filled.

Traditionally, retailing was geographically tied and retailers were embedded in their local market. But this has been changing in the last two decades. In the early 1990s, the orthodox retail geography was re-theorized by Wrigley, Lowe, and a few other European economic geographers, and a new geography of retailing was advocated to reflect a series of important changes in the global economy. The main concern of the new geography of retailing is the grounding of global flow of retail capital and its geographical expressions. It also calls for much more serious treatment of regulations because they are important forces influencing corporate strategies and geographical market structures.

The new geography of retailing is theorized in the context of the Western market economies. Its testimony in the emerging markets is still limited. The current book follows this innovative approach in the case study of China—the world's largest emerging market resulting from extensive economic reforms in the last three decades. The book fills a void in the English literature on this important topic.

Unlike the existing books, this book moves away from the "firm centric" approach and focuses on the forces and the process of retail change in post-reform China, along with the geographical outcomes. Specifically, this book is written to achieve three broad objectives. First, it provides a comprehensive assessment of the changes in consumption patterns in China, the current size of the Chinese consumer market, and the regional variations, to establish the context of *demand*. Second, it presents a systematic interpretation of the progressive retail *de-regulation* and *re-regulation* process to provide the legal context for the understanding of the retail changes. Third, it delivers a systematic analysis of the transformation of China's retail sector to gauge the changes in the *supply* side. This includes the entry and expansion of foreign retailers, the development of indigenous retail chains as a national strategy to modernize China's retail industry, and the more recent pattern of capital groundings in commercial real estate developments that create new consumption spaces.

This book results from decade-long observations and study of China's retail economy. I made extensive field studies in China in the last 10 years, including visiting every shopping center and commercial node in Beijing and Shanghai, and interviews with key retailers and relevant government officials. The book is not just packaged with information and data. The information and data are processed and analyzed to reconstruct the process of change and growth, and to reveal the impact and consequences. It should not only be a useful reader for university students and faculty researchers, but also be an informative reference for international retailers and transnational real estate developers, who complete business and investment opportunities in China.

While this book is comprehensive in scope, it does not include every aspect of China's vast retail economy. Research gaps remain, which hopefully will be filled by other interested researchers.

Shuguang Wang
Department of Geography
Center for the Study of
    Commercial Activity
Ryerson University

Acknowledgments

I wish to thank the following individuals and institutions for their support and assistance in producing this book:

Mr. Paul Du, GIS Analyst at Ryerson University's Center for the Study of Commercial Activity, made all the maps. His excellent cartographic skills greatly enhanced the quality of the presentation of the research results.

Dr. Yongchang Zhang of East China Normal University assisted me in my site visits, interviews, and data collection in Shanghai in the last 8 years.

Dr. Chongyi Guo of Beijing Technology and Business University assisted me in my site visits, interviews, and data collection in Beijing several times.

The Society of Asian Retailing and Distribution at the University of Marketing and Distribution in Japan provided me with opportunities to test most of the chapters during its annual workshops.

The Office of Dean of the Faculty of Arts at Ryerson University provided a special project grant to help produce the final draft of the manuscript.

My wife Feng Wang did my share, as well as hers, of the household chores in the last twelve months, so that I could concentrate on writing the book during all my non-teaching hours.

1 Introduction

The retail sector is an integral part of a nation's economy. From the political economy point of view, all consumer goods have surplus values locked up in them; the surplus values are not realized until the consumer goods are purchased by consumers through various distribution channels (Blomley, 1996). As such, retailing is the essential link between production and consumption, and the accumulation of capital is achieved through "repeated acts of exchange" between consumers and retailers (Ducatel & Blomley, 1990, p. 218). The dynamics of a nation's economy therefore cannot be fully understood without a good understanding of its retail sector (see Figure 1.1).

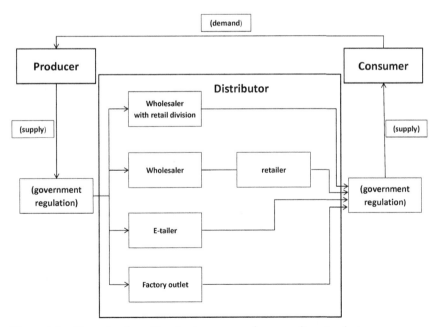

Figure 1.1   The role of retailing in the system of commodity circulation.

(Retailing is carried out by a variety of distributors. They link forward with consumers, and backward with producers/suppliers. Governments regulate the circulation system and the relationships both between distributors and producers and between distributors and consumers.)

Retailing is especially important in the urban economy. Cities are not only centers of power and prestige; they are also centers of consumption and concentrations of retail businesses. Distribution of goods between retailers and consumers is among the chief economic activities of urban areas (Hartshorn, 1992). Knox (1991) even had the view that "the whole of the [urban] landscape is geared toward consumption." Whereas retail activities occupy only a small proportion of the developed urban land, they play several important roles including the generation of large amounts of retail employment while serving as the centers of consumption (Yeates, 1998). As production firms become more mobile, the success of cities hinges more and more on the role of cities as centers of consumption (Glaeser et al., 2000).

In the last three decades, a series of revolutionary changes have taken place in the retail industry worldwide amid the process of globalization of the world economy. Most of these changes originated in the Western capitalist economies, but they quickly spread to the emerging markets in Asia, Latin America, and, to a lesser extent, Africa. Among the emerging markets, China has been the new frontier for much of international business, and the transformation of its retail economy should be the most profound, including the disengagement of the state in operating retail stores, the entry of international retailers, and the emergence of non-state enterprises.

Despite its importance, there has been a lack of attention to the restructuring and transformation of China's retail sector in the large body of literature concerning economic reform and regional development in China. For one example, among Routledge's publications of its *Contemporary China Series* and its series of *Studies on China in Transition* (over 60 titles in total), no book deals with China's burgeoning retail economy. The four existing books printed by other publishers all focus on one aspect of China's retail economy—retail internationalization—and their studies are "firm centric" (see Zhen, 2007; Chevalier & Lu, 2010; Gamble, 2011; Siebers, 2011). This book is written to fill the gap. It goes beyond retail internationalization and moves away from the "firm-centric" approach. The book aims to achieve three broad objectives. First, it provides a comprehensive assessment of the changing consumption patterns, the current size of the Chinese consumer market, and the regional variations within the vast country. This assessment of "demand" establishes the fundamental context for a subsequent examination of the changes in the "supply" side. Second, the book delivers a systematic interpretation of the transformation of China's retail economy in the last three decades. This includes the entry and expansion of foreign retailers, the development of indigenous retail chains as a national strategy to modernize China's retail industry, the changing retailer-supplier relations, and the resultant structural changes in the retail sector. Third, it examines the changes in the regulatory system and the corresponding policy initiatives. While all major retail corporations (both domestic and foreign) have their own *geo-strategies*, their geo-strategies are largely dictated by the *state spatial strategies* of the Chinese government.

The book is written with the approach of the new geography of retailing advocated by Lowe and Wrigley (1996) and using the economic transition process for post-socialist states, as generalized by Bradshaw (1996), as a theoretical framework, for a deep understanding of the transformation of China's retail economy. The changes in China are also analyzed and interpreted in contrast to the characteristics and recent trends of the contemporary capitalist retail economy.

CHARACTERISTICS OF THE CONTEMPORARY CAPITALIST RETAIL ECONOMY AND RECENT TRENDS

From the vast literature on retail structure and structural changes in the Western capitalist economies, it is possible to generalize the following major characteristics and trends.

> 1. *Private ownership predominates in the retailer sector, but government intervenes through regulatory measures.*

Within the capitalist market economy, retailing is defined as private sector activities that provide goods directly to consumers (Simmons & Kamikihara, 2003). Governments rarely own or operate retail businesses, except for a few selected consumer goods (i.e., non-merit goods such as alcoholic beverages and cigarettes). For example, in the Province of Ontario in Canada, all liquor stores are owned and operated by the Liquor Control Board of Ontario—a provincial government enterprise. Whereas corporations and individual entrepreneurs enjoy a high degree of freedom in business decision making, governments do intervene in the retail industry with regulatory measures, often in the form of public policies, to mitigate negative impacts (see Figure 1.1). In turn, these policies, which are supposed to reflect the values of society, impose limits on the retailer's freedom to deal with competitors and conduct business with suppliers and consumers, thus affecting retail operations and the overall market structure.

Dawson (1980) has generalized five types of public intervention that commonly exist in the Western capitalist economies: (1) **location restriction** through land use planning and zoning bylaws to minimize spatial externalities; (2) **price control** to protect consumers from inadequate advertising and predatory selling practices, and to generate revenues for governments; (3) **optimization of business structure** through fair competition laws to prevent monopoly and encourage innovation; (4) **promotion of business efficiency** by controlling new entries into a market to avoid excess retail capacities and waste of economic resources; and (5) **protection of consumer well-being and safety** through licensing/inspections and compulsory labeling. Dawson (1980) also pointed out that whereas direct policies toward retailing are few, indirect policies that aim at other sectors but impinge on retailing are abundant. The various types of public intervention are often imposed by different levels of government and implemented at different spatial scales (Jones & Simmons, 1993).

2. A planned hierarchy of shopping centers is common in metropolitan cities.

This is perhaps the most conspicuous in North American cities, where "there are more shopping centers than movie theatres; and there are more enclosed malls than cities" (Kowinski, 1985, p. 20). The rapid progress of suburbanization in the late 1950s and the 1960s required that cities be planned following "the principle of hierarchical organization" (Wang & Smith, 1997). Accordingly, a hierarchy of shopping centers was incorporated in this form of planning, consisting of neighborhood, community, and regional shopping centers. Each type of shopping center had a clearly prescribed tenant mix, trade area size, and even physical form (Urban Land Institute, 1985). In the 1970s, a newer and larger type of shopping center—the super-regional shopping center—began to be built. These centers often combine entertainment and recreation with shopping under one roof, becoming a new palace of consumption. Typical examples are the West Edmonton Mall in Canada (493,000m^2) and the Mall of America in the United States (466,000m^2). As suburbanization continued, the metropolitan city became multicentric, and a network of retail nodes evolved to serve the expansive city. Each regional and super-regional shopping center became a node, spatially distributed in a hierarchical fashion analogous to central places in Christaller's Central Place Model (Yeates, 1998).

3. Big box stores and power centers have emerged to become new leading retailers.

By the late 1980s, retailing re-emerged as an important and dynamic economic sector in many developed nations. In addition, major technological innovations took place in the distribution system. The highly computerized goods-tracking systems and inventory control enabled direct communications with, and direct shipping from, manufacturers (Hughes & Seneca, 1997). In the process, it spawned urban shopping environments and led to the emergence of a new retail format, known as 'big box' stores. At first, such stores were freestanding outside shopping centers; but eventually several big box stores began to cluster together at one location in the form of a planned plaza, commonly called a 'power center' (also known as a retail park). In less than ten years, this new format has been adopted by a variety of retail businesses. The big box stores and power centers have become leading retailers in the Western retail system (Jones & Doucet, 1999; Hernandez & Simmons, 2006) and have been widely blamed as the cause of the 'graying' of regional and super-regional shopping centers and the demise of department stores in North American cities (Kmitta & Ball, 2001; Doucet, 2001). These new retail spaces have been created and manipulated by the innovative retailers and commercial real estate developers to induce consumption.

   4. *Retail chains continue to be the most important form of retail concentration, but significant restructuring and reshuffling have been taking place in the retail industry.*

With no exception, all retail giants are chain operators, as the retail chain provides a way of introducing scale economies while avoiding the restrictions of market size (Jones & Simmons, 1993). Retail chains often account for 70 percent or more of the total retail sales in a metropolitan market. The 1990s and the 2000s witnessed significant restructuring of retail chains, leading to concentration of retail capital into the hands of a few "super leagues" (Marsden & Wrigley, 1996). Some sought to acquire, or merge with, others to consolidate resources and rose to the status of global corporations. For example, in 1991, the French firm Carrefour took over two other domestic hypermarket chains: Euromarche and Montlaur. In 1999, it merged with Promodes to create the largest European food retailing group and the second largest worldwide.

   In 2002, the American electronics retailer, Best Buy, expanded by acquiring Future Shop, a Canadian retail chain. Big capital retailers are better able to invest heavily in information technology and centralized distribution systems, the use of which enables the retailers to more effectively perform their competitive functions of reducing the turnover time of commodities (Hughes, 1996). Meanwhile, many other chains were not as fortunate and subsequently went under. Eaton's, a Canadian department store chain with a history of more than 100 years, was one such victim.

   5. *The retailer-supplier relationship has tipped toward retailers.*

For many years, producers of consumer goods effectively dictated brands and types of products being sold as well as their price in the retail market. Since the 1980s, retailing has been shifting from being the sales agent for manufacturing and agriculture to being the production agent for consumers, and the balance of the retailer-supplier relationship has tipped toward the large retail chains (Dawson, 2008). The significant retailers are no longer passive receivers of consumer goods supplied to them by producers. While still mediating between consumers and producers, they are no longer neutral mediators. Instead, they influence consumers by selecting goods with larger profit margins (Foord et al., 1996). They erode manufacturers' share of the surplus value by influencing patterns of consumption in their own favor and by using their bargaining power to lock manufacturers into retailer-led supply situations (Hughes, 1996, p. 99). They also aggressively develop "own-label" products as a competitive strategy. With their significant purchasing and bargaining power, they manage to exploit "negative working-capital cycles" by negotiating for extended credit payment periods, to reduce circulation costs and to accelerate accumulation of capital (Marsden & Wrigley, 1996). Pressure is often placed on suppliers to develop just-in-time production programs and factory-to-warehouse distribution systems to match the demands of the retailers.

6. *Internationalization of retailing has intensified.*

As their home markets became saturated, large retail chains were motivated to explore foreign markets, using a variety of paths ranging from licensing and franchising to joint ventures and wholly-owned subsidiaries. Almost every successful large retail chain has been seeking possibilities for expansion into other countries (Simmons & Kamikihara, 1999). Initially, they chose markets that had the least physical and cultural distances in order to minimize cost and the degree of uncertainty about sourcing and operation. In recent years, the major international retailers have increasingly turned their attentions to the 'emerging markets' in Asia and Latin America (Nakata & Sivakumar, 1997; Wrigley, 2000). Wal-Mart became an international company in 1991. By 2012, it has more than 5,000 stores in 26 countries, including 370 in China (Wal-Mart China, 2012). Carrefour, which went international in the 1970s, has also intensified its overseas operations since the late 1980s. It now operates 9,500 stores in 32 countries, including 361 in China (Carrefour Corporate Website, 2012). Revenue from their overseas operations has become an increasingly important part of business success, or even survival, for many multinational retailers.

7. *E-tailing has been gaining increased popularity.*

In the early 1990s, a new agent of retailing and a new form of retail space—online shopping and web stores—came into being. This led to the creation of the famous Amazon in 1995 and eBay in 1996. Online shopping is one form of electronic commerce, whereby consumers purchase goods (or services) from a seller over the Internet, without having to visit a brick-and-mortar store. Shoppers must have access to a computer connected to the Internet and a method of electronic payment—typically a credit card. Once a payment is received (usually through a third-party e-commerce business that facilitates online money transfer between consumers and retailers, such as Paypal), the goods can be shipped to a prescribed address via post or courier services, or they can be picked up by the consumer from a nearby store.

Most people tend to think that web stores are virtual space, but the e-(re)tailers do need to set up such physical facilities as warehouses and regional distribution centers by either constructing new buildings or leasing existing spaces, thus requiring heavy monetary investment. These facilities are necessary in order for online retailers to reduce delivery time and cost.

Initially, online shoppers were deterred by fraud and privacy concerns, such as risks of cyber theft to steal credit card numbers and identity. In recent years, such risks have been greatly reduced by the use of Secure Sockets Layer (SSL) encryption and firewalls, and e-tailers improved their refund policies. As a result, more and more consumers are encouraged to shop online for the benefits of convenience and saving, as the web stores are open all year round with no after-business hours and with no restrictions by location and distance.

The increased popularity of online shopping is leading to another revolution in the retail industry. In the new world order of retail, shoppers have become more tech savvy, even using smartphones to shop, order, and pay; or they go to a store to look at and feel a product, and then buy it online from Amazon, turning the brick-and-mortar stores into show rooms. Not all merchandise have the same level of suitability for sale online. Yet, e-tailers have been expanding their offerings, taking market shares away from the brick-and-mortar retailers. Amazon continues to be on the march, successfully moving into merchandise that Wal-Mart traditionally has sold. In the 2011 fiscal year, Amazon posted an impressive 41 percent revenue growth, compared with 8 percent at Wal-Mart, putting pressure on Wal-Mart to fix its lagging e-commerce operation (Welch, 2012). In response, Wal-Mart is investing heavily to revamp and expand its online shopping system with a new motto, "Anytime, Anywhere." To reduce overall cost to consumers, Wal-Mart aims to use its stores as pickup centers, instead of shipping the products from a distribution center. More retailers responded to the new shopping pattern by offering both multi-channel retailing (sell both in store and online in parallel) and cross-channel retailing (order online but pick up in store).

THE NEW GEOGRAPHY OF RETAILING: A PARADIGM SHIFT

Retailing is a subject of study by two schools of scholars and students— business management and geography—but they approach the subject from different perspectives. The former concentrates on firms and business organizations, including logistics, merchandising, marketing, consumer behavior, in-store display, and customer service; whereas the latter traditionally focused on selection and determination of business locations and delimitation of trade areas in localized markets.

Retail geography (originated as marketing geography, but lately called business geography by some) was created as a separate field of study in the mid-1950s in the United States. William Applebaum is widely regarded as the chief architect of this field of study. He emphasized that marketing geography should be viewed essentially as an applied, rather than as a purely academic, subject (Applebaum, 1954), and he considered that the best place to develop the field of marketing geography is in business itself. Marketing geography was further developed and advanced by such leading geographers as Brian Berry and David Huff. In its first 40 years, retail geography was primarily concerned with the identification (i.e., areal expression) of the demand for various goods and services and with the spatial arrangements for supplying them (i.e., areal structure of the system of supply) through an efficient distribution network (Davis, 1976). In general, this orthodox retail geography, as it is called by some contemporary retail geographers, was founded on a predictive and instrumentalist epistemology, and most of its ontological presumptions are linked to the neoclassical economic view of the world, such as the Central Place Theory, Gravity Model, and Distance-Decay function, which conceive space as a neutral container, at most affecting transportation costs (Clarke, 1996). Further, it maintained a focus primarily on the retailer rather than on the commodity channel as a whole, and was restricted to concentrating on the geography of stores and neglecting the geography of such important trends as the centralization of retail distribution operations. The traditional maxim of location, location, location was well reflected in orthodox retail geography as a study focus.

The early 1990s witnessed a paradigm shift in the study of retail geography: orthodox retail geography was reconstructed and re-theorized by Wrigley, Lowe, and a few other European economic geographers (Lowe & Wrigley, 1996), and a new geography of retailing was advocated to reflect the series of important changes in the global economy as highlighted in the preceding section of this chapter. The new geography of retailing has a number of important differences when compared with orthodox retail geography.

First of all, it takes a political economy approach, seeing retail capital as a component part of a larger system of production and consumption (Blomley, 1996). As such, its study scope extends to include production spheres in the system of circulation activities, particularly the production-commerce interface, namely the changing relations between retailers and suppliers. Aided by advanced technologies, retailers have developed logistically efficient stock-control systems and centrally controlled warehouse-to-store distribution networks. These systems permit shorter and more predictable lead time, with important implications for configuration of new retail space as well as reconfiguration of existing retail spaces.

Second, it concerns the geography of retail restructuring and the grounding of global flows of retail capital (i.e., sinking of capital into physical assets in overseas markets) and its geographical expressions (i.e., spatial outcomes) in the form of retail facilities of different formats. Innovative retailers, teamed up with developers, create differentiated spaces of retailing in the same market or different markets, and premeditate them to induce consumption (Ducatel & Blomley, 1990).

Third, it calls for much more serious treatment of regulations because the regulatory state is an important force influencing both corporate strategies and geographical market structures. In the view of Lowe and Wrigley (1996), orthodox retail geography was remarkably silent about regulation and the complex and contradictory relations of retail capital with the regulatory state. With the exception of a discussion concerning the constraining influence of land use planning regulations, the transformation of retail capital appeared to take place in a world devoid of a macro-regulatory environment that would shape competition between firms and the governance of investment. The new geography of retailing distinguishes two types of regulations: public-interest intervention and private-interest interventions, with the former concerning the relations between retailers and consumers, and the latter concerning relationships between retailers and producers/suppliers (see Figure 1.1).

THE DIMENSIONS OF THE ECONOMIC TRANSITION PROCESS FOR POST-SOCIALIST STATES

While most retail innovations originated in the Western developed countries, they spread, through the process of retail internationalization, to the emerging markets, many of which are post-socialist states. The post-socialist states were referred to as transitional economies before being called emerging markets, meaning that these states had been undergoing the shift from a planned economy to a market economy (Gregory & Stuart, 1994). Based on the experiences of the former Soviet Union and the Eastern and Central European countries, Bradshaw (1996) theorized a model of economic transition for the post-socialist states. While not retail specific, this model provides a useful framework for examining the retail transformation in China. In this theorization, Bradshaw identifies four dimensions in the economic transition process: macroeconomic stabilization, economic liberalization, privatization, and internationalization. These dimensions have no particular sequence and often take place simultaneously.

Macroeconomic stabilization refers to the need to bring the economy into balance with two components: to balance the level of income with the supply of goods, and to balance the difference between government expenditures and revenues. The planned economy had typically been characterized by a shortage of consumer goods. This often resulted in a certain level of personal savings, which Bradshaw (1996) describes as "repressed inflation." A major corrective action in the transition process is to improve the supply of consumer goods and, at the same time, implement controlled wage increases.

Economic liberalization refers to the gradual removal of government restrictions on economic activities in general and on price control in particular. Initially, the process of price liberalization may produce a severe price shock; but in the end, it makes the inefficient state-owned enterprises no longer economically viable and leads to the creation of new and more efficient enterprises (Nakata & Sivakumar, 1997).

The third dimension, which is closely related to liberalization, is to legalize private economic actors and to eventually create a private sector. *Privatization* is achieved in two ways: by selling off state-owned enterprises (usually starting from small- and medium-sized enterprises) and through the creation of new, privately owned businesses. Privatization gives companies the freedom in business decision making, necessary for the transition toward a market economy.

In need of economic stabilization, and due to international pressures as they strive for membership in international treaties or trading blocks, post-socialist states have begun to open their national borders to foreign direct investment (FDI) to capture the opportunities afforded by the globalization of the world economy. *Internationalization* enables these states to obtain much needed capital, technology, managerial know-how, as well as high-quality consumer goods. Through innovation diffusion, foreign investors play a catalytic role in the economic transition process for the post-socialist states (Lever & Daniels, 1996; Dawson, 2003).

It should be emphasized that accompanying economic transition is a fundamental change in the role of the state, manifested by the replacement of antiquated socialist economic policies with pro-market economy policies, and by the shift from owning enterprises and setting prices to regulating business operations by legal means. The challenges for the governments of the post-socialist states include establishing new rules and new institutions for stronger governance (United Nations Development Programme, 1999), balancing between public interest and private interest (Wrigley & Lowe, 1996), and minimizing the various impacts of the economic transition on the well-being of their citizens (Green & Ruhleder, 1995). Local governments within a state are also forced to be much more competitive with one another as they attempt to protect their economic base and exploit a new competitive edge with which to attract global financial capital and foreign technologies. This intergovernmental competition has bred so-called "entrepreneurial cities" (Knox et al., 2003), or in a few cases, "global islands of prosperity" (Heredia, 1997).

In his examination of the urban transformation in China, Ma (2002) put forth two arguments. First, China's economic transformation should be viewed as a prolonged process of change with unpredictable consequences, instead of as a transitory short phase leading to a Western capitalist system of production and consumption. He further points out that China has no desire to copy Western capitalism. Instead, what China has been trying to achieve is a new form of socialism with Chinese characteristics. Second, unlike other former socialist countries, where the political structures have been fundamentally altered by the demise of communism in the late 1980s, China's economic reform has been carried out in a stable political environment. Therefore, no mature theories have been developed that can adequately account for the complexity of socialist transition in general. Whereas these arguments seem to have direct implications for the appropriateness of the aforementioned conceptual framework in the Chinese context, they should not be used as a basis to reject the Bradshaw model in this China analysis.

As noted by Gregory and Stuart (1994, p. 306), "transition implies the shift from one set of system arrangements to another (for example, the replacement of government plan by market orientation), while reform implies change in an existing system (for example, attempts to make the socialist system work better)." By the account of Bradshaw (1996), the attempt of reform in the former Soviet Union failed and it is now accepted that the only solution is to replace the entire system, hence the transition to the market economy. China has been focusing on building a new form of economy with Chinese characteristics (hence reform), but even the Chinese government itself admits that the new form of economy should be market-driven with much-reduced state intervention. It is the interpretation of the author of this book that the eventual destination of the reform is a full-flung market economy similar to that prevailing in the capitalist countries. What is unpredictable lies in the exploration of the path leading to the destination (i.e., in the words of China's former leader Deng Xingping, "groping for stones to cross the river"). In fact, the notion of Chinese characteristics is touted simply to defend the legitimacy of the communist party as the sole governing body, and the Chinese characteristics may only represent transitory phases of a long process of economic transition. In this sense, the reference in this book to the typical characteristics of the contemporary capitalist retail economy is appropriate. It is against such a reference that the so-called Chinese characteristics can be revealed clearly.

Ma (2002) is right in that there are a variety of transitional economies and China's economic transformation is not necessarily the same as that of the former Soviet Union and the Eastern and Central European countries. However, there must also be some commonalities among all socialist countries in the course of economic transition. As Lin (2004, p. 18) states, "[the] different trajectories of departure from socialism have not, however, totally eliminated the common legacies of social urban development shared by China and its socialist counterparts elsewhere." In several studies that examined the growth and change of the service economy in certain Chinese cities (Gong, 2002; Lin, 2004; Yang, 2004), all the researchers situated their inquiries in the context of Chinese cities being transformed from the Soviet-style socialist cities (which emphasized industrial production) to post-socialist cities (whose growth is driven by a combination of secondary and tertiary activities including retailing). Of the four factors that these researchers have identified as the driving forces for accelerated 'tertiarization' in the Chinese cities, three can be explicitly accounted for by the Bradshaw model: (1) rising income and increasing consumer purchasing powers as a result of macroeconomic changes; (2) liberalization of state policies including marketization and privatization; (3) FDI as a consequence of internationalization. The only exception is the factor of urban planning. Because no China-specific theories have been developed as yet, it is fitting to use the Bradshaw model as a convenient framework for examining China's retail transformation, though this does not mean that the model is endorsed for its universality. In fact, Bradshaw (1996) acknowledges that each of the post-socialist states confronts a unique set of circumstances: whereas the general process of economic transition may be similar, the place-specific responses are most likely to be different.

ORGANIZATION OF THE BOOK AND MAJOR DATA SOURCES

The book is organized into 10 chapters. After this **Introduction** chapter, which sets up the research context and the theoretical framework for the entire book, **Chapter 2** deals with "the geography of demand," in which the size of the consumer market is measured with the two benchmark indicators: population size and disposable income. Because increase in income has led to significant changes in consumption patterns, detailed expenditure breakdowns are also analyzed. Regional variations are first exhibited between urban and rural areas, and then among cities of different tiers. A classification of cities is developed particularly for this purpose to facilitate the analysis of regional variations and geographical patterns. **Chapter 3** analyzes the progressive process of retail deregulation and re-regulation in China in the past three decades, to set up the legal context for the understanding of the formation of the new retail economy. In **Chapter 4**, the trajectories of growth and the resultant changes of the retail sector are depicted. It reveals, albeit in a succinct way, how the retail sector has been transformed from a centrally-planned industry into a market-driven business, and how the traditional state-owned department stores have been challenged by the new format stores and have lost their supremacy and monopoly. It also illustrates how retail businesses have been concentrating into the hands of a few players—a typical characteristic of retail structure in the Western capitalist market economies.

Chapter 5 is devoted to two areas of investigation. First, it explores how foreign retailers adopted unconventional entry paths to bypass the regulatory barriers and penetrate the China market before the country was admitted to the WTO. Second, it examines how and where they have grounded their retail capital (i.e., their corporate geo-strategies) and what geographical outcomes this has entailed (spatial expression). **Chapter 6** recounts how the national strategies were devised and implemented to nurture national champions to defend against foreign competition, and what effects these strategies have had on the growth of domestic heavyweights. Through a case study of Best Buy in China, **Chapter 7** confirms two important points in the literature of retail internationalization: (1) any firm entering a new market will face some degree of disadvantage compared with the local firms (Borgström et al., 2008); and (2) the major issue for internationalization of retailing is one of *standardization* versus *adaptation* (Sternquist, 2007). **Chapter 8** examines the patterns of shopping center development, including the role of foreign capital, the emergence of domestic developers, and the impacts on urban development.

Having realized that it is increasingly difficult to compete with their Chinese counterparts on price, many foreign retailers turned to selling quality, instead of quantity, leading to a new wave of retail internationalization characterized with luxury goods retailing. Associated with this new development are a series of new issues and concerns. **Chapter 9** discusses these issues and the need of managing luxury retailing in China. Finally, in **Chapter 10,** conclusions are drawn from the various topical chapters, and remarks are made on opportunities and challenges in future development of the Chinese retail economy for both domestic and foreign retailers.

The opportunity to write this book has been afforded by the availability of a number of new data sources. For many years, retailing, wholesaling, and catering (restaurants) were lumped into one sector in Chinese statistics—commercial activity—with no separate statistics for retailing. In 1988, China began to publish the *Almanac of China's Commerce*. In 1994, it was renamed *Almanac of China's Domestic Trade*. Each issue is composed of three main parts: major events; policy initiatives and regulations introduced in that year; and separate statistics for retailing, wholesaling, and catering.

In the late 1990s, major cities began to collect and publish detailed data for commercial activities in their own city, especially Beijing and Shanghai, both of which conducted a census of commercial activity in 1999 and published detailed data in special volumes, including district-level dissemination. The municipal census of commercial activity is useful in two ways: it separates retailing from other commercial activities, thus permitting retail-focused studies; and it allows cross-tabulation of the retail data in a number of dimensions (such as number of stores, employment, floor area, retail sales, etc. vs. business ownership, store format, and districts).

In 2000, China for the first time published the *China Chain Store Almanac*. The first issue covers 10 years: 1990–2000. Since then, this almanac has been published every year. The *Almanac* is a comprehensive and particularly useful source of information for the study of retail chains in China. While its organization changes slightly from year to year, the *Almanac* is typically organized with the following sections: speeches of state leaders about chain development; selected essays by experts and government officials; reports of chain development by retail format, region, and key enterprise; FDI in retail chains; state policies and regulations; and statistics of the top 100 retail chains (including their total sales and number of stores). By analyzing these data, it is possible to reconstruct the growth patterns in terms of business volume, structure, and geographical distribution.

In more recent years, a number of government agencies have established permanent websites to disseminate news and information about retail development. Again, Shanghai and Beijing take the lead in the country. Shanghai Commerce Information Center (under the auspices of Shanghai Commission of Commerce) launched a well-maintained website to report the latest news of commercial activity development in Shanghai. The site is updated almost daily. The information is current and the news informative. One other reputable website is Retailer Link at http://www.linkshop.com. cn/. This retail-specific website posts timely reports on major developments and events, and the reports have proved highly reliable.

China Statistical Yearbook and *China City Statistical Yearbook* are not new data sources, but they now have separate chapters on retailing and consumption. They not only report wages (China's population census never collects data on family income), but also document consumer spending on various types of consumer goods (through annual household surveys), therefore permitting study of consumption patterns and changes.

It should be pointed out that there have been known issues with the quality and accuracy of the official statistics in China. Alteration of data by either companies or local governments is common. For example, the total retail sales reported by the top 100 chains to China Chain Store Association for 2011 was 2 trillion yuan, but nearly 20 percent of it was non-retail-related sales (Zheng, 2012). The State Bureau of Statistics issued a stern circular in 2012, ordering the major companies and real estate developers (about 700,000 of them) to report their business data directly to the State Bureau or to the state-authorized provincial data centers, to eliminate the opportunity of "interference" by local officials (Zhu & Lu, 2012). The data must be reported via the Internet and using a standard template, making manipulation of aggregation easily visible to the auditors.

This book draws information and data from all the above sources. It is however not just packaged with information and data. The information and data are processed and analyzed to reconstruct the process of change and development, and to reveal the impact and consequences—both economic and geographical. The book should be a useful and valuable reader not only for university students and faculty researchers in business management and economic geography, but also for international retailers and commercial real estate developers, who contemplate business and investment opportunities in China.

2 The Consumer Market
Size, Consumption Patterns, and Regional Variations

For nearly 30 years before economic reform began in 1978, the planned economy of China resulted in a shortage of consumer goods. Between 1952 and 1978, China adopted a fiscal policy that emphasized high national accumulation and low wages and salaries. Beginning in the early 1980s, economic planning shifted to address a greater balance between state accumulation and personal earnings, with the aim to raise the standard of living for ordinary citizens and to also stimulate production through increased domestic demand for consumer goods. The three decades of reform and economic stabilization have nurtured an affluent consumer market, a necessary condition for retail growth. This chapter establishes the geography of demand. The consumer market size is measured with such benchmarks as population size and income. Since rise in income has led to significant changes in consumption patterns, expenditure breakdowns are also examined. Regional variations are first contrasted between urban and rural areas, and then exhibited among cities of different tiers. A classification of cities is developed specifically for this purpose.

MARKET SIZE AND CONSUMPTION PATTERNS

Mainland China consists of 31 provincial-level administrative divisions, which include five autonomous regions and four municipalities directly under the state government (Figure 2.1). According to the 2010 national census, China has a total population of 1.34 billion, a 7.8 percent increase from the previous decennial census (see Table 2.1). In 2011, the urban population for the first time surpassed the rural population, accounting for 51 percent of the national total (Chinese Academy of Social Sciences, 2012a).

The largest three provinces by population are Guangdong, Shandong, and Henan, each accounting for 7 percent of the national total. The three long-standing municipalities of Beijing, Shanghai, and Tianjin all witnessed tremendous population growth: at 44.5 percent, 40.3 percent,

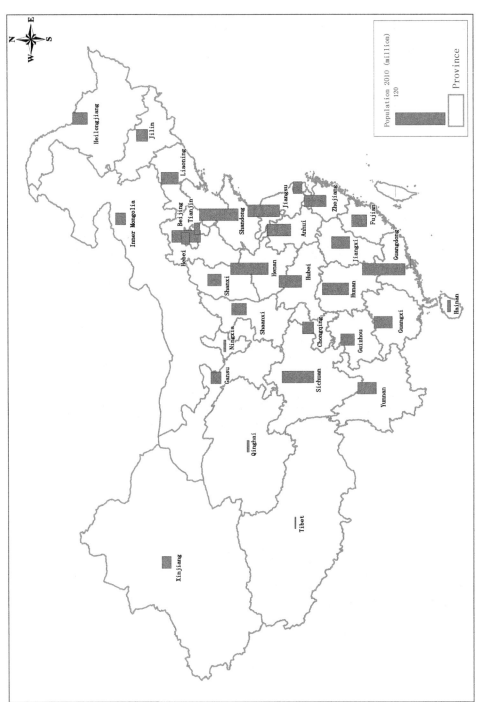

Figure 2.1   Administrative division of China with population distribution, 2010.

Table 2.1   Administrative Division of China and Population Distribution, 2010

Region	Province	Population (in millions)	% of national total	2000–2010 change (%)	Number of cities by tier				
					mega	1st	2nd	3rd	4th
North China	Beijing**	19.61	1.46	44.5	1				
	Tianjin**	12.94	0.97	31.4	1				
	Hebei	71.85	5.36	7.8			2	3	6
	Shanxi	35.71	2.67	10.0			1	2	8
	Inner Mongolia*	24.71	1.84	6.0			2	2	5
Northeast China	Liaoning	43.75	3.27	4.6		2	1	5	6
	Jilin	27.46	2.05	2.5		1	1		6
	Heilongjiang	38.31	2.86	5.7		1	1		10
East China	Shanghai**	23.02	1.72	40.3	1				
	Jiangsu	78.66	5.87	7.7		3	4	5	1
	Zhejiang	54.53	4.06	18.7		2	1	6	2
	Anhui	59.5	4.44	0.8			1	3	13
	Fujian	36.89	2.75	8.2			2	2	5
	Jiangxi	44.57	3.33	10.3			1	2	8
	Shandong	95.79	7.15	6.5		2	4	7	4
Central-South China	Henan	94.02	7.02	3.0			1	3	13
	Hubei	57.23	4.27	-3.8		1		2	9
	Hunan	65.68	4.9	3.8		1		4	8
	Guangdong	104.3	7.79	22.4	2	2	4	3	10
	Guangxi*	46.03	3.44	5.0			1	1	12
	Hainan	8.67	0.65	14.7				1	1
Southwest China	Chongqing**	28.85	2.15	-5.4		1			
	Sichuan	80.42	6.0	-2.3		1		2	15
	Guizhou	34.75	2.59	-1.4				1	3
	Yunnan	45.97	3.43	8.5			1	1	6
	Tibet*	3	0.22	14.5					1
Northwest China	Shaanxi	37.33	2.79	5.6		1		1	8
	Gansu	25.57	1.91	1.8			1		11
	Qinghai	5.63	0.42	16.8				1	
	Ningxia*	6.3	0.47	14.8				1	4
	Xinjiang*	21.81	1.43	18.1			1	1	
Others	Armed forces	2.3	0.17						
	Transient population	4.65	0.35						
Country total		1339.72	100.00	7.8	5	18	30	59	175

Source: National Bureau of Statistics of China, 2011a.
*Autonomous region ** municipality directly under the state government

and 31.4 percent, respectively. As stipulated in the *Beijing General Plan 2004–2020* (Beijing Planning Commission, 2004), the city's population should be capped at 18 million by 2020. Yet the number of permanent residents in Beijing had already reached 17.5 million in 2010, plus another 2.1 million migrant workers, for a total of 19.6 million. Drawing migrant workers from interior provinces, the coastal provinces of Zhenjiang (on the Yangtze River Delta) and Guangdong (on the Pearl River Delta) also experienced significant population increases, with gains of 18.7 percent and 22.4 percent, respectively. Only four interior provinces—Sichuan, Chongqing, Hubei, and Guizhou—experienced a negative population change, attributed to emigration. This largest national population in the world, along with sustained income improvement, has made China the largest emerging consumer market for retailers, both domestic and international.

As is shown in Table 2.2, per capita income increased 11.6 times in urban areas and 7.6 times in rural areas in the 20-year period 1990–2010. Wage and salary, which used to be the only source of income for the Chinese urban consumers, now account for only 65 percent of total income (see Table 2.3). As the population is aging, pension income has increased to 24.2 percent of total income. Business earnings and capital gains from investment are now new sources of income, accounting for 8.2 and 2.5 percent, respectively. In the meantime, the country has nurtured a swelling middle class and even a new class of social elites. The steady improvement in income has fueled a continued rise in consumer demand, which in turn greatly boosted retail sales and led to massive investment in the retail sector.

Increase in income has led to changes in lifestyles, which in turn led to new consumption patterns. Between 1990 and 2010, per capita expenditure increased 9.5 times in urban areas and 6.5 times in rural areas (see Table 2.2). During the same 10-year period, fixed-base CPI (1978=100) increased progressively, by 354 percentage points in urban areas and 238 percentage points in rural areas, reflecting high levels of inflation. (In recent years, the highest levels of inflation occurred in costs of food, housing, and health care; see Table 2.3). Minus the inflation effects, however, disposable income still increased impressively, and the Engel coefficient continued to decline (see Table 2.2), indicating that as income rises, the proportion of income spent on food falls, even if actual expenditure on food rises. That is, the increase in expenditure on food products in percentage terms has been less than the increase in income, reflecting a higher standard of living and more disposable income available for discretionary purchase.

Consumption patterns have gone through some significant changes in the past three decades. In the 1980s and the early 1990s, a rapidly increasing disposable income was spent mainly on better food, higher-quality

Table 2.2   Change in per Capita Income, Expenditure, and Ownership of
Consumables, 1990–2010, Urban vs. Rural*

Income, expenditure, and savings (in Chinese RMB yuan)	1990	2000	2010	1990–2010 change (%)
Income (disposable income for urban areas; net income for rural areas)	1,510 (686)	6,280 (2,253)	19,109 (5,919)	1,165 (763)
Expenditure	1,279 (585)	4,998 (1,670)	13,471 (4,382)	953 (649)
Balance of saving deposits**	623	5,076	22,619	
Fixed-base CPI (1978=100)	222.0 (165.1)	467.6 (314.0)	576.3 (403.5)	354.5 (238.4)
Household Engel's coefficient	54.2 (58.8)	39.4 (49.1)	35.7 (41.1)	-18.5 (-17.7)

Consumables (number of units per 100 households)

Automobile		0.50 (-)	13.07 (-)	
Motorcycle	1.9 (/0.9)	18.8 (21.9)	22.5 (/59.0)	
Cell phone		19.5 (4.3)	188.8 (/136.5)	
Color TV	59.0 (4.7)	116.6 (48.7)	137.4 (111.8)	
Computers		9.7 (0.5)	71.2 (10.4)	
Washing machine	78.4 (9.1)	90.5 (28.5)	96.9 (57.3)	
Fridge	42.3 (1.2)	80.10 (12.3)	96.6 (45.1)	
Hi-fi		22.2 (-)	28.1 (-)	
Camera	19.2 (0.7)	38.4 (3.1)	43.7 (5.1)	
Air conditioner	0.3 (-)	30.8 (1.3)	112.1 (16.0)	
Water heater		49.1 (-)	84.8 (-)	
Camcorder		1.3 (-)	8.2 (-)	
Microwave oven		17.6 (-)	59.0(-)	
Fitness equipment		3.5 (-)	4.2 (-)	

Source: National Bureau of Statistics of China, 2011a.
* numbers in parentheses are for rural areas
** separate data for urban and rural areas are not available
- data not available

Table 2.3   Income, Expenditure, and Disparities in Urban Areas of China, 2010

Survey item	Total/ average		Lowest income group		Highest income group		CPI 2009 = 100
Sample size (no. of household)	65,607	100%	6,569	10.0%	6,548	10.0%	
Average HH size (in persons)	2.9		3.29		2.51		
Average number of persons employed	1.5		1.32		1.54		
Per capita income (yuan)	21,033	100%	6,704		56,435		
Salary/wage	13,707	65.2%					
Business income	1,713	8.2%					
Income from property and investment (interest/rent/stock)	520	2.5%					
Transfer	5,092	24.2%					
Disposable income	19,109		5,948		51,431		
Consumer expenditure (yuan)	13,471	100.0%	5,472	100.0%	31,762	100.0%	
Food	4,805	35.7%	2,525	46.2%	8,535	26.9%	107.2
Apparel	1,444	10.7%	514	9.4%	3,149	9.9%	99.0
Housing	1,332	9.9%	656	12.0%	3,014	9.5%	104.5
Household consumables/ service	908	6.7%	288	5.3%	2,381	7.5%	100.0
Health care	872	6.5%	405	7.4%	1,843	5.8%	103.2
Transportation and communication	1,984	14.7%	448	8.2%	6,770	21.3%	99.6
Education/recreation/ Entertainment	1,628	12.1%	503	9.2%	4,515	14.2%	100.60
Miscellaneous consumer goods/ services	499	3.7%	132	2.4%	1,554	4.9%	-

Source: National Bureau of Statistics of China, 2011a.

apparel, and such durable goods as watches, bicycles, color TVs, sewing machines, refrigerators, and washing machines (Sun, 1997). A number of subsequent policy changes diverted a considerable amount of household spending from retail stores.

As a result of housing reform, government agencies and state enterprises stopped providing free or subsidized housing to their employees. New housing has been commercialized and must be purchased at market price. Until 1996, post-secondary education was largely free and accessible only to those who were able to pass the national entrance exam. In 1997, all universities and colleges (except normal universities and teachers' colleges) began to charge full tuition. Some institutions also accepted students who did not pass the entrance examination but could afford to pay a differential fee on top of full tuition. When the entrance exam was reinstated in 1977, only 5 percent of the examination takers were admitted to a university or college. The acceptance rate surpassed 50 percent in 1999, and exceeded 72 percent in 2011 ("Statistics of high education applications and enrolment", 2012). Increasingly, families are spending, or are saving, a large proportion of their income to support their children for college or university education.

Compared to 30 years ago, consumers now spend larger shares of income on housing (10%), household appliances (7%), transportation/communication (15%), education/recreation/entertainment (12%), and health care (7%; see Table 2.3). Between 1990 and 2010, a total of 25.6 billion square meters of living space were built across the country, with 10.5 billion in urban areas and 15.1 billion in rural areas. Per capita living space increased from 24.5 m^2 in 2002 to 31.6 m^2 in 2010 in urban areas, and from 26.5 m^2 to 34.1 m^2 in rural areas. As families moved into new and more spacious apartments, many of them spent heavily on interior furnishings and decorations. Households are also replacing their old appliances with new models. New purchases include flat screen/high definition TVs, smartphones, digital cameras, and laptop computers. Appliances such as color TVs, cell phones, washing machines, refrigerators, microwave ovens, and air conditioners are now ubiquitous in urban households (see Table 2.2). In 2011, sales of new electronic products through the trade-in program was 92.5 million units and 342 billion yuan; another 100 million units were sold in rural areas through the popular program of offering rebates on purchases of electronics and appliances, both being government-subsidized programs (Zhang, 2012). Mainly due to demand from the swelling middle class and the new elite class of consumers, China has now surpassed the United States to become the world's largest automobile market with annual sales of 18 million cars. Automobile ownership in urban areas increased from 0.5 percent in 2000 to 13.1 percent in 2010 (see Table 2.2), and further to 18.6 percent in 2011 ("Reading China with Statistics", 2012). SUVs and CUVs have become new status symbols among the affluent professionals and the social elites. At the 2012 Beijing Auto Show, all Western brand manufacturers were present with new models. GM Chairman and CEO Dan Akerson announced on site that GM plans to increase its Chinese dealership network from 2,900 in 2011 to 3500 by the end of 2012 (Leblanc, 2012).

It should be pointed out that with widening gaps in income and social disparity, purchasing powers and consumption patterns vary greatly among different income groups. The annual Survey of Household Spending distinguishes seven income groups. The highest income group enjoys 8.6 times as much income as the lowest income group (56,400 yuan vs.

6,700 yuan). The lowest income group spends 46 percent and 12 percent of their total expenditure on food and housing (i.e., the necessities), while the highest income group spends only 27 percent and 9.5 percent, respectively (see Table 2.3). In addition, the highest income group spends 21 percent of their total expenditure on transportation (mainly in the form of private automobiles) and 14 percent on both communication (internet and smartphones) and education/recreation/entertainment, compared with only 8 and 9 percent by the lowest-income group. The differences in terms of *yuan* are more pronounced.

To reduce the gaps between the rich and the poor, the state government continued to raise minimum wage for the low-income workers. Between 2006 and 2010, minimum wage increased by an average of 12.9 percent annually. In the next five years (2011–2015), the government plans to continue increasing minimum wage at the same annual rate. The level of minimum wage varies in different regions. Shenzhen has the highest minimum wage at 1,500 yuan per month, while Qingdao has 1,100 yuan (Lu, 2012). The increase in minimum wage has put pressure on employers to raise wages for other employees as well. Since 2005, the Chinese government has raised pensions several times for the gray consumers (i.e., retirees). At the 12th National People's Congress held in March 2013, Premier Wen Jiabao announced that pension would be raised again by another 10 percent, from an average of 700 yuan per month in 2004 to 1,700 yuan in 2013. This will translate into an additional 1,700 yuan per year for each retiree, giving the gray consumers more money to spend (Xiao, 2013).

Facing reduced international demand for exports from China, resulting from the economic crisis in the Euro Zone and the sluggish economy in the U.S., the state government took measures to encourage domestic consumption and stimulate retail sales. Recently, the government further lowered personal income tax for the low- and middle-income earners. Beginning on September 1, 2011, the basic personal amount, at which personal income tax kicks in, was raised from 2,000 yuan per month to 3,500 yuan, an increase of 75 percent. This has resulted in a significant reduction in the number of income tax payers by 60 million: from 84 to 24 million (Zhou, 2012a; Liang, 2012). The reduction will retain more cash in the pockets of more consumers.

Gift-related consumption has become a big part of business for retailers in China. In the 1980s, gift giving was limited to such things as candy and tea. Over time, it has gone beyond occasions of celebration and congratulation. Nowadays, expensive gifts are often given for favors from friends and relatives who help with career promotion, acceptance of a child to a preferred school, or even introduction to a medical doctor for treatment of illness. Retailers are well aware of this special area of demand and are aggressively marketing a variety of merchandise as gifts, including but not limited to health products, cosmetics, jewelry, high-end cigarettes and wine (sold for more than 1,000 yuan per carton or bottle), luxury bags, and even cash in the form of prepaid gift cards. According to an estimate by the China Institute for Gift Business Research, the total market of gift purchasing in the country is 768 billion yuan a year (Zhao, 2012a).

Besides individual and household consumption, institutional and corporate purchases account for a significant portion of retail sales, though there are no data to substantiate this portion of consumption accurately. According to an estimate by the China Institute for Gift Business Research, 34 percent of the total market of gift purchasing is made by corporations, institutions, and government agencies (Zhao, 2012a). The use of prepaid purchase cards is the main means of exchange in institutional and corporate purchases. Two types of prepaid purchasing cards are in circulation to facilitate transactions. The first is issued by non-banking institutions and can be used at different retail outlets and chains, and even in different regions (known as "multi-purpose and trans-sectoral cards"). The second type is issued by retailers themselves and is retailer specific. For retailers, prepaid cards greatly speed up circulation of cash and guarantee a certain amount of sales with virtually no risk. According to a research report by iResearch—a marketing research firm headquartered in Shanghai—sales of prepaid purchase cards are estimated at 96.5 billion yuan in 2010, and may reach 300 billion yuan in 2013 ("Sales of multi-purpose, pre-paid purchase cards reach 96.5 billion yuan in 2010 in China", 2011). Officials of the Municipal Bureau of Commerce of Yangzhou City estimated that annual sales of prepaid cards in their city have reached several hundred million yuan (Zhu et al., 2012).

All prepaid purchase cards will eventually be redeemed at retail stores with purchase of goods. For many retailers, the prepaid cards have become their lifelines. Shanghai-based Hualian Supermarket Inc. issues a prepaid card (named the "Hualian OK Card"), which has become one of the most popular in Shanghai and the surrounding region. According to Hualian's 2011 mid-year report, its prepaid card-related liability was 8.3 billion yuan, equivalent to nearly 60 percent of the sales in the first six months of 2011 (Li, 2012b). Many retailers have even set up a separate web page to provide instructions specifically for corporate purchasers, including incentives. The incentives offered by Wu-Mart, a Beijing-based supermarket chain, include a 20 percent cash rebate for a single purchase of 50,000 yuan or over. If a "customer" purchases prepaid cards worth 50,000 yuan or more, the cards will be delivered to the purchaser, without the purchaser needing to be present at a store. These offers are obviously intended for corporate and institutional purchasers because few individual consumers would purchase a prepaid card with a face value of 50,000 yuan or more from a supermarket. As Wu-Mart promotes on its website, its purchase cards are "the best choice for giving to friends, relatives, employees [as a bonus], and clients [for doing business with you]." Another retailer, Wuhan Zhongbai, is more direct on its website: "we provide group purchase service to institutions, corporations, universities and colleges in both retail and wholesale, including selling of pre-paid VIP purchase cards."

In sum, the economic reform has created an affluent, but also disparate, consumer market in China. In 2012, total retail sales in the country reached 20,716 billion yuan (or US$3,341 billion), a 12 percent increase from the previous year after price adjustment (National Bureau of Statistics of China, 2013). This is only 23 percent less than the total retail sales in the United States in the same year, which is reported as US$4,355 (YCharts, 2013). As well, the "digital wallet" has moved closer to the Chinese consumers: according to China People's Bank, 3.69 billion credit cards and debit cards have been issued in the country, with an average of two cards per citizen ("Number of credit cards and debit cards issued in China has reached 3.69 billion" , 2013). More importantly, the consumer market has become more segmented and more individualized than ever. In addition to the wealthy elites, the children of the baby boomers, commonly known as the "post-1980s" in China, have become a distinct group of consumers; they have a tendency of pursuing fashion and new products, can afford them, and are not as money conscious as their parents and grandparents. Indeed, consumer segmentation and differential marketing have never been as relevant in China as they are now. Retailers need to respond to the various segments of the consumer market, including the complex institutional and corporate consumptions, by offering different merchandise mixes through a diverse array of distribution channels.

REGIONAL VARIATIONS AND TIERS OF URBAN MARKETS

Modern retailing, characterized by retail chains and large format stores, is largely an urban phenomenon. Cities are not only centers of power and prestige; they are also centers of consumption and concentrations of retail businesses. As such, the distribution of goods between retailers and consumers is a primary economic activity in urban areas. The main commercial districts of a city shape the city's image: its prosperity, diversity, sophistication, and innovation. As Yeates (1999) has observed, foreign retailers are attracted to large wealthy urban markets and to metropolitan areas with high market densities and strong commercial nodes. The level of retail development also reflects the standard of living in the host city. In the study of retail geography, cities are treated as dynamic and multi-layered consumption spaces, where shopping, selling, and buying activities interact. Urban development stimulates retail growth in two ways: opening up new consumption spaces (new business locations and sites) and reinforcing accessibility to the new retail facilities by providing efficient transportation networks.

While China is customarily referred to as the largest emerging market in the world, many of its large urban centers have in effect become mature markets. Beijing, Shanghai, Tianjin, Guangzhou, and Shenzhen, for example, are by no means less mature than the typical urban markets in the Western economies, and they are already saturated with retailers of all formats and caliber. International retailers have long recognized the complex urban hierarchy in China and the associated regional disparities. They devised, and continue to revise, their geospatial business strategies accordingly. In China, cities, especially the large cities, are "islands of prosperity." While the level of urbanization is still relatively low (currently at 51 percent, compared with 70–80 percent in the Western developed economies), a disproportionate amount of retail sales are generated in cities, where the growing accumulation of wealth endows urban dwellers with high purchasing powers and consumption capabilities (see Table 2.2).

Due to the vast variations in population size, settlement patterns, economic structure, and wealth accumulation among the Chinese cities, levels of demand and market size differ significantly within the nation's urban system. When international retailers plan to penetrate the China market and execute their spatial business strategies, they invariably enter large urban markets first before branching out to smaller cities. They often use such names as first-, second-, and third- tier cities to describe and label the Chinese urban markets of various size and potential. For retailers, knowledge of regional or local markets is more meaningful and useful than the general picture of the national market.

While a hierarchy of cities can be a useful framework for retail diffusion, no systematic classification of Chinese cities has ever been developed and applied for the study of retail geography. Even the China Chain Store Association, the national council of retailers, ambiguously defines Tier 1 cities as those including metropolitan cities, large cities, and other economically advanced cities; it defines Tier 2 cities as those consisting of medium- and small-sized cities with a population less than 2 million (China Chain Store Association, 2010, p. 51). As one blogger puts it pointedly, "We often hear of China's first or second or third tier cities; yet, what actually makes a city tier? The terms are so often used, yet there is actually no official formula for determining what tier a city falls in. Instead, everyone makes up their own rules" (Barry, 2011).

In the literature of urban geography, hierarchies of cities are constructed primarily on the basis of population, but the cities' economic, social, and administrative importance is also taken into consideration. The first classification of cities in the United States was proposed by the urban geography pioneer Chauncy Harris in 1943 on the basis of two sets of figures that described the principal activities in each U.S. city: occupation and employment (Harris, 1943). Another classification of U.S. cities was developed by H. J. Nelson in the mid-1950s, looking at proportions of the labor force of a city engaging in different services (Nelson, 1955). Both of these early systems were functional classifications, differentiating cities by the level of specialization in economic activities, or more exactly, in production activities. A contemporary metropolitan hierarchy of the United States was constructed in the 1990s and was adopted widely in urban geography textbooks (see Hartshorn, 1992; Yeates, 1998). This contemporary urban hierarchy, which is based not only on population size and labor force concentration, but also on a variety of social, economic, and political institutions, consists of three orders: international metropolis, national metropolis, and regional metropolis, with New York City being the lone member of the international metropolis class.

Similar classifications and designations of Chinese cities exist, which differentiate the urban centers into provincial-level cities (i.e., the cities directly under the state government), sub-provincial cities, provincial capitals, prefecture- and county-level cities, and Special Economic Zones (SEZ).[1] Four of the sub-provincial cities, Dalian, Qingdao, Ningbo, and Xiamen (along with Shenzhen), are also delegated provincial-level autonomy in economic planning, and share revenue with the state government, instead of with their respective provincial governments. These political classifications and designations, however, are not conducive to the study of retail geography. The references to provincial capitals and other political criteria are only marginally useful for comparing cities within their own provinces. From the viewpoint of retailers, the paramount and the most relevant attributes of an urban center are the market's size and its associated purchasing powers, typically measured by population size (or number of households) and level of disposable income. As such, the capital city of a western province in China may be far less important to retailers than a medium-sized city in an eastern coastal province.

Surprisingly, discussions of city tiers are all initiated and suggested by business and real estate consultants. There seems to be a total lack of interest among, and contributions from, academic researchers. In February 2007, a group of large institutional property companies gathered in the city of Chongqing for a conference. The purpose of the conference was to formulate a set of standards for differentiating Chinese cities into tiered markets by business opportunities (McMillian, 2007). There seemed to be a consensus among the participants that the top-tier cities were obvious: Beijing and Shanghai are definite members, but Guangzhou and Shenzhen might be included as well. However, finding Tiers 2 and 3 is difficult and confusing. Xavier Wong, Head of Research at the Knight Frank real estate office in Hong Kong, suggested that, to be considered in the second tier, a city should have a population of about 3 million and a minimum GDP that is equivalent to US$2,000 per capita. In addition to the simple population and income guides, the cities should also have a strong history of exports, a robust record of foreign direct investment, and good policy initiatives (McMillian, 2007).

RightSite Asia, an industrial property consulting company specializing in real estate search and brokering in China, proposed its own set of criteria to organize Chinese cities into tiers (Cole, 2009). In addition to population and economic output, the criteria include economic growth, transportation, and even historical and cultural significance. Yet, RightSite did not provide an account of how the various parameters can be operationalized to produce a systematic classification scheme.

To fill the void in academic literature, the author of this book has developed a multivariate classification scheme of the Chinese cities, specifically for the study of retail geography. Nine variables, as listed in Table 2.4, are chosen to construct the classification scheme. The first five are indicators of demand, purchasing power, and size of the retail economy. Ideally, disposable income should be used in favor of wage because wage is not the only source of disposal income. However, income (both total and disposable) is never a part of the Chinese population census. Although income is reported in the annual Survey of House Spending, the survey data are solicited from only 65,607 urban households and 68,190 rural households in the entire country (National Bureau of Statistics of China, 2011a), and reported for the nation as a whole with no regional differentiations. For this reason, total wage by city is used as a proxy to reflect relative purchasing powers in different urban markets. Average wage is also used in the classification scheme to signify the level of affluence at individual levels in different cities. GDP indicates not only a city's ability to develop and provide retail-related infrastructures, but also the potential of institutional and corporate purchases, which account for a significant portion of retail sales in China, as mentioned earlier in this chapter.

Table 2.4   Classification Variables

Variable	Pearson correlation coefficient r with retail sales (all coefficients are significant at $\alpha = 0.01$)
Total population	0.867
GDP	0.979
Retail sales	1.000
Total wage	0.938
Average wage	0.627
Internet subscriptions	0.864
Cell phone users	0.934
Number of buses	0.900
Population density	0.216

The four remaining variables are facilitating factors. For example, more and more urban consumers use the Internet and cell phone not only to search for product features, availability, and price, but also to make purchases (and have them delivered to their homes). Both the Internet and the cell phone represent reciprocal use of business information technologies on the consumer end. According to a recent report released by the China Internet Network Information Center (2011), the number of internet users in the country reached 513 million in 2011, about 40 percent of the total population; 356 million users obtain information from the Internet via their cell phones. The number of IP addresses reached 2.3 million, many of which have been set up by retailers or by third-party ISPs providing services to retailers. It is not clear what percentage of cell phone subscribers use smartphones, but it is safe to assume that the proportion is significant and still on rise, especially among the young generation of consumers. A recent U.S. study confirms the role of smartphones in transforming the shopping process. It found that smartphones have significantly changed the way Americans shop and make purchase decisions: 96 percent of smartphone owners use mobile devices to research product and service information; 35 percent intentionally have smartphones with them to compare prices and find product information while on the go, and 32 percent have actually decided against purchasing a product while in a store as a result of smartphone research (Pham, 2012). Indeed, smartphones are making consumers smarter shoppers and are influential at the point of purchase (Kopun, 2012). Similar influences are being felt in China.

Retailers typically favor cities with high population density, as high density means compact trade areas with high sales potentials (i.e., an agglomeration effect). For retailers, a high density urban structure provides a concentration of potential purchasing power that can compensate for low income and consumption levels. Private automobile ownership is an important indicator of consumer mobility. Unfortunately, this information is not available at the city level in official statistics, though the Survey of Household Spending suggests that private automobile ownership had reached 13 percent of all households in 2010. In the absence of automobile ownership data, the number of buses is used to differentiate cities with regard to levels of mobility. A number of cities have also built extensive subway and light rail transit (LRT) lines, but systematic information on this type of transportation is not available. Indeed, public transportation in China is critically important to retail locations. Five Star Electronics, now a wholly-owned subsidiary of Best Buy (China), has the following location requirements posted on its corporate website for commercial property brokers: "[we seek to lease commercial buildings that have] floor areas between 2,500 and 15,000 m², extending from the ground floor up to 4 storeys; *buildings must be reached by multiple lines of public transit including both buses and subways*" (Five Star, 2012; emphasis added). Ikea looks for store locations with the same principles (Burstedt, 2011). Where public transit services are inadequate, retailers are often seen providing free shuttle buses (at their own cost) to bring in shoppers.

Given the large number of urban centers in China, only the provincial-, sub-provincial-and prefecture-level cities, a total of 287, are included in this multivariate classification exercise. The county-level cities are not included. The data are extracted from the *2011 China City Statistical Yearbook* (National Bureau of Statistics of China, 2011b). Statistics for the selected cities are reported for two levels of geography: the administrative city region and the city proper. For the classification exercise in this study, data are used for the city proper instead of the city region, because many city regions include large rural-like areas and populations. For example, 57 percent of these city regions have 70 percent or more of their populations living outside the city proper; another 23 percent of these cities have 50–70 percent of their populations living outside the city proper. In one extreme example, the City of Chongqing has a total population of 32.3 million in its city region, twice as large as the populations of Beijing and Shanghai. However, only 15 million of its inhabitants live in the city proper. Several other regional cities, including Linyi (in Shandong Province), Nanyang (in Henan), Baoding (in Hebei), and Zhoukou (also in Henan), have populations of more than 10 million in their respective city regions, but only 10–25 percent of them live in the city proper. The decision to use statistics for the city proper, however, should not diminish the importance of the urban markets: after all, 42 of the 287 cities have more than 2 million people living in their city proper; another 81 have populations between one and two million people, and 109 others have more than half a million, living in their city proper.

Figure 2.2 illustrates the rank-size relationship among the 287 cities on the basis of their population size. Instead of showing a regular rank-size relationship in the form of a straight line (with city rank shown on the x-axis and population shown on the y-axis), the relationship of the Chinese urban system shows a downward curvilinear pattern, known in the urban geography literature as a "primate city-size distribution" (Jefferson, 1939; Berry, 1961; Haggett, 1965). That is, a few very large cities (particularly Chongqing, Beijing, and Shanghai) dominate all other cities. A sound and comprehensive explanation of the conditions associated with such a distribution does not exist (Hartshorn, 1992). However, several generalizations were suggested by Berry (1961) as possible explanations, according to which, the primate city-size distribution typically occurs in less developed countries with a shorter history of urbanization. This suggestion seems to fit the China situation, where the history of urbanization has been relatively short, except in the capital city of Beijing and in the colonial cities of Shanghai, Tianjin, and Guangzhou. The "primate city-size distribution" also suggests that the small number of large cities is likely to form single-case clusters, with a large number of smaller cities lumping in one huge cluster.

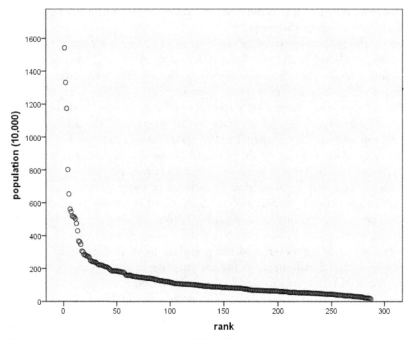

Figure 2.2 Rank-size relationship of the Chinese cities.
(This distribution suggests that the small number of large cities is likely to form single-case clusters, with a large number of smaller cities lumping in one huge cluster.)

As the correlation coefficients in Table 2.4 show, retail sales in the 287 cities are highly correlated with all variables, except population density. This suggests that the choices of variables are appropriate for classifying the Chinese cities for the study of retail geography.

K-means cluster analysis is performed to classify the 287 cities into different clusters, or tiers, on the basis of similarities and dissimilarities in the nine chosen variables. The details of the classification procedure are explained in Appendix 1. All 287 cities are grouped into five tiers for the purpose of this study. Fifteen cities could not be classified due to missing data in at least one of the nine variables. These include the provincial capitals of Harbin, Wuhan, Chongqing, Xian, and Lhasa.[2] They are assigned to the closest cluster by visually inspecting the attributes for which data are available. The five tiers are labeled as mega urban markets, Tier 1, Tier 2, Tier 3, and Tier 4 (see Table 2.5).

As Table 2.6 shows, the market size and conditions vary significantly among the different tiers, revealing conspicuous regional variations in China. In general, the market size and the size of the retail economy decrease progressively from the mega urban markets and Tier-1 cities down to the lower-tier cities. However, within each tier, some attributes also exhibit wide ranges. These within-tier variations have resulted from the multivariate classification exercise, as cities in each cluster are differentiated from others by distances between their cluster centers.

Table 2.5 City Tiers

Tier	Member cities
Mega urban market(5 cities)	Beijing[1]; Shanghai[1]; Guangzhou[2,3]; Shenzhen[3,4]; Tianjin[1]
Tier 1 (18 cities)	Changchun[2,3]; Changsha[2]; Chongqing[1,*]; Chengdu[2,3]; Dalian[3]; Dongguan; Foshan*; Hangzhou[2,3]; Harbin[2,3,*]; Jinan[2,3]; Nanjing[2,3]; Ningbo[3]; Qingdao[3]; Suzhou; Shenyang[2,3]; Wuhan[2,3,*]; Wuxi; Xian[2,3,*]
Tier 2 (30 cities)	Anshan; Baotou; Changzhou; Daqing; Dongying; Fuzhou[2]; Hefei[2]; Hohot[2]; Huizhou; Jilin; Kunming[2]; Lanzhou[2]; Linyi; Nanchang[2]; Nanning[2]; Nantong; Shantou[4]; Shijiazhuang[2]; Taiyuan[2]; Tangshan; Urumqi[2]; Wenzhou; Xiamen[3,4]; Xuzhou; Yangzhou; Yantai; Zibo; Zhengzhou[2]; Zhongshan; Zhuhai[4]
Tier 3 (59 cities)	Guiyang[2]; Haikou[2]; Yinchuan[2] (See Appendix 2 for others)
Tier 4 (175 cities)	Guilin; Lhasa[2*]; Lijiang; Sanya; Zhangjiajie (See Appendix 2 for others)

[1]. provincial-level city; [2]. provincial capital; [3]. sub-provincial city; [4]. Special Economic Zone; * with missing data

Table 2.6 Market Conditions of Different City Tiers

Attributes	Mean and Range				
	Mega	Tier 1	Tier 2	Tier 3	Tier 4
Total population (10, 000)	842.0 246–1,332	438 179–1,543	201.7 83.3–503.4	118.2 25.3–274.5	74.0 15.3–204.2
Population density (person/km²)	1,514 964–2,583	1,543 592–3,606	1,315 243–5,324	1,090 <100–3,405	805 <100–4,554
GDP (billion yuan)	1,010.0 703.0–1,487.6	319.8 205.3–489.2	128.7 76.8–192.9	50.3 12.2–74.1	17.7 2.7–35.0
Retail sales (billion yuan)	327.5 227.9–521.2	130.0 76.2–196.9	51.3 20.7–97.1	17.8 1.7–36.6	7.1 0.5–28.7
Total wage (billion yuan)	160.7 78.7–318.3	31.5 9.5–66.6	13.9 5.1–27.2	5.8 2.0–15.5	2.3 0.4–9.9
Average wage (1,000 yuan)	53.0 45.2–63.5	39.6 31.5–45.1	35.2 25.5–44.3	31.3 20.9–47.0	26.7 12.7–43.2
Cell phone subscription (million)	17.4 9.9–21.1	7.0 3.5–14.1	2.8 0.3–5.2	1.1 0.1–3.1	0.5 0.1–1.2
Internet subscription (million)	5.6 2.5–12.5	1.1 0.6–2.0	0.53 <0.1–1.9	0.2 <0.1–4.5	0.1 <0.1–3.5
Number of buses (1,000)	16.0 7.9–25.3	4.9 1.4–8.1	2.1 0.6–5.3	0.8 0.1–2.5	0.4 <0.1–1.8

The five mega urban markets of Beijing, Shanghai, Tianjin, Guangzhou, and Shenzhen have the largest populations, with an average of 8.4 million people living in their city proper. Both Beijing and Shanghai have more than 10 million residents. These cities also command the highest levels of GDP and retail sales, particularly Beijing and Shanghai. Although Shenzhen has a population of only 2.5 million, the smallest of the five, both its GDP and retail sales are larger than those of Tianjin, meriting its inclusion in this elite group.

Coincidently, the same five cities were chosen by Sun (1997) as China's leading consumer markets in his study of 15 years ago. Indeed, no cities in any other tier have achieved retail sales higher than the lowest of the mega urban markets (which is 228 billion yuan). The very high retail sales in the mega markets should be attributed to the high levels of wages and the various facilitating factors. Both total wage and average wage in the five mega urban markets are much higher than in any other city. On average, there are twice as many cell phone users in these five cities as those in the Tier 1 cities, and there are five times as many internet subscribers. In addition to the large number of buses, these cities are known for high automobile ownership. All five cities also have extensive subway/LRT networks. By the end of 2010, Beijing had 330 km of subway/LRT track in operation; Shanghai, 410 km; Guangzhou, 220 km; Tianjin, 72 km; and Shenzhen, 60 km. The expanded transportation network has also created many accessible locations for construction of large retail facilities, adjacent to subway stations.

Eleven of the 18 Tier 1 cities are provincial capitals, including the provincial-level city of Chongqing. Twelve of them, including nine provincial capitals, hold "sub-provincial" status with a high level of autonomy in economic planning—a status higher than ordinary provincial capitals. These cities also have very favorable market conditions. The average population is 4.4 million, with the highest being Chongqing's 15 million residents. Both total wage and average wage are much higher than those in the lower-tier cities, with average wage close to 40,000 yuan per year. Similarly, the numbers of cell phone and internet subscribers are much higher in the Tier-1 cities than in cities of the lower tiers. In addition to the relatively large number of buses, two of these cities, Chengdu and Shenyang, already have subway lines in operation, and another 13 have subway lines under construction.

Although Chongqing's population is larger than that of Beijing and Shanghai, it is placed in Tier 1 because its GDP, retail sales, and the numbers of internet subscribers and city buses are all smaller than the lower bound of the respective ranges for the mega urban markets. Dongguan in Guangdong Province is the smallest Tier 1 city with a population of only 1.8 million. It is pushed into this tier mainly because of its high GDP and retail sales volume. The average wage in Dongguan stands at 42,600 yuan, ranking fifth among the 18 Tier 1 cities. Similarly, Guangdong's Foshan City has a much higher GDP and higher retail sales than the group average, making it a Tier 1 city as well. It should be noted that the Tier 1 cities are not limited to the eastern coastal provinces. There are five of them in central China and two in northeast China (see Figure 2.3).

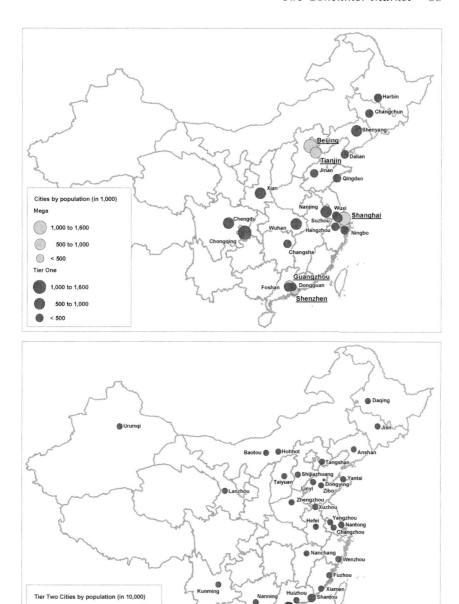

Figure 2.3 Geographical distribution of mega urban markets and Tier 1 and Tier 2 cities.

(The map on the top shows the mega urban markets and Tier 1 cities; the map at the bottom shows the Tier 2 cities.)

Thirty cities are classified as Tier 2 urban markets. This group includes 11 provincial capitals and three SEZs (Xiamen, Shantou, and Zhuhai). Most other Tier 2 cities are regional urban centers with relatively high levels of economic development. Except for the interior provincial capitals, a large number of cities in this group are situated in three coastal provinces— Shandong, Zhejiang, and Guangdong—with four in each province. This reflects high levels of economic development in these provinces and the coastal region in general (Figure 2.3). The market conditions of the Tier 2 cities are not as favorable as those of the Tier 1 cities. Their average population size and retail sales, 2 million and 50 billion yuan respectively, are both half of those of Tier 1 cities, indicating much weaker total purchasing powers. Largely due to their smaller populations, these cities also have much smaller numbers of cell phone and internet subscribers. Of the 30 cities in this group, none has subway trains in operation, and only six of them (Fuzhou, Xiamen, Changzhou, Zhengzhou, Nanchang, and Nanning) are constructing subway lines. Still, their market conditions are distinctly superior to those of the Tier 3 and Tier 4 cities: their average population size, GDP, and retail sales are all twice as large as those of the Tier 3 and Tier 4 cities (see Table 2.6).

The Tier 3 and Tier 4 cities are mostly smaller municipalities of regional importance, with only four provincial capitals (Guiyang, Haikou and Yinchuan in Tier 3, and Lhasa in Tier 4). Accordingly, they have a much smaller population size and much lower GDP values and retail sales. None of them have subways in operation or even under construction. Of the 59 Tier 3 cities, only 36 have populations of 1 million or more. Among the smallest are Xinjiang's Karmay and Inner Mongolia's Eerduosi, both with less than 400,000 people living in their city proper. It should be noted that the Tier 4 cities include several popular tourist destinations, such as Sanya, Guilin, Lijiang, and Zhangjiajie. These cities may bring in considerable numbers of tourists, who contribute to local retail sales. (For the complete membership of the Tier 3 and Tier 4 cities, see Appendix 2.) Despite their lower status in the urban hierarchy, these smaller cities should not be neglected by the international retailers. After all, most Tier 4 cities still have more consumers than some major urban centers in North America and Western Europe. Their small market size may currently limit their ability to attract FDI. As income increases further, however, demand for consumer goods will multiply.

In a final note, Chinese cities are not necessarily locked into the same tier for a long time. Their status may change over time, even in the near future.

3 Building a Modern Regulatory Regime

Regulation is an important part of the modern retail environment, and is a significant force "shaping competition between firms, the governance of investment, the use of labor, and the overall extraction of profit from retailing of goods" (Lowe & Wrigley, 1996, p. 13). Further, the regulatory environment varies greatly, or is in various stages of development, from country to country. As explained in Chapter 1, in the Western capitalist economies, retailing is largely a private sector, and both retail corporations and individual entrepreneurs enjoy a high degree of freedom in business decision making. Nonetheless, governments do intervene in the retail industry with regulatory measures, as generalized by Dawson (1980).

In the former socialist countries characterized by a centrally planned economy, retail, like all other economic sectors, was typically a public enterprise. With all retail operations being owned by the state, public intervention in the form of regulations was considered irrelevant and therefore did not exist. After these countries embarked on economic reform, moving toward a market-driven economy through privatization of state enterprises, they began to feel the consequences of the policy void: chaotic development, unfair competition, misleading marketing, and deceptive sales practices. Additional effects were brought about by international retailers after these countries opened up their domestic market to FDI and allowed foreign retailers to set up business operations. Dawson (2003) summarizes the following types of impact that are often caused by international retailers: (1) new changes in competitive structure within the retail sector, which may lead to merger and acquisition of domestic retailers; (2) social and cultural influences on consumer behavior and the process of consumption; (3) changes in relationships between retailers and supply chains; and (4) challenges to existing regulatory systems. The compound effects of these impacts can be enormous for a host country to cope with.

Before the launch of economic reform in 1978, China virtually had no rules and laws regulating the retail sector. The only law, which was enshrined in the Constitution, was the prohibition of private ownership and operation of retail stores. Since the economic reform began, China has made considerable progress in building a modern regulatory system congruent with a market economy. While an affluent consumer market is a necessary condition for sustained retail growth and since urban development opens up new consumption spaces, it is the implementation of reformative policies and progressive changes in the role of the regulatory state that has been the driving force for the transformation of China's retail economy. In other words, deregulation accounts for much of the retail liberalization, privatization, and internationalization in China.

A series of policies were developed progressively to achieve five purposes: to diversify retail ownership; to open up the domestic market to foreign retailers but maintain conventional barriers; to continue restraining the entry and expansion of foreign retailers after China's admission to the WTO, but with new forms of regulations; to balance the retailer-supplier relations; and to regulate internet retailing and build up consumer confidence. The emerging regulatory system now covers almost every aspect of retailing, from location restrictions and price control to competition, business efficiency, and consumer protection.

This chapter reconstructs the evolution of the contemporary regulatory state of China. Specifically, the chapter examines and interprets the major policy developments in the regulatory regime, which have defined the competitive space for retail capital and shaped China's new retail economy in significant ways. The policy initiatives before 2004 can be called *deregulation*; those introduced and implemented after 2004, when China became a "full" member of the WTO, are more appropriately described as *re-regulation*.

RETAIL DEREGULATION (1978–2004)

Ownership Reform

In essence, ownership reform was the most fundamental catalyst for China's retail transformation. Shortly after 1949, the communist government of China began to establish a state-owned distribution system. Initially, the old capitalist modes of ownership (such as private and family-run businesses) were permitted to coexist with the newly established state-owned enterprises. But beginning in 1952, the state government quickly moved to reform all non-state-owned businesses and forced them to form cooperatives, either in partnership with state enterprises, or among themselves to be called 'collectives.' Within five years, all capitalist modes of distribution were virtually eliminated. This policy became most extreme during the Cultural Revolution (1966–1977), when the state government declared the collectively-owned cooperatives an alternative form of public ownership but banned all country fairs and urban markets throughout the country.

After 1978, but particularly after 1992, a series of policy changes were instituted by the state government and retail deregulation began to occur (Sun, 1997, 2002; Wang & Jones, 2001, 2002). As the very first step, the state government permitted (re)entry of individual retailers in the distribution system and reintroduced retail marketplaces in cities and rural areas as fundamental parts of the distribution system. As a result, family-owned and individually-run retail establishments mushroomed all over the country.[1] In addition to providing self-employment for the store owners themselves, the reemergence and proliferation of private retail ownership helped to expand the coverage of the commodity distribution system in the country, and resulted in convenience shopping for both urban and rural consumers. In the meantime, the state government began to gradually withdraw from its direct involvement in the retail sector, gave up its monopoly in procurement of commodities, and relaxed price control. In the four years between 1979 and 1983, the number of state-regulated agricultural products was reduced from 46 to 21, and the number of state-controlled manufactured consumer goods was reduced from 136 to 26 (Wan, 1999).

The next significant policy initiatives were taken in 1984 with three major changes (Wan, 1999). First, both farmers and manufacturers were allowed to set their own prices for the commodities that were no longer under state regulation, moving toward a market-driven system. This provided incentives to producers to increase production, variety, and quality, which in turn improved the supply of consumer goods in retail stores. It also gave retailers the much needed autonomy and freedom in fundamental business decision making. Second, the state government eliminated the state-dictated three-level wholesale distribution system, to greatly shorten the channels linking producers, wholesalers, and retailers. Third, many small state-owned stores were either contracted or sold to private operators (either individual operators or groups of individuals), who were obligated to pay a portion of their profit to the government, but were responsible for their own business losses. This was similar to the responsibility system initiated in rural China in the late 1970s and subsequently endorsed by the state government in 1982.

In December 1993, at its 5th Plenary Meeting, the Standing Committee of the 8th People's Congress passed the Company Law of the People's Republic of China, which both encouraged and legitimized the transformation of large and medium-sized, state-owned retail enterprises into joint-stock companies. In order to take advantage of the favorable political environment created by the state deregulations, many local governments wasted no time and spared no effort in reforming their obsolete retail system. In 1993 alone, the government of Shanghai made a number of significant changes, including a comprehensive ownership reform of state- and collectively-owned retail enterprises (Shanghai strives to become an international city of commerce", 1994). Specifically, it granted autonomy in business decision making to 700 or so large and medium-sized enterprises, and either sold or contracted all small retail stores to private operators. It also authorized the formation of 19 joint-stock retail companies.

Opening up the Domestic Market to Overseas Retailers

After the economic reform began to bring improved income to its ordinary citizens in the mid-1980s, China became a dream market for international retailers. However, China did not allow foreign retail operations, either as sole foreign ownership or in joint ventures, until 1992. This was nearly 10 years after its manufacturing and agricultural sectors were opened to foreign direct investment. Since then, China has made a series of policy changes to open up its consumer market to international retailers. The entire process is marked by four distinctive phases of retail deregulation.

Phase One: 1992–1995

In July 1992, China designated six cities and five Special Economic Zones (SEZ) to open to overseas retail investment for experiment. The six designated cities were Beijing, Shanghai, Tianjin, Guangzhou, Dalian, and Qingdao (four would become mega urban markets and two would become Tier 1 cities, as classified in Chapter 2). The five SEZs were Shenzhen, Zhuhai, Shantou, Xiamen, and Hainan, all located in the eastern coastal region. Overseas retailers were differentiated into two categories: retailers from foreign countries and those known as overseas Chinese-invested enterprises based in Hong Kong and Taiwan. The latter were, and still are, treated by the Chinese government as de facto foreign investment, and governed by the same regulations and laws that apply to the former, even though Hong Kong, Taiwan, and Macau are all claimed by the state government as territories of China.

To control the experiment process effectively, the Chinese government cautiously imposed a series of restrictions on the entry and operation of foreign retailers, ranging from geographical limitations to restrictions on capital participation, business format, and sourcing (Editorial Board of *Science and Technology Think Tank*, 1997). For example, only the 11 designated cities and SEZs were allowed to participate in the experiment, and each of them was permitted to host only one or two overseas retailers. The entry of foreign retailers had to be approved by the state government; local governments were prohibited from admitting foreign retailers independently. Approved foreign retailers had to operate in joint ventures with at least one Chinese partner; whole foreign ownership was prohibited. In joint ventures, foreign investors' stakes had to be less than 50 percent. With regard to format, joint ventures were strictly limited to single-store retailing; retail chains and wholesaling were prohibited. While foreign retailers were allowed to import certain types of merchandise for retailing, total import could not exceed 30 percent of their total sales, meaning that at least 70 percent of the merchandise had to be purchased from domestic manufacturers and suppliers.

With the designation of the 11 cities and SEZs for experiment, the state government approved 15 foreign retailers to establish joint ventures in China (Beijing Intelligence Tapping and Management Consulting Ltd., 1997b). Wang & Jones, 2001). These first 15 joint ventures were all department stores, which were what China had to offer at that time to form joint ventures with overseas capital. This initial opening up enjoyed only limited success. The 15 joint ventures were not necessarily the retailers most wanted by China. The majority were Asian-based retailers from Hong Kong, Japan, Malaysia, Singapore, and Thailand. Domestic industry leaders contended that what China really needed were the large retail corporations from North America and Western Europe, and that the selection of the first 15 overseas retailers simply wasted the government quotas.

Phase Two: 1995–1999

In October 1995, the state government took the second step to open its retail sector, but only slightly wider. This time, it authorized Beijing to experiment with expanding joint ventures from single store operations to retail chains. It also allowed the expansion of foreign participation from retailing to wholesaling, and from general merchandise to food products. Two international retailers were subsequently approved to form chains in Beijing. The first linked Japan's Ito-Yokado to the China Sugar-Liquor Corporation, while the second linked the Netherlands' Makro to China Native Products Import/Export Corp. Both Chinese partners were directly affiliated with government ministries: Interior Trade and Foreign Trade, respectively.

As a measure of precaution, the state government still insisted that partnership with Chinese retailers was mandatory, and that the Chinese partners must have a controlling ownership. In addition, the length of the business contract was limited to 30 years or less.

Overseas retailers wanted to enter the Chinese market due to its large size and business potential. Conversely, Chinese retailers were eager to form a partnership with foreign retailers to access capital, technology, marketing and merchandising expertise, and high-quality goods. Despite strict government controls, the number of overseas-invested retailers in China increased rapidly. According to government official statistics, there existed a total of 1,697 foreign-invested and 1,088 overseas, Chinese-invested, retail stores in China in 1996 (National Bureau of Statistics of China, 1997).

How did so many overseas retailers bypass government regulatory barriers and gain entry in this highly protected market? According to various reports, the penetration of overseas retailers took a number of different routes. Many municipal and provincial governments were not content with the slow pace of opening up and the restrictions imposed by the state government. Some, including Beijing and Shanghai, took the liberty of approving foreign investors independently. Things progressed to a point that the state government had to issue an urgent circular to reiterate that local governments had no authority to approve any joint ventures in retailing ("Local governments are prohibited from approving foreign invested retail enterprises", 1997). Interestingly, the state government did not take punitive actions against the local governments that approved joint ventures for their own jurisdictions. To save face, the State Planning Commission, Ministry of Foreign Trade, Ministry of Interior Trade, and State Bureau of Industry and Commerce Administration joined forces to scrutinize 277 joint retail ventures that did not have state approval. Consequently, 41 were ordered to close; 42 were given state approval retroactively; and 194 were told to "reorganize" while waiting for after-the-fact approval (Government of Beijing, 1999).

Phase Three: 1999–2004

To speed up its negotiations with the WTO, the state government in June 1999 made its third major move with further and more significant deregulations (State Economic and Trade Commission & Ministry of Foreign Trade, 1999; "China further opens its circulation sector", 1999). The experiment was expanded geographically to include all provincial capitals and those municipalities that were designated to be independent of their province in economic planning (most of which later became sub-provincial cities). Sole foreign ownership was still prohibited, but majority foreign ownership was allowed in retail chains that would purchase large quantities of domestically made products and export these products through their own distribution channels, as a relaxation of restrictions on foreign ownership. While all joint ventures were allowed to engage in wholesaling as well as retailing, more stringent criteria were set forth for the selection of foreign retailers and Chinese partners (Wang, 2003). In correspondence with the country's newly-devised national strategy of "Developing the West," preferential treatment was offered to those joint ventures that were willing to set up business operations in Western China.

Evidently, the new policies aimed at raising the entry bar and selecting only large international retailers as future entrants. These policies were expected to bring to China its much needed capital, information technology, merchandising techniques, and managerial know-how. At the same time, the new policies were meant to ensure that only the large domestic retailers that had adequate resources and experience would become partners. This would also raise the level of participation by the Chinese retailers in business decision making, so that their role in joint ventures would not be reduced to a liaison or messenger between the foreign retailer and the government.

Phase Four: 2004

After 15 years of prolonged negotiation and numerous concessions, China was finally admitted to the WTO in December 2001. However, it was given a three-year "grace period" to gradually remove all trade barriers to FDI. In April 2004, as the three-year "grace period" was about to end, the state government announced further policy changes with regard to the participation of FDI in commercial sectors including retailing, marking the end of the 12-year-long experiment. The new policies, released by the Ministry of Commerce in its Document No. 8 titled *Regulations on Foreign-Invested Enterprises in Commercial Sectors* (Ministry of Commerce, 2004a), lifted virtually all remaining restrictions and promised a fully-open retail market to international retailers for fair competition. The key points of the new policies are highlighted as the following:

- With the exception of solely foreign-owned enterprise and the foreign-controlled large joint ventures,[2] provincial governments are delegated the autonomy to approve future entrants and opening of new retail outlets in their respective jurisdictions.
- The life span of business contracts for foreign-invested enterprises is limited to 30 years (or 40 years if the business operation is set up in Western China).
- Business plans of foreign-invested enterprises must conform to the local municipal plan and to the commercial activity development plan of the host city. Land for building new business premises must be obtained through public bidding on the land market in a transparent process.
- Foreign-invested enterprises must agree to accept annual inspections with audited financial reports. Those that fail to pass the inspections will not be allowed to open new stores, or may be ordered to close their existing operations.
- The above policies apply equally to retailers and investors from Hong Kong, Macau, and Taiwan.

These policy changes had several important implications. Domestic retailers, large and small, from the eastern coastal region to the western interior, were fully exposed to foreign competition, and were pressured to improve operating efficiency, product quality, and customer services. In other words, they had to learn how to "dance with wolf" in order to survive. For the first time, regulatory powers became decentralized and shared with provincial and municipal governments. Specifically, provincial governments were permitted to approve foreign-invested retail enterprises and outlets (up to a certain limit), and municipal governments were given the responsibility of making commercial activity plans. A vertically-integrated and power-sharing regulatory system was in the making. Through offering incentives, the state government hoped to direct more FDI to the interior west as part of the country's new geo-strategy to address the long-standing issue of regional inequality.

These policies were particularly welcomed by the big international chains, whose operations expanded rapidly through both organic growth (i.e., opening of new stores) and acquisition of existing retailors, posing new challenges to the emerging Chinese regulatory system. With the removal of unconventional barriers, China began to shift to regulating foreign retailers by legal means commonly acceptable to the WTO members, as alluded to in the aforementioned 2004 policies.

RETAIL RE-REGULATION (2004 AND AFTER)

The policies implemented before China's admission to the WTO were mainly dictated and imposed by the state. Local governments were given little autonomy and had little to say in the regulation-making process. For a less developed country like China with a weak retail economy, the initial protective policies were necessary, as they provided breathing time for the domestic retailers to absorb the impacts while transforming themselves into modern enterprises. The removal of the unconventional trade barriers after China's admission to the WTO, however, was by no means to eradicate the need for regulations. Rather, it meant that China had to shift to other forms of regulation that were less likely to be challenged and disputed by the member countries of the WTO. Indeed, what appeared initially to be deregulation was in reality merely a changing form of regulation (Marsden & Wrigley, 1996).

Regulating Retailing Through Land Use Planning

Rapid expansion of foreign operations and the reactions of domestic retailers to their increased presence inevitably led to intensified competition and chaotic developments. The battlegrounds were spreading to the second- and even third-tier cities, and the state government realized that conflicts and issues are better handled by the municipal governments, while the state government retains the highest level of control. To establish a legal framework and empower local governments to regulate retail developments, the Ministry of Commerce issued two related documents in 2004. The first (Document No. 180 of 2004) provides guidelines for preparation of municipal plans for commercial activity development (Ministry of Commerce, 2004b). Specifically, the document requires that (1) each municipality prepare its own commercial activity development plan and related land use bylaws that are in conformation with the municipal General Plan; (2) the plan explicitly specify the retail structure, total amount of supply, projected scales, and spatial distribution, in consistency with the city's market size; and (3) the plan ensure harmonious coexistence of large and small retailers. The second document (Document No. 390 of 2004), a companion to the first, provides standard definitions of the various retail formats and types of facilities (Ministry of Commerce, 2004c). Municipalities across the country are expected to follow these definitions when preparing their own commercial activity development plan and when approving future development proposals.

These guidelines were fairly broad, but they represent a significant policy shift toward institutionalizing retail development with legal means. The stated purpose is to rationalize the retail network by achieving optimal business structure, spatial distribution, and development scale relative to the local market size, thus avoiding overdevelopment and waste of economic resources. The unstated purpose is for the state government to use these planning tools to limit future entry and expansion of foreign retailers in the already congested urban markets, and encourage them to set up stores in smaller cities.

The state government was therefore very serious about the implementation of these policies and insisted that municipalities complete their plans on time, because without such plans in place, the ability of the state government to regulate future entry and expansion of foreign retailers would be limited. Unhappy with the slow pace of implementation, the Ministry of Commerce issued a second document in 2005 to reiterate the importance and urgency of commercial activity planning (Ministry of Commerce, 2005a). In this document, the state government required that all municipalities spare no effort to complete their plan by the end of 2005. Where a municipal government lacked expertise, external consultants should be brought in to do the job—but the municipal government was expected to foot the bill. It also required that provincial governments assume the responsibility of monitoring the progress in their own jurisdictions.

With no previous experience and a lack of financial resources, many municipalities found it difficult to deliver the plan by the deadline. In 2006, the Ministry of Commerce issued yet another circular. This time, it even named the municipalities that either had not started the process or were making slow progress, and demanded that they submit their plans within one month from receiving the circular (Ministry of Commerce, 2006a). This was not only an ultimatum, but also a public humiliation, for the local officials. More seriously, it warns that the Ministry of Commerce and its provincial counterparts would not approve any foreign business applications in the cities that do not have a plan approved yet—an implicit confirmation of the unstated purpose of the new policies.

The implementation of the commercial activity plan needed the support of other measures. One of these measures was the introduction of a public hearing as part of the approval process to be implemented at the municipal level. Shanghai was the first municipality to institutionalize the public hearing in the form of a bylaw (Shanghai Commission of Commerce & Shanghai Commission of Economic Development and Planning, 2001); it was ahead of the game, as the bylaw was adopted three years before the state called for such regulations. According to the bylaw, all developers of future hypermarkets (10,000 m² or larger; most foreign operations were in this category at that time) had to go through this process. The Shanghai Association of Retail Chains was delegated the authority to preside over such hearings; pertinent government officials, industry leaders, interested retailers, and representatives of the affected communities were invited to comment on the business proposal.

The public hearing is a democratic exercise common in most Western cities, but the Shanghai bylaw has at least three fundamental differences. First, public hearings are presided over by a business association, instead of the municipal planning authority. Second, the general public cannot attend these public hearings freely; only "selected representatives" are admitted to such meetings. As well, attendants at these meetings must keep business "secrets" in confidence, and cannot share meeting discussions with others who are not at the meetings, thus depriving the general public of the opportunity to be informed about the development plan. Third, the Adjudication Committee decision is final; there is no mechanism for appeal. This is in striking contrast to the practice in North American cities. In the City of Toronto in Canada, for example, public hearings are advertised in local newspapers to notify the entire community. Both individuals and incorporated groups are invited to such meetings and can make their views known regarding a development proposal. If an individual or incorporated group has filed an appeal of a decision of the City Council (through either oral submissions at the public meeting or written submissions before the meeting), but the city, after the public meeting, still adopts the zoning bylaw amendments to accommodate the development proposal, an appeal can be made to a provincial adjudication panel—the Ontario Municipal Board.

Evidence shows that even the Municipal Government of Shanghai itself has not implemented the bylaw wholeheartedly. According to a report (Guo, 2006), Shanghai held only seven to eight public hearings between 2001 and 2006, and all the business proposals heard at these meetings were from foreign retailers for new development of hypermarkets. It should be noted that the public hearing in Shanghai was applied to hypermarkets only, which was the most contested market by foreign retailers. Development of shopping centers was exempted, even though they were much larger than typical hypermarket. The 10th Five-Year Plan for Commercial Activity Development in Shanghai (announced in 2000) called to cap the number of hypermarkets at 60 for the entire city, including suburbs, but by the end of 2004, the actual number had already reached 249 (Shanghai Economic Commission, 2005).

Preventing Foreign Monopoly

The battle among foreign retailers for a bigger share of the Chinese market had also heated up. The French Carrefour withdrew from Japan (in 2005) and South Korea (in 2006) to focus on China (Chen, 2006). Wal-Mart gave up its interest in South Korea (in 2006) to concentrate on the China market. Tesco sold it business interest in Taiwan to Carrefour in 2005 to focus on its growth in mainland China. During an interview in 2007, Terrence Cullen, vice president of Wal-Mart's China operation, disclosed that Wal-Mart planned to more than double its stores in China in the next five years and aimed to garner 20 percent of China's retail market ("Wal-Mart to double outlets in China," 2005). In the meantime, a number of foreign retailers were moving toward "independence" in an effort to consolidate their resources and decision-making power (Zhen et al., 2005; Ma, 2006). In 2005, Carrefour formed a wholly-owned subsidiary in Haikou of Hainan Province; it also bought out its Chinese partners in Kunming, Urumqi, and Changsha. In the same year, the German Metro increased its China ownership from 60 to 90 percent. Similarly, the Thai-based Lotus opened its first wholly-owned store in Jinan, and bought out its Chinese partners in Beijing, Tianjin, and Shanghai. It is important to note that mergers among overseas retailers began to occur as well. The French Auchan teamed up with the Taiwanese RT-Mart by exchanging one third of ownership in their respective China operations in 2000 (Gu, 2006). The British Tesco entered a joint venture agreement with the Taiwanese Hymart in 2004 by acquiring 50 percent of the latter ("British supermarket giant Tesco lands in China", 2004). Its share of ownership increased to 90 percent in 2006 (*China Chain Store Association, 2007*). Similarly, Wal-Mart in 2006 acquired 35 percent of the ownership of Trust-Mart—another Taiwanese retail chain. In the same year, the American Best Buy and Home Depot both entered China through acquisition of domestic retailers: the former acquired a 56 percent ownership of Five Star Electronics; the latter acquired the entire ownership of Home World—a home furnishing and building material retailer. It was anticipated that a new wave of merger-and acquisition-driven consolidation would take place in China's retail sector in the next 5–10 years—a phenomenon that happened in many other countries in the late 1990s (Currah & Wrigley, 2004). Foreign retailers, especially the Western retailers, were poised to become powerful players, reshaping the corporate and physical landscape of retailing in China.

To prevent foreign monopoly, the Ministry of Commerce issued *Regulations on Foreign Merger and Acquisition of Enterprises in China* in 2006. While not retail specific, these policies apply equally to retailing. According to the regulations, the foreign retailer (or investors), if planning to acquire or merge with a domestic Chinese enterprise, must in any of the following circumstances apply to both the Ministry of Commerce and the National Bureau of Industry and Commerce Administration for approval (Ministry of Commerce, 2006b):

- the foreign retailer's gross sales exceed 1.5 billion yuan in the year of application;
- the foreign retailer has already merged more than 10 domestic retailers (large and small) within one year;

- the foreign retailer's market share in China has reached or exceeded 20 percent;
- the foreign retailer's market share in China will reach or exceed 25 percent after the proposed merger or acquisition.

Similar regulations were announced for acquisition and mergers among foreign retailers that have business operations in China. Specifically, the regulations stipulate that foreign investors (including retailers) must also apply to the Ministry of Commerce and the National Bureau of Industry and Commerce Administration for approval if:

- the acquirer owns capital assets of 3 billion yuan or more in China;
- the acquirer's gross sales in China exceed 1.5 billion yuan in the year of application;
- the acquirer's market share in China has already reached or exceeded 20 percent;
- after acquisition or merger, the foreign retailer's market share in China will be 25 percent or higher;
- after acquisition or merger, the foreign retailer and the business entity, of which the acquirer is a shareholder, will have more than 15 enterprises.

The Ministry of Commerce and the National Bureau of Industry and Commerce Administration will then hold, within 90 days of receiving the application, a public hearing meeting to be attended by "relevant government agencies, affected enterprises, and other interest groups" (Ministry of Commerce, 2006b). Depending on the consultation results, the state government can either approve or reject the merger or acquisition application.

Most other countries have such regulations, but the Chinese regulations seem to be stricter than those in other countries. For instance, the Canadian federal government's Bureau of Competition Policy, whose power derives from the *Competition Act*, has set up a series of internal criteria for retail competition and mergers. All mergers involving "significant retailers" (defined as holding 10 percent or more of a market) must be approved by the Bureau, and the approval process permits a variety of competitors, consumer groups, and labor unions to raise questions about the merger implications. However, undue concentration in Canada is defined as a post-merger market share greater than 35 percent (Competition Bureau of Canada, 2004), which is 10 percent higher (or looser) than the Chinese regulations.

Regulating Retailer-Supplier and Retailer-Consumer Relations

From the beginning, foreign retailers brought about, along with retail capital, unfamiliar business practices to China, including new forms of relationships with suppliers and new marketing methods. Under the planned economy, there had never been conflicts between retailers and suppliers, as retailers were simply supplied by state-owned and designated wholesalers, and sold whatever they were supplied with (Sun, 1997, 2002). They had no need, nor bargaining power, to negotiate with suppliers for better prices. Foreign retailers, however, deal with suppliers very differently and rather aggressively. They not only push suppliers to the very limit in accepting low purchase prices due to their considerable purchase leverage (Lowe & Wrigley, 1996), but also dictate product specifications to the suppliers (Hughes, 1996, p. 106). They also levy a variety of fees that never existed in China before. These fees were charged for selling a product in their store, product promotion, and merchandise display (which varies depending on shelf prominence inside the retail store). Some foreign retailers even demanded suppliers to send their own employees to work in the retail stores to help promote their own products, but at the supplier's expense. Carrefour was the most notorious for charging such fees. These practices were quickly copied and adopted by domestic retailers.

Some retailers abused their powers to delay payments to suppliers. In other words, they were supplied on credit and took the advantage of "operating on negative working capital cycles" (Wrigley, 1992). They often used the delayed payments to finance opening of new stores. In a number of cases where these retailers went bankrupt (intentionally or unintentionally), suppliers had to rush to the stores to grab whatever merchandise they could. This type of "merchandise repossessing" has caused violence, threatening both social and political stabilities. Pricemart (China) is a typical example. A franchisee of the American PEI (Price Enterprises Inc.), Pricemart (China) expanded aggressively and irregularly using "negative working capital cycles." In the nine-year period from 1996 to 2005, it opened 46 hypermarkets in 30 cities (Shi et al., 2005). In 2005, it suddenly went bankrupt, owing 800 million *yuan* (US$100 million) to thousands of suppliers and another 1.2 billion yuan (US$150 million) to banks.

In September 2005, four ministries and national bureaus—the Minstry of Commerce, the Ministry of Public Security, the State Bureau of Taxation, and the State Bureau of Industry and Commerce Administration—joined forces to announce the *Administrative Measures to Rectify Unethical and Unfair Dealings of Retailers with Suppliers* (Ministry of Commerce et al., 2005). One year later, in October 2006, the same ministries and bureaus, plus the State Commission of Economic Development and Reform, issued the *Regulations on Fair Trade between Retailers and Suppliers*, this time, in legal terms (Ministry of Commerce et al., 2006). According to the regulations, retailers are not permitted to use their purchasing powers to coerce suppliers into accepting unfair trade terms (including breaking of promises and alteration of contracts). Nor are retailers permitted to interfere with suppliers in conducting business with other retailers. Outstanding balances must be paid to suppliers within 60 days of receiving the merchandise. Further, retailers are not permitted to request suppliers to send workers to work in their stores, unless agreed upon by the suppliers. If workers from suppliers are needed to help promoting the suppliers' own products in retail stores, the retailer is responsible for the workers' compensation. Neither are retailers permitted to unilaterally charge suppliers for sponsoring grand openings of new stores, store-wide promotions, festival celebrations, and store renovations/decorations, unless the fees are used exclusively for promoting and selling the merchandise from the same suppliers. As for suppliers, the regulations prohibit them from forcing retailers to buy unwanted products, or restricting retailers from procuring from other suppliers. Clearly, the regulations aim mainly to regulate retailers and protect suppliers, and are necessitated by the shift of power away from suppliers to retailers.

Protection of consumers is also an important part of retail regulation making. In 2005, the same five ministries and bureaus issued regulations to prevent deceptive marketing practices often employed by retailers during merchandise promotion (Ministry of Commerce, 2005c; Ministry of Commerce et al., 2007). In principle, retailers are expected to abide by laws, assume social responsibilities, and respect the rights of consumers. Specifically, the regulations stipulate:

- when holding promotion sales, retailers must provide sufficient information regarding the terms of the promotion, including the types of merchandise included, the duration of the promotion, and the attached conditions;
- all promises must be honored, and all forms of advertisement and communications with consumers must use explicit language;
- merchandise on promotion must be of the same quality as before the promotion, and retailers must honor the same post-sale service and warranty; if the merchandise on promotion has defects, retailers must inform the consumers;
- Sufficient quantity should be made available during the promotion; if quantities are limited, the retailer must inform the consumers in their advertisements.

In another area of consumer protection, the state government has imposed a ban on "multi-level marketing (MLM)" in China. Also known as "network marketing," MLM is a business distribution model that allows a parent multi-level marketing company to market their products directly to consumers. Independent, unsalaried salespersons, referred to as distributors, represent the parent company and are rewarded a commission. Individual distributors develop their network by either building an active customer base or by recruiting a down line of distributors who also build a customer base to expand the overall network. Commissions are paid to distributors according to the company's compensation plan and relative to the volume of the product sold through the effort of each distributor. The U.S.-based Amway, arguably the largest multi-level marketing network in the world, entered China in the 1990s, but it has not been allowed to do business using the same model as it does in the United States. After many years of lobbying with the Chinese government, a compromise was reached in 2005, when the State Council issued two documents simultaneously. In the first, it reiterates China's position of prohibiting MLM in China (State Council, 2005a). In the second, it permits "direct marketing"—a modified form of network marketing with only one level of distributors, but requires that companies that sell consumer goods via direct marketing abide by the following regulations (State Council, 2005b):

- Direct marketing firms must have brick-and-mortar stores at fixed locations, where consumers can view merchandise samples and inquire about prices, and can get a refund if they wish to return the products.
- Individual distributors are limited to one layer, but the following groups of people cannot be recruited as distributors: youngsters under 18 years of age; full-time students; teachers; medical professionals; soldiers in active service; non-permanent residents of China.
- Direct marketing firms cannot enter a franchising relationship with individual distributors, and cannot ask distributors to pay a membership fee or buy a certain amount of products from the company; contracts can be cancelled within 60 days. After 60 days, cancellation is still allowed with 15 days of advanced notice; commission paid to distributors cannot exceed 35 percent of the sales achieved by the distributors.
- Direct marketing firms must pay a deposit of 20 to 100 million yuan to the government (as a bond); the money is to be used for resolving disputes between the company and the individual distributors, or between distributors and consumers.

EFFECTIVENESS OF THE MODERN REGULATORY REGIME

The competitive structure in China's retail market has been altered significantly since its admission to the WTO. So have the business behaviors of retailers and retailer-supplier relations. The various types of impacts that Dawson (2003) summarized have all been felt in China. A comprehensive regulatory system is needed not only for protecting domestic retailers, suppliers, and consumers, but also for maintaining China's economic sovereignty. In the meantime, power transfer, albeit limited, has taken place from the state to provincial and municipal governments.

The examination of the public policies in this chapter shows that most regulations are mimicked from those of the Western countries, but some of them apparently privilege the capital of domestic retailers. To make the domestic market internationally contestable, it is necessary for foreign retailers to receive "national treatment and right of establishment, and also for them not to be subject to discriminatory domestic policy in a variety of fields" (Rugman & Gestrin, 1997, p. 27). China has begun to give them such treatment, and the retail environment is no longer as hostile to foreign retailers as before. Yet, as has been revealed, China still has many regulations specifically directed to foreign retailers, such as stricter regulations on mergers and acquisitions involving foreign retailers. The formation of some regulations even involved the Ministry of Public Security. These regulations have led to a different retailer-regulatory state relationship for the foreign retailers in China than in the foreign retailers' home countries.

Having regulations in place is one thing; to implement them effectively is another. All the regulations that are described in this chapter not only stipulate what can and cannot be done by retailers and, to a lesser extent, by suppliers, but also contain terms of punishment. In general, violators are dealt with in three ways: (1) punishment according to law if criminal activities are involved (as was the case with Pricemart); (2) the issue of warnings or suspension of new store openings if no criminal activities are found; and (3) monetary fines. While some regulations (such as municipal planning bylaws and public hearings) have not been implemented effectively, others are being used to punish violators. For one example, after entering China in 2006 through acquisition of the domestic retail chain of Five Star Electronics, the American Best Buy in the first couple of years opened one store (in Shanghai) under its own banner and nearly 50 stores under the Five Star banner. It was alleged that appropriate state approval was not obtained for the opening of these stores, and that Best Buy therefore violated the state regulations (i.e., *Regulations on Foreign-Invested Enterprises in Commercial Sectors.*) When Best Buy applied to open a second store in Shanghai, the application was denied and Best Buy was asked to "clean up its own house" first. ("Ministry of Commerce demands Best Buy to rectify its erroneous business deeds," 2008). In fact, the new policies and regulations have not stopped foreign retailers from entering and expanding in China. They only slowed down the process and bought more time for the Chinese government and the domestic retailers to deal with the resultant economic and social conflicts and to cope with the intensified competition. Foreign retailers were well aware of that, and they continued to lobby the Chinese government to achieve their business goals. The State government has used these regulations to leverage the foreign retailers to agree to certain conditions that would increase the "net benefit" to China, such as high percentages of domestic ownership (thus more profit sharing for domestic retailers), management technology transfer, protection of employees, contribution to local infrastructure improvement (roads and utility, etc.), and purchase of domestic products for both retail and export. This is also what many Western countries have been doing with regulations. For example, while Canada has similar restrictive regulations, the Canadian government rarely denies any foreign proposal. Instead, it often requests that foreign retailers revise their plans to increase contributions to Canada in the above-mentioned terms.

In a final note, the regulatory system in China is still evolving, and regulations are expected to be revised and amended over time to suit the political, economic, and social changes both within and outside China.

4 Trajectories of Growth and Changes in Retail Structure

For nearly 30 years before the economic reform began in 1978, retailing in China was a simple yet rigid distribution system, limited to the distribution of necessities to consumers. Within a planned economy and with a shortage of consumer goods that were distributed with ration coupons, retailing was a passive activity, and any response by merchants to consumer preference was out of the question. No competition existed, in direct contrast to the competitive nature of a market economy. Private business ownership was banned and all retail market places were eliminated. The entire retail system was either state owned or collectively owned. The department store was the predominant retail format, and retail chains were nonexistent.

After 1978, the retail sector underwent an enormous transformation with profound changes. Store ownership diversified considerably; foreign retailers were allowed to enter the country; and almost all new retail formats that were invented in the Western economies were introduced. These included supermarkets, shopping centers, factory outlets, warehouse membership clubs, and retail chains. Chinese scholars likened these changes to a "revolutionary storm" that totally altered the retail structure and landscape in China (Li, 1997a). In essence, the sector has moved away completely from a centrally-planned, toward a market-oriented, retail economy. Retailers currently not only respond to changing consumer demands but also induce consumption by manipulating consumer tastes and preferences. As in many post-industrial Western societies, retailing in China now plays a prominent role in job creation and regional economic development.

This chapter interprets the changing structure of China's new retail economy. Since the new retail economy has many facets, the chapter focuses on the aspects that best reflect the extent of the retail transformation: ownership change, retail format diversification, and the emergence of retail chains.

CHANGES IN OWNERSHIP STRUCTURE

In the study of retailing, structure is typically described with reference to different types of retail activity and associated retail formats. In China, however, retail structure must be described by ownership as well, because changes in ownership have been a conspicuous aspect of transformation in the country's retail economy, and the reform in retail ownership has been the catalyst for most other changes in the retail structure. Changes in ownership structure have been marked by three distinctive characteristics: permission of individual entrepreneurs to enter the circulation system, retreat of the state from the business of retailing, and the entry of overseas retailers. The driving forces for the ownership changes have been explained in Chapter 3.

In 1996, after separate statistics began to be published for the retail sector, 14 million retail establishments were reported, of which 92 percent were individually- or family-owned businesses; they also provided 70 percent of the country's total retail employment (National Bureau of Statistics of China, 1997, p.558–559; Ministry of Interior Trade, 1997a). Since the late 1990s, however, official statistics shifted to report only the large retailers that meet the statistics threshold set by the National Bureau of Statistics, because the large retailers are considered the key retail enterprises constituting the mainstream of the country's new retail economy. The vast numbers of smaller enterprises were no longer included. In any case, without an institutionalized income tax filing system in place, the accuracy of data collected for the individually-owned and family-run businesses was questionable. To meet the new statistical threshold, a retailer must have achieved annual sales of 5 million yuan or more, and have at least 60 employees. The analysis of ownership change is therefore limited to these large retailers.

In 2010, there were 52,306 such key enterprises in the country, employing 5 million workers (see Table 4.1). These represented a 414 percent increase in key enterprises, and a 144 percent increases in employment, from 2000. However, the average number of employees per retailer decreased by 55 percent. There are three explanations for this decrease. First, many of the new key retailers are possibly smaller operations. Second, and more importantly, it is now common that the large stores (especially department stores) either lease spaces to independent retailers, or have workers from producers to work in their stores to promote and sell the producers' own products, as mentioned in Chapter 3. Third, Chinese retailers now also employ part-time workers, who are often not included in their workforce statistics. The actual number of workers in the stores of the key enterprises should be much larger than what is reported in the official statistics. In 2010, the 52,306 key retailers generated 5.8 trillion yuan (or US$913 billion) in retail sales.

The traditional state-owned and collectively-owned enterprises have declined from an absolute monopoly to a much smaller proportion, due to the expansion of other types of ownership. In 2000, they still represented 45 percent and 25 percent of the total key retail enterprises. By 2010, they declined to 5.8 percent and 5.4 percent, respectively.

Table 4.1 Changes of Key Retail Enterprises by Ownership, 2000 and 2010

Status of registration (type of ownership)	2000			2010						
	Number of companies	Number of employees (1,000)	Average number of employees	Number of companies	Number of employees (1,000)	Average number of employees	Sales (billion yuan)	Sales per employee (million yuan)	Profit (billion yuan)	Profit per employee (1,000 yuan)
Domestic	9,984	2,070.4	207	50,820	4,408.9	87	4,998.4	1.13	445.3	101.0
State-owned	4,616	910.0	197	3,046	332.5	109	439.3	1.32	37.2	111.9
Collective	2,510	324.0	129	2,820	166.1	59	113.4	0.68	11.9	71.7
Co-operative/ joint ownership	560	89	159	780	57	73	55.6	0.98	4.7	82.5
Limited liability	1,059	275.4	260	13,235	1,587.4	120	1,781.0	1.12	163.3	102.9
Stock companies	651	392.8	603	1,948	569.3	292	877.2	1.54	71.9	126.3
Private	588	78.1	133	28,201	1,642.4	58	1,687.0	1.03	151.8	92.4
Foreign-invested	89	50.8	571	836	364.9	436	454.4	1.25	54.3	148.9
Overseas Chinese-invested (from HK, Macao, and TW)	101	44.8	444	650	239.1	368	298.7	1.25	37.1	154.9
Total	10,174	2,166.1	212.9	52,306	5,012.9	96	5,751.5	1.15	536.7	107.1

Note: the average size of some types of enterprises is less than 60 employees. This indicates that some of them were actually smaller than the minimum requirement, and suggests a problem of data compilation in government statistics.

Source: National Bureau of Statistics of China, 2011a

The fastest growing, and now the largest, category is private ownership: from nonexistence in 1978 to 5.8 percent in 2000, and to a significant 54 percent in 2010. This is a fundamental indicator of the retail transformation in China from a socialist planned economy to a capitalist market economy. The other categories that are new to China are the limited liability companies and the stock companies, many of which were transformed from state-owned enterprises. The former now account for a quarter of the total key enterprises. While the latter are much smaller in number, they are the largest among all types of domestic enterprises, as reflected by the average number of employees: 292 per company. In addition to their high job-creation capability, both stock companies and limited liability companies are high performers: per employee sales at stock corporations was 1.54 million yuan in 2010—the highest among all categories of retailers; per employee sales at limited liability companies was 1.12 million yuan, only slightly lower than that of the state-owned enterprises among all the domestic retailers. This explains why these new types of companies have been promoted by the state government as a new means of capital raising for retail growth and development.

The number of key retail enterprises with foreign investment increased steadily as well. In the last decade alone, it increased by 747, from 89 in 2000 to an impressive 836 in 2010. The number of overseas Chinese-invested key enterprises also increased substantially, from 101 in 2000 to 650 in 2010. A partial explanation for their significant increases is that after China's admission to the WTO, it legalized all those that were approved by local governments only. Both the foreign-invested and the overseas Chinese-invested firms include joint ventures as well as those of sole ownership. They are the largest companies in terms of average number of employees, with 436 for the former and 368 for the latter: both significantly larger than the domestic companies, including the stock companies. This reflects their dominance in large-format retailing in the form of retail chains.

While neither the foreign-invested nor the overseas Chinese-invested companies are the most productive and efficient, as measured by retail sales, they seem to be the most profitable. As shown in Table 4.1, although their per-employee sales are lower than those at the domestic stock and state-owned companies, their per-employee profit is much higher, suggesting that they are able to work with a low cost structure. Of the various types of domestic companies, the stock companies are the most productive and profitable.

RETAIL FORMAT DIVERSIFICATION

Closely associated with ownership reform has been the diversification of retail format. Until 1978, all stores in China belonged to one of seven types: department stores, grain/flour stores, grocery stores, hardware stores, bookstores, stationery/sports goods stores, and coal stores. This was a typical retail structure of a less developed economy, where food, clothing, and daily-use consumer goods constitute the largest proportion of consumption.

In the early stages of the economic reform, a considerable amount of effort and capital were invested in upgrading the department stores, which traditionally performed the highest order retail functions and served as anchors of the various retail nodes and high streets in Chinese cities. The growth of department stores was fueled by ineffective government planning. For example, the Beijing Planning Commission in 1993 launched a city-wide project to build 100 large department stores of 10,000 m² or larger in floor space by 2000 (Sun, 1993; Li, 1998). Back in 1987, Beijing had only six department stores with floor space over 10,000 m². By 1994, the number had increased to 40. In 1996, the total had grown further to 70, of which 17 were opened in 1996 alone (Beijing Almanac Compilation Committee, 1997). The Beijing Plan was formulated without sufficient understanding of the extent of market change and therefore contributed to an oversupply of department stores. The new developments emphasized high-end, air-conditioned, department stores that focused on exclusive merchandise (Jin, 1998; Li, 1997b, 1998). By 1998, Beijing already had 130 full-line department stores in the city proper, more than in Singapore, New York, or London, even though the citizens of Beijing had significantly lower purchasing power (Li, 1998; Wang & Jones, 2002). These fashionable department stores attracted large numbers of curious shoppers, but there were more window shoppers than actual buyers due to high prices at the time. Some analysts noted that the pace of retail development was too fast and resulted in too many department stores. Others contended that the problem was not "too many," but a lack of diversity (Jin, 1998). The new department stores typically offered a similar product mix. From a locational perspective, the department stores tended to concentrate in the central area of the city and cluster on a few busy commercial streets. Their product similarity and spatial concentration all contributed to an excess of competition. Similar problems of overdevelopment happened in Shanghai and many other cities (Wang and Zhang, 2005).

With the entry of overseas retailers and the rapid development of new-format retailing, the ensuing competition resulted in a series of price wars. In order to increase or even maintain their market share, large department stores spent heavily on advertisements in all forms of news media. While consumers benefited, retailers were forced to lower their profit margins, with many suffering losses, and with some being pushed to the brink of bankruptcy (Su, R., 1998). During the two-year period from 1995 to 1997, more than 20 large department stores in the country were closed due to declining sales (Wang, 1997). According to information compiled by the Beijing Commission of Commerce, 30 department stores in Beijing suffered losses in 1998 and 19 made no profit at all ("Will wholesale of high-grade goods be profitable?", 1999). For 40 years after 1949, the Shanghai No. 1 Department Store was the city's largest retailer with the most sales. In 1999, it lost the title to a supermarket chain, Lianhua, despite having been transformed into a joint-stock business group in 1992. Beijing's Wangfujing Department Store, once the nation's largest and iconic retailer, suffered the same fate. It should be noted that during the period of rapid department store expansion in the Chinese cities in the late 1980s and the 1990s, the department store as a long-standing format in most Western countries was experiencing significant decline and lost its supremacy. Unfortunately, the Chinese planners could not foresee that, as new-format retailers began to enter the China market, the position and dominance of the traditional department store would inevitably be put under increased pressure and suffer significant declines in their market shares.

The loss of market share by department stores has been transferred to new-format stores. In particular, supermarkets, hypermarkets, and specialty stores have all sprung up in large numbers to nibble at the market shares of department stores. In many cases, the new-format stores are operated as big-box stores, and in almost all cases, they are organized in the form of retail chains. These contemporary formats are all introduced and transplanted to China by foreign retailers, an obvious benefit of retail internationalization. The big-box format has since been copied by domestic retailers for its high efficiency.

In the mid-1990s, the state government began to back off from its efforts in revitalizing the traditional department store as the backbone of China's distribution system. Instead, it shifted support to the development of indigenous retail chains as a means to modernize China's retail industry, because chains were recognized as the most efficient form of retail organization in a modern market economy (Li, 1997c; Gu, 1998). From a business point of view, retail chains have a number of advantages (Jones & Simmons, 1993). Their stores at different locations collectively serve large markets. They are able to use a variety of media to advertise. The cost of administration, location analysis, and advertising can be spread over a number of store facilities. Major chains also have enormous bargaining power in negotiation with suppliers. Moreover, because of their greater financial resources, retail chains are able to carry unproductive stores until the market grows, or until a network of stores is completed.

The first and primitive domestic retail chain was created in 1990, when Meijia Supermarkets was formed in Dongguan City of Guangdong Province, through a merger of several state-owned stores. After Meijia, domestic retail chains were created in other cities and provinces, such as Shanghai and Beijing. Grocery chains in Beijing began in the mid-1990s. Some of the state-owned stores, mainly those selling grains, vegetables, meat, and cooking oil, were reorganized into chain stores. Early developments were all local initiatives. Not until 1994 did the state government begin to be involved in the planning and development of nationwide retail chains.

In March 1994, the Ministry of Interior Trade (MIT) established a task force to monitor and coordinate development of retail chains. By June 1995, the MIT issued the *Blueprint for Development of Retail Chains in China.* This document gave new impetus to the establishment of retail chains in a number of provinces. In January 1996, a permanent government agency—the Office of Commercial Chains Administration—was created under the auspices of the MIT. In March 1997, the MIT issued the *National Standards for Operation and Management of Commercial Chains* in an attempt to streamline this new form of retail organization in China (Ministry of Interior Trade, 1997b). Chains that did not meet these national standards would not be recognized by the state government and therefore would not be eligible for preferential tax deductions, government loans, and import/export autonomies. To supplement the *National Standards for Operation and Management of Commercial Chains*, the MIT in November 1997 issued the *Operation Guidelines for Commercial Franchising.*

By the end of 1997, the number of retail chains in China reached 1,000, which consisted of approximately 15,000 stores and accounted for 42 billion yuan in sales, or 7.8 percent of all retail sales in the country (Office of Commercial Chains Administration, 1998). Most of the domestic chains were in the subsectors of supermarket and convenience stores. There were a few department store chains, but none of them consisted of more than 10 outlets. The two largest chains at that time, Hualian (China United) and Lianhua (United China), were both headquartered in Shanghai. Hualian started in January 1993, well before the state government advocated this form of retail organization. In its first year of operation, Hualian reported a loss of 5.4 million yuan, but it continued to open new stores. Only after its 18th store was opened did the firm begin to make a profit (Beijing Intelligence Tapping and Management Consulting Ltd., 1997a). In1996, Hualian merged with Lawson—a Japanese convenience store chain—to create a sub-chain, named Hualian-Lawson CVS. By mid-1998, Hualian had expanded to 250 stores, with a total of 100,000 m² of retail space and 510 million yuan of capital assets (Office of Commercial Chains Administration, 1998). While centered in Shanghai, Hualian also opened stores in the adjacent provinces of Jiangsu, Zhejiang, Anhui, Jiangxi, and Henan.

Not all early domestic chains were as fortunate as Hualian. Some expanded too rapidly and suffered fatal blows as a consequence. The Asia Group and the Red Apple Group, both private enterprises, are examples of such failures. The Asia Group was formed in the late 1980s with its headquarters in Zhengzhou City of Henan Province. By 1993, the management of Asia Group established an ambitious plan to build a nationwide network of department stores (He, 1998). To realize the plan, the Asia Group tried to raise capital from the stock market. Its attempt to go public failed, yet the implementation of the plan for expansion went ahead. In a short period of three years, the chain opened 11 large department stores in several cities, including Shanghai, Guangzhou, and Beijing. Unfortunately, most of the stores suffered heavy losses. By the summer of 1998, its operations in Guangzhou and Shanghai had to be closed, and its store in Beijing was struggling (Su, Z., 1998).

The Red Apple Group was established in November 1995 in Beijing as a mini-market chain (Li, 1997c). Within one year, it opened 42 stores, with 35 opened on the same day—June 1, 1996. It cost 50 million yuan to open these stores, and another 20 million to purchase POS (point of sale) cash registers and related computer facilities. Only in its second year, it reported a debt crisis, which turned into a credit crisis, as suppliers refused to continue providing merchandise to the Red Apple stores. In July 1997, the Beijing Bureau of Industry and Commerce intervened and appointed an independent accounting and auditing firm to manage Red Apple's day-to-day operations.

The slow pace of retail chain development in the 1990s was attributed to such factors as the inflexible political environment, regional barriers, and a lack of human and capital resources. While the government encouraged the development of national chains, the political environment at the time did not provide the necessary incentives for full participation by competent managers (Xu, 1998). The majority of the chains remained state owned, rooted in organizations where business decisions were usually made by the local governments, and managers as government appointees were decision takers, not decision makers. Because their autonomy in business decision making was limited and their pay was not tied to sales performance, the store managers often felt powerless and were not motivated to run the business wholeheartedly. Furthermore, competent managers were frequently recruited by Sino-foreign joint ventures, which offered considerably higher salaries and bonuses. Many chains were formed by simply merging existing state or collectively-owned stores under local government directives, as that was considered the most expedient way of creating and expanding a chain. In many cases, however, these stores were merged against their will. The longtime store managers did not want to lose their independence because they would lose certain personal benefits. Often, they resisted the merger and only passively participated in coordinated operations of the company. In other cases, local governments forced "arranged mergers" that integrated poor performers or near-bankruptcy stores with high performers, in order to save jobs. That policy had actually transformed some high performers into slow-growth enterprises (Office of Commercial Chains Administration, 1997).

Regionalism, which was often reinforced by local governments, frequently required the protection of local retailers, even within a city. This tendency made interregional expansion of chains and market penetration extremely difficult. Even the most successful chains, including Shanghai's Hualian, were mainly regional players. Beijing's Wangfujing Department Store had planned to establish a national chain and opened directly-owned stores in such urban centers as Guangzhou (South China), Chengdu

(Southwest China), Wuhan (Central China), Nantong and Suzhou (East China) (An, 1998; Zheng, 1998). Similarly, the Shanghai No.1 Department Store Group opened branch stores in Huaiyin and Hefei (East China), Wuhan (Central China), Chongqing (Southwest China), and Xi'an (West China). Both chains met great resistance from local governments and local retailers. As a result, Shanghai No.1 had to close all stores outside Shanghai (according to personal interviews with Shanghai No. 1 managers in the summer of 2000).

Perhaps the most significant obstacles to the development of domestic retail chains had been the lack of competent managers and the lack of capital to purchase state-of-the-art technology necessary for a centralized information system that was crucial for monitoring, coordinating, and managing a chain's operation. Even limited expansion in the area of information technology quickly exceeded the human and capital resources that were available in the 1990s. Since it was not easy to obtain financial loans from banks, this lack of resources continued to be a major problem for the development of the Chinese retail economy for quite some time.

Most domestic chains had not established either centralized procurement or distribution systems before 2000. Some chains (such as Hualian) did have distribution centers, but those facilities could not supply the stores outside their home provinces. Most chains remained geographically confined to the provinces or even cities where their headquarters were based. As a consequence, no true national chains emerged until the country entered the 21st Century.

The state government had promised to gradually reduce the amount of central intervention in retail business decision making and operations, while maintaining its role of providing policy guidelines. The state government also continued to push for the transformation of state-owned chains into stock companies as an effective means of raising business capital and to facilitate the breaking down of barriers associated with trans-regional and trans-sectoral retail chain expansion. It was not until the emergence of the modern types of enterprises in large numbers that these obstacles were overcome progressively.

There are three routes to chain expansion: organic growth, acquisition and merger, and franchising. In consideration of China's particular situation, the state government also encouraged franchising as a means to fast-track the development of domestic chains. From a consumer's point of view, franchised outlets appear like other chain stores: they offer standardized products and similar decor and merchandising techniques, but they have the advantage of using existing facilities and local market knowledge without investing heavily in development of new retail sites or extensive training of store managers. At the same time, franchising allows store owners to retain a certain level of independence and control. Many retailers have taken the low-cost and low-risk route of franchising for rapid expansion. The Shanghai-based Hualian adopted this growth strategy and began recruiting franchisees in the late 1990s. In 2004, 70 percent of Hualian's stores were actually franchised subsidiaries.

The state government also provided preferential assistance to the large, high-performing chains. In 1997, the state government selected 60 chains as recipients of the State Technology Improvement Foundation Grants, and gave 19 of them permission to import and export their own merchandise—the same privilege that had previously been granted only to foreign retailers. In line with the state program, the China Bank of Industry and Commerce (CBIC) provided six billion yuan in loans to support the growth of major Chinese-based chains (Office of Commercial Chains Administration, 1997).

In anticipation of accelerated expansions of foreign retailers through acquisition of domestic retailers and through mergers among themselves, the Chinese government felt the urgent need to nurture its own retail heavyweights to combat foreign competition, so that the national market would not become dominated by international retailers. In June 2004, the Ministry of Commerce released the country's post-WTO retail development strategies in the document titled *National Strategies for Reform and Development of China's Distribution System* (Ministry of Commerce, 2004d). A key strategy is to nurture, in a period of five to eight years, 15 to 20 domestic retailers capable of competing with the international retail superpowers in China.

Consistent with the national strategies, the Ministry of Commerce announced the selection of 20 domestic retailers to form the "national team," to which the Chinese government was prepared to provide special support to assist in their growth and expansion. No criteria were publicly announced for the selection of the retailers, but most of them were former state-owned enterprises, of which the state was still the largest stakeholder, even after these enterprises had been transformed into joint-stock companies or company groups. On the top of the list was the Shanghai-based Bailian Group, created by the Shanghai Municipal Government in 2003 through the merger of four stated-owned company groups. A close examination of the 20 members of the national team also reveals a geo-spatial consideration: they are not only based in Beijing, Shanghai, and the coastal provinces of Liaoning, Shandong, and Guangdong, but also in the interior provinces of Hubei and Anhui and in the western city of Chongqing. In addition, the national team members include both state-controlled companies and privately owned enterprises.

An important form of state assistance was special bank loans. In 2005, the Ministry of Commerce and China Development Bank (2005) jointly announced the provision of 50 billion yuan (US$6 billion) to assist the selected domestic retailers to grow and expand. While all enterprises could apply for financial assistance, the members of the national team were given top priority to receive the special loans. The loans could be used not only for development of new stores but also for expansion through merger and acquisition. In 2007, both the ministry and the bank made a second announcement to expand the program (Ministry of Commerce & China Development Bank, 2007).

At almost the same time, the state government announced two other initiatives as supplements to the *National Strategies for Reform and Development of China's Distribution System* to help modernize the distribution system in rural China. The first was announced in February 2005 to nurture 250,000 chain stores in tens of thousands of villages and towns (Ministry of Commerce, 2007); the second, announced in February 2006 and dubbed "The Double-Hundred Project," was to foster 100 large wholesale markets and 100 large retailers of agricultural products (Ministry of Commerce, 2005b). That mandate was given to All China Federation of Supply and Marketing Cooperatives—a government body directly under the State Council.

While the preferential policies were seemingly directed at assisting domestic retailers, they indirectly affected foreign retailers' ability to gain market dominance in China, particularly in the mega urban markets of Shanghai, Beijing, Guangzhou, and Shenzhen—homes to the largest domestic retailers. It has not been observed that similar public policies are administered by the governments of the Western capitalist economies. If Canada had such government programs, Eaton's, a 130-year-old domestic department store chain with 90 department stores across the country, perhaps would not have gone into bankruptcy in 1999, and the Hudson's Bay Company—another Canadian retailer that owned both the Bay and the Zeller's department store chains—would not have fallen into the hands of an American investor in 2006. The government support in China could have been subjected to complaints to the WTO by foreign retailers.

Despite the early upheavals, and with persistent government support, retail chains continued to grow, expand, and mature in the last decade. As of 2010, there existed 2,361 retail chains in China, operating 176,972 stores and employing 2.3 million individuals (Table 4.2). Retail chains of different types can be examined and compared with four indicators: number of stores, employment, sales, and floor areas as selling space.

By ownership, most of the chains are limited liability, stock companies, or privately owned. Together, these three types account for 80 percent of all retail chains in China. Foreign-invested and overseas Chinese-invested account for nearly 10 percent. The largest chains are those of stock companies with 176 stores per chain. The second largest are the foreign-invested, with 100 stores per chain. Surprisingly, the state-owned chains are the best performers, with retail sales of 33,500 yuan per m^2 of floor space. This is followed by the stock companies with 23,000 yuan per m^2. Foreign-invested chains are below average, with only 18,500 yuan per m^2, indicating that not all of them are high-volume sellers. However, statistics also show that they are the most profitable (see Table 4.1). Notably, most chains have

Table 4.2 Retail Chains by Ownership and Format, 2010

Type of chain	Number of chains	Number of stores	Number of stores per chain	Average store size (m²)	Retail sales per unit area (1,000 yuan/m²)	% of procurement through centralized distribution system
By ownership						
Domestic	2,134	158,196	74	-	21.7	74%
State-owned	171	15,497	91	-	33.5	85%
Collective	34	3,099	91	-	8.9	64%
Co-operative/ joint ownership	43	2,585	60	-	11.5	69%
Limited liability	838	55,696	66	-	17.3	76%
Stock companies	260	45,632	176	-	23.0	70%
Private	788	35,687	45	-	13.2	75%
Foreign-invested	141	14,217	101	-	18.5	71%
Overseas Chinese-invested (from HK, Macao, and TW)	86	4,379	51		22.9	51%
By format						
Convenience store	94	14,202	151	75	230	50
Discount store	3	701	234	306	169	68
Supermarket	400	32,818	82	586	144	83
Hypermarket	158	6,322	40	2,916	158	50
Warehouse club	7	272	39	2,001	316	21
Department store	97	4,239	44	3,493	180	47
Specialty store	1,269	84,678	67	798	255	78
Franchised store	294	27,641	94	163	238	77
Building material store	13	108	8	5,786	90	71
Factory outlets center	4	66	17	613	87	100
Others	22	5,745	261	92	392	97
Total	2,361	176,792	75		21.5	72%

Source: National Bureau of Statistics of China, 2011a

achieved high levels of centralized purchase and delivery of goods by their own distribution centers: above 70 percent, which is an essential element to efficient and profitable operations in modern retailing. The overseas-Chinese invested chains have the lowest level of centralized procurement and delivery of goods, at only 50 percent.

By format, the largest category is specialty store chains, with a total of 1,269 chains. However, this category is so broad and internally so diverse that it is hardly meaningful to compare it with other types of chains. Except specialty store chains, there are more supermarket and hypermarket chains than any other type: 400 supermarket chains and 158 hypermarket chains. In addition, there are 97 department store chains and 94 CVS chains. The hypermarket is a combination of a supermarket and a discount department store selling both foodstuff and general merchandise. It quickly became a popular and competitive format in China because such stores provide a wide assortment of consumer goods at competitive prices and take market shares from both the traditional department stores and the smaller scale supermarkets.

THE TOP 100 RETAIL CHAINS

Since 2000, when China Chain Store Association began to publish the *China Chain Store Almanac*, the sales and size of the top 100 chains (ranked by sales) have been reported annually. These large chains represent the highest level of retail development in China, but the membership of this elite club has changed frequently in the last 10 years, with some being edged out and replaced by new players. For example, of the top 100 chains in 2000, only 18 remained on the list by 2010. Therefore, the changes in the top 100 chains in the last decade are also telling with regard to the rapid growth and change in the retail sector.

In 2000, the top 100 chains consisted of 7,706 retail outlets, with combined sales of 98.2 billion yuan. Nineteen of them were headquartered in Beijing; 13 in Shanghai; and another 15 in Guangzhou, Shenzhen, and Tianjin. In other words, 47 percent of the top 100 chains were based in the five mega urban markets alone. The largest three chains were all Shanghai-based supermarkets: Lianhua (with 950 stores), Hualian (682 stores), and NGS (146 stores). Together, they accounted for 23 percent of all the stores operated by the top 100 chains, and also 23 percent of the total sales. Only three overseas retailers were included in the top 100 chains: the German Metro (ranked 7th but with only 8 stores), the Taiwanese RT-Mart (ranked 34th with only 2 stores), and the Hong Kong-based PARKnSHOP (ranked 37th with 18 stores). All of them had food retailing as their core business.

Five years later in 2005, the top 100 chains consisted of 38,368 stores—a 398 percent increase from 2000. Their combined sales were 701 billion yuan—a 615 percent increase. The largest chain was Bailian Group, but as explained in Chapter 3, it is a business conglomerate created by the Shanghai Government, with business operations spanning across several categories: from department stores to hypermarkets, supermarkets and convenience stores. Its subsidiary companies of Lianhua, Hualian, and Quick CVS are among the largest chains in their respective sub-sectors. Two domestic electronic retail chains—the Beijing-based Gome (with 426 stores) and the Nanjing-based Suning (with 323 stores)—ascended to the second and third largest chains by sales. Those with overseas investment increased to 14 (excluding Yum and MacDonald's, both of which operate quick-service restaurants.)

In 2010, the top 100 chains operated 150,211 outlets, with combined sales of 1.66 trillion yuan. The New Cooperation Joint Stock Trade Chain Co. Ltd. (ranked the 13th) is an anomaly: it reportedly operated 99,000 outlets (66 percent of the total number of stores operated by the top 100 chains), but its sales were only two percent of the total sales of the same chains. In fact, this is a loose chain created by the All China Federation of Supply and Marketing Cooperatives. The mandate of this company is to promote and facilitate the formation of retail chains in the vast rural areas of China. Specifically, it coordinates the existing cooperative stores, and recruits individually-owned stores via franchising, to form a nationwide chain supplied by a network of distribution centers. Excluding this anomaly, the total number of stores of the remaining 99 chains is still 7 times as many as in 2000, and their sales are 17 times as high as in 2000. Similar to the 2000 list, 46 percent of the top 100 chains in 2010 are based in the mega cities: 17 in Beijing, 15 in Shanghai, 10 in Shenzhen, and four in Guangzhou.

Bailian Group is no longer the largest chain: although the group has many more store locations, it was surpassed by both Suning and Gome in sales. NGS, once the third largest chain in 2000, was pushed down to 15th place, though it expanded to operate 3,204 stores in 2010. More impressively, 19 of the top 100 chains in 2010 are overseas invested (excluding Yum and MacDonald's). They represent only 4.5 percent of the total store locations operated by the top 100 chains, but their combined sales account for 19 percent. Notably, the foreign retailers focus heavily on retailing of fast moving consumer goods (FMCG), and they now effectively dominate the sub-sectors of hypermarkets and large-format supermarkets in most large urban markets. The foreign chains that focus on FMCG through hypermarkets and supermarkets are the French Carrefour and Auchan (ranks 7 and 35), the American Wal-Mart (9), the British Tesco (31), the Korean Lotte and E-Mart (33 and 73), Lotus of Thailand (34), the German Metro (40), the Taiwanese RT-Mart and Trust-Mart (6 and 27), and the Hong Kong-based PARKnSHOP (75). Their recent expansion has been achieved through a mix of organic growth and acquisition. Not all of the overseas-invested retail companies have had the same level of success; some failed miserably. Their stories of success and setbacks will be told in Chapters 5 and 7.

In addition to Bailian, several other top chains are created by local governments, with their respective government (either provincial or municipal) still being a key stakeholder. Most of these chains are multi-format retailers, or even mixed business groups with retailing being only part of their business operations. More analysis and discussion of these government-created retail firms will be presented in Chapter 6.

It is also worth mentioning that 35 of the top 100 retail chains operate department stores, either as their core business or as part of their overall business operations. Department stores continue to be squeezed by specialty stores at one end and by hypermarkets at the other. Consequently, most department stores have stayed away from selling electronics and furniture, but have had an increased focus on fashion—a trend observed in the Western countries as well. Newly developed department stores tend to be larger. It is now typical for department stores to lease floor space (known as "brand counters") to individual retailers, who rent the space to sell apparel of a particular brand. In the Parkson department stores, only 32 percent of the total income is derived from direct sales; 52 percent is derived from the leasing of floor spaces (China Chain Store Association, 2011).

REGIONAL VARIATIONS

In a country as vast as China, where population distribution is uneven and economic disparities are rampant, geographical variations in retailing are not only anticipated but are also a reality. Table 4.3 shows the expected and familiar pattern of regional variations at the provincial level. In general, the level of retail development and the relative importance of the retail industry decline from the eastern coastal region towards the western region. Four characteristics can be easily generalized. First of all, the five coastal provinces of (from south to north) Guangdong, Zhejiang, Jiangsu, Shandong, and Liaoning have the largest shares of the key enterprises and associated retail employment, the number of retail chains, and the number of chain stores. Specifically, these five provinces account for 41 percent of the key retail enterprise, and are home to 35 percent of all the retail chains and 45 percent of the chain stores. This clearly shows that retailing is the most developed in the eastern coastal region. Second, compared with the other provinces, Beijing and Shanghai—the two largest mega urban markets—also have larger shares of retailers and retail stores, relative to their share of the national population. While they account for only three percent of the national population, they are home to eight percent of the key retail enterprises and 11 percent of the retail chains, and host 15 percent of the chain stores in the entire country. This is hardly surprising because they are wealthy urban markets and contain no poor rural areas. Third, six interior provinces have larger shares of retail enterprises and chain stores than the other interior provinces in China. These are: Henan, Anhui, Hubei, Hunan, Sichuan, and Chongqing. Fourth, even after 30 years of economic reform and despite the recent actions taken by the state to develop the west, the retail sector in the western provinces of Xinjiang, Qinghai, Gansu, Ningxia, Inner Mongolia, and Tibet is still the least developed, though these western provinces also have the smallest populations in the country, meaning the smallest consumer markets.

Table 4.3   Regional Variations in Retail Supply, with Reference to Population
Shares, 2010 (All in Percentage)

Region	Province	Population	Number of key enterprises	Retail employment	Retail chain	Chain stores
North China	Beijing	1.5	5.8	5.9	6.3	3.9
	Tianjin	1.0	1.5	1.8	1.7	1.1
	Hebei	5.4	2.8	3.4	3.9	2.4
	Shanxi	2.7	2.7	2.8	1.7	1.1
	Inner Mongolia	1.8	1.6	1.7	0.8	1.0
Northeast China	Liaoning	3.3	4.7	4.2	3.9	3.2
	Jilin	2.0	1.5	1.3	1.1	0.5
	Heilongjiang	2.9	1.7	2.1	1.3	0.6
East China	Shanghai	1.7	2.6	5.3	4.2	10.9
	Jiangsu	5.9	8.4	8.2	7.3	10.1
	Zhejiang	4.1	5.5	5.3	9.7	13.7
	Anhui	4.4	3.0	3.2	2.8	4.6
	Fujian	2.8	3.3	3.2	5.3	1.7
	Jiangxi	3.3	1.4	1.4	2.8	1.6
	Shandong	7.2	13.2	10.8	4.9	5.2
South China	Henan	7.0	8.4	5.9	6.5	3.6
	Hubei	4.3	4.4	4.8	4.2	2.8
	Hunan	4.9	3.4	3.4	3.8	2.1
	Guangdong	7.8	8.8	9.6	8.7	13.1
	Guangxi	3.4	1.5	1.4	2.2	1.9
	Hainan	0.6	0.6	0.5	0.2	0.1
Southwest China	Chongqing	2.2	2.4	2.4	3.5	6.0
	Sichuan	6.0	3.6	4.0	3.9	3.6
	Guizhou	2.6	0.9	0.8	1.1	0.4
	Yunnan	3.4	1.8	1.8	1.8	1.8
	Tibet	0.2	0.1	0.1	<0.1	<0.1
Northwest China	Shaanxi	2.8	2.2	2.7	1.1	0.3
	Gansu	1.9	0.8	0.9	1.1	0.5
	Qinghai	0.4	0.2	0.2	0.5	0.1
	Ningxia	0.5	0.4	0.4	0.8	0.8
	Xinjiang	1.6	0.9	0.8	3.0	1.4
		100.0*	100.0	100.0	100.0	100.0

* 0.5 percent of the national population are army soldiers in active service and are floating/
transient people, not tied to a particular province at the time of the census

Source: National Bureau of Statistics of China, 2011a

While the provincial variations are easy to identify, variations at city level are more meaningful for retailers and retail planners, because even the not-well-off provinces may have cities that are "islands of prosperities." Geographical variations by retail firms are also useful for analysis of competition. Such analysis can allow researchers to infer the geo-spatial strategies of different retailers, which are typically not public information. These more detailed geographical variations will be presented in subsequent chapters with various case studies.

5 Penetrating the Great Wall and Conquering the Middle Kingdom

For international retailers seeking foreign markets for expansion, China was perhaps the most challenging. Before its admission to the WTO, China retained a great wall of barriers to the entry and expansion of international retailers. Nonetheless, the international retailers were determined to conquer the Middle Kingdom (the name of China in Chinese). Even after China became a full member of the WTO, the challenges persisted, though in different forms, as discussed in Chapter 3. Some international retailers have been much more successful than others. Their experiences in China present interesting case studies of the retail internationalization process.

The process involving retail internationalization is complex. Any move toward multinational operations has to acknowledge that culture varies through space (Dawson, 1994). Dawson (2003, p. 4) proposes a four-phase model to describe the complex process: stability, consolidation, control, and dominance. Initially, there is considerable fluidity as the firm gains understanding about the new market. In the second phase, the firm adjusts to new conditions, consolidating its position. After that, it begins to try to exert control over vertical and horizontal channel relationships. When the retailer becomes established in the market, mature strategies seeking market dominance, similar to those used in the home country, are applied. Dawson also points out that few firms pass through the complete cycle; many fail to achieve their objectives and decide to withdraw from the market at some stage. The failures of four high-profile international retailers in Chile (namely, the American Home Depot and J. C. Penney, the French Carrefour, and the Dutch Royal Ahold) and their subsequent withdrawal from that country are a testimony of the challenges of retail internationalization ("Globalization's Winners and Losers," 2006). The reasons for their failures vary, and the "standardization versus adaptation" debate continues in the study of international business.

With reference to another model developed by Vida and Fairhurst (1998), the direction and pace of the retail internationalization process is influenced by both firm characteristics and the external retail environment. The key characteristics internal to the firm are resource availability and commitment, and its differential advantages. The retail environment factors include market conditions, consumer affluence and cultural prefer-ence, competition, and regulation. They serve as promoters or inhibitors for whether a firm will initiate international retail activities, maintain a constant level of involvement, increase or decrease its involvement, or com-pletely withdraw from the international market.

While there have been many studies of 'direction of international retail expansion,' most of these studies focused on market reorientation from the advanced economies in North America and Western Europe to the emerg-ing markets in Asia and Latin America. Few have examined the direction of intra-national expansion within a host market, leaving a research gap to be filled. This chapter discusses international retailers in China with stories of success and setbacks. It extends beyond the points of entry to consider the subsequent development of the foreign operations. The chapter first exam-ines the process and direction of market penetration and the performance of the international retailers, and then compares their business models and corporate strategies.

MARKET PENETRATION AND PERFORMANCE OF INTERNATIONAL RETAILERS

The success of international retailers is assessed with two typical indicators: the degree of market penetration (i.e., geographic scope of activities), and the level of business performance. The former is measured not only by the num-ber of stores but also by their geographic distribution, because a wider geo-graphic distribution indicates success over local protectionism and cultural barriers. The latter is measured by retail sales and profit levels. Because data on profit are not available for individual firms, retail sales are used as the sole indicator of performance, though retailers with high sales volumes may not yet be making a profit. For convenience of analysis, the major international retailers are separated into three groups: Western retailers (including both North American and European retailers), Japanese retailers, and those from Southeast Asia (see Table 5.1). The retailers from Taiwan and Hong Kong are included among Southeast Asian investors in consistency with China's trade and investment policies. This separation of international retailers is useful because the retailers have developed in different institutional contexts.

Western Retailers

In general, the Western retailers, particularly the food and general mer-chandise (GM) retailers, have achieved higher levels of market penetration in China than other foreign retailers. By the end of 2010, Wal-Mart had opened 219 stores in 95 cities; Carrefour 182 stores in 58 cities; Tesco 109 stores in 38 cities; Metro 48 stores in 34 cities; and Auchan 41 stores in 21 cities (see Table 5.1). It should be stressed that much of their expansion

Table 5.1 Major Foreign Retailers in China, 2010

Home region/ country	Retailer	Year of 1st store opening	Category*	Format	Market penetration		Performance	
					Number of stores	Number of cities	Total sales (billion yuan)	Per store sales (million yuan)
Western	Wal-Mart (U.S.)	1996	G. M. & food	Hypermarket	219	95	40.0	182.6
	Carrefour (France)	1995	G. M. & food	Hypermarket	182	58	42.0	230.8
	Auchan (France)	1999	G. M. & food	Hypermarket	41	21	13.5	329.3
	Tesco (U.K.)	2004	G. M. & food	Hypermarket	109	38	15.9	159.0
	Metro (Germany)	1996	G. M. & food	Warehouse/membership	48	34	11.7	243.8
	Ikea (Sweden)	1998	Furniture	Warehouse	8	8	4.3	537.5
	B&Q (U.K.)	1999	Home improvement	Warehouse	40	17	-	-
	Home Depot (U.S.)	2006	Home improvement	Warehouse	7	3	-	-
	Best Buy (U.S.)	2006	Electronics	Big box/specialty store	277	36	27.0	97.5
	H&M (Sweden)**	2007	Apparel	Specialty store	114	47	-	-
	Zara (Spain)**	2006	Apparel	Specialty store	60	31	-	-
Japan	Jusco	1996	G. M. & food	Department store	27	14	6.6	245.4
	Isetan	1993	Department store	Department store	4	4	-	-
	Ito-Yokado	1998	G. M. & food	Supermarket	12	2	7.1	588.5
	Uniqlo**	2002	Apparel	Specialty store	170	41	-	-

(continued)

Table 5.1 (continued)

Home region/country	Retailer	Year of 1st store opening	Category*	Format	Market penetration		Performance	
					Number of stores	Number of cities	Total sales (billion yuan)	Per store sales (million yuan)
S. E. Asia	Lotus (Thailand)	1997	G. M. & food	Hypermarket	74	23	13.6	183.78
	Parkson (Malaysia)	1994	Department store	Department store	47	30	16.6	352.3
	RT-Mart (Taiwan)	1997	G. M. & food	Hypermarket	143	88	50.2	351.2
	Trust Mart (Taiwan)	1997	G. M. & food	Hypermarket/superstore	104	33	16.5	158.6
	PARKnSHOP (H.K.)	1994	Food	Supermarket	44	5	3.9	88.3
	New World (H. K.)	1994	Department store	Department store	37	17	17.9	483.8
	Lotte Mart (S. Korea)	2008	G. M. & food	Hypermarket	80	33	14.4	180.6
	E-Mart (S. Korea)	1997	G. M. & food	Hypermarket	16	4	4.0	148.1

* G. M. = general merchandise ** 2012 data

Sources: China Chain Store Association, 2011; corporate annual reports and websites.

has been achieved since 2001 when China was admitted to the WTO, particularly after 2004, when the grace period ended and China had to remove all trade barriers in accordance with the WTO rules. For example, 80 percent of the Wal-Mart stores and 70 percent of the Carrefour stores opened after 2004. Also exemplified by Wal-Mart and Carrefour, market penetration of the Western retailers has taken place in two directions simultaneously: from the eastern coastal region to the western interior, and from large urban centers to smaller cities (see Figures 5.1 and 5.2). Wal-Mart now has 38 percent of its stores in Tier 3, Tier 4, and other lower tier cities, as shown in Table 5.2. Carrefour has 9 percent of its stores in Tier 3, Tier 4, and other lower tier cities. Although Tesco has fewer stores in China than Carrefour, it has more stores in the lower tier cities than Carrefour. Relatively speaking, both Auchan and Metro have a lower level of market penetration than Wal-Mart, Carrefour, and Tesco. Unlike the hypermarket operators, the German Metro is in the business of a warehouse membership club. Its big box clubs are engaged in business through both retailing and wholesaling of a wide assortment of merchandise including foodstuff. Due to its wholesaling nature, Metro is not expected to have as many store locations as the hypermarket operators, and it is not surprising that Metro still focuses on cities of higher tiers, where car ownership, among other facilitating factors, is high. While it opened only three stores in three separate Tier 3 cities, it has not bothered to penetrate the Tier 4 cities at all.

Makro—a Dutch warehouse format retailer—entered China in 1996, with its first two operations established in Guangzhou and Shantou in Guangdong Province. One year later, it moved to Beijing and opened two stores in 1997 and 1998 respectively. However, it was not able to resume expansion until 2003, when it opened one store each in Tianjin, Shijiazhuang, and Shenyang. In 2004, when it obtained state approval to engage in wholesaling, Makro decided to divest from its Guangdong operations and focus on expansion in Northern China. Sadly, its expansion met with serious setbacks: both its Shenyang and Shijiazhuang stores were closed in less than a year due to heavy losses (Du, 2004). This forced Makro to retreat to Beijing and Tianjin, where it opened two new stores in 2006. In 2008, it sold its entire China operation to the South Korea-based Lotte Mart.

The furniture and home improvement retailers have achieved much lower levels of market penetration. The Swedish Ikea, which specializes in operation of large-format furniture and décor stores, opened only eight stores in 12 years, with less than one store opening per year. The first two Ikea stores were opened in Shanghai (in 1998) and Beijing (in 1999) respectively. While both stores later moved into larger facilities, Ikea closed both original stores in these two largest urban centers. Instead, it opened its third store in the distant city of Guangzhou in 2005 and its fourth store in Chengdu in 2006. In the following two years, Ikea was

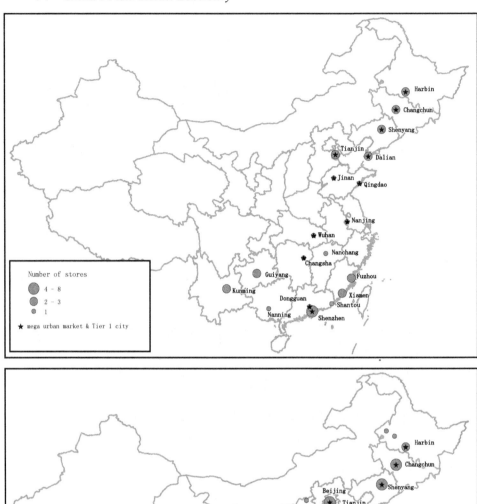

Figure 5.1 Distribution of Wal-Mart stores in China, before and after WTO.

(The map on the top shows Wal-Mart stores before 2005; the map at the bottom shows Wal-Mart stores in 2010.)

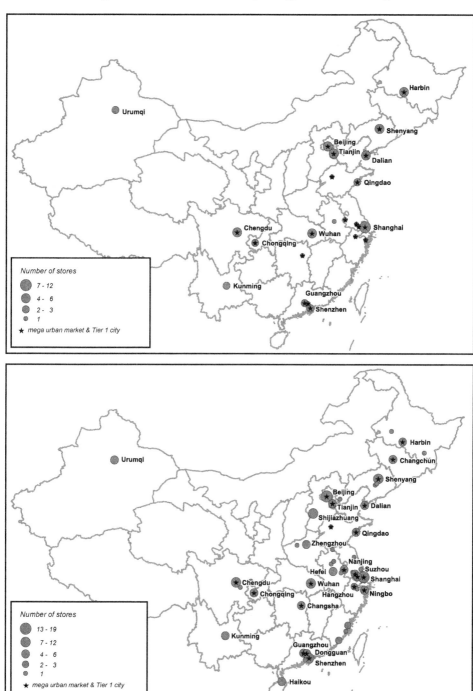

Figure 5.2   Distribution of Carrefour stores in China, before and after WTO.
(The map on the top shows Carrefour stores before 2005; the map at the bottom shows Carrefour stores in 2010.)

Table 5.2   Geographical Distribution of Foreign Retailers by City Tiers, 2010 (All in Percentage)

Home region/ country	Retailers	City by tier						Total
		Mega	*1*	*2*	*3*	*4*	*Other*	*Total*
Western	Wal-Mart	13.8	31.3	16.9	16.9	15.9	5.1	100
	Carrefour	30.6	43.3	17.2	6.1	2.2	0.6	100
	Auchan	22.5	40.0	12.5	25.0	0	0	100
	Tesco	34.4	34.4	8.9	12.2	6.7	3.3	100
	Metro	27.1	50.0	18.7	4.2	0	0	100
	Ikea	50.0	50.0	0	0	0	0	100
	B&Q	52.5	40.0	7.5	0	0	0	100
	Home Depot	57.1	28.6	14.2	0	0	0	100
	H&M	24.6	50.0	16.7	3.5	2.6	2.6	100
	Zara	47.0	34.8	12.1	3.0	3.0	0	100
Japan	Aeon (Jusco)	48.1	25.9	18.5	7.4	0	0	100
	Ito-Yokado	88.9	11.1	0	0	0	0	100
	Isetan	50.0	50.0	0	0	0	0	100
	Uniqlo	48.2	31.1	11.8	3.5	5.3	0	100
S. E. Asia	Lotus	45.7	28.4	12.3	7.4	3.7	2.5	100
	RT-Mart	14.1	25.4	19.0	13.4	9.2	19.0	100
	Trust Mart	n/a	n/a	n/a	n/a	n/a	n/a	100
	Lotte Mart	13.2	10.8	16.9	45.8	13.2	0	100
	E-Mart	87.5	12.5	0	0	0	0	100
	PARKnSHOP	n/a	n/a	n/a	n/a	n/a	n/a	100
	Parkson	16.7	35.4	31.2	12.5	4.2	0	100
	New World	43.6	41.0	10.2	5.1	0	0	100

largely dormant and did not open any new stores. Between 2008 and 2012, it resumed expansion and opened six stores in six different cities, including a second store in Shanghai. All the Ikea stores concentrate in the mega urban markets and Tier 1 cities. It has not even attempted to set up stores in Tier 2 cities. However, this makes business sense because the Ikea furniture is styled to the liking of the young urban professionals and is pricey to ordinary Chinese consumers. It may not sell well in smaller urban markets.

The British B&Q, which specializes in home improvement and building materials, entered China in 1999, one year after Ikea. At the end of 2010, it was operating 40 stores in 17 cities, representing a much higher level of market penetration than that of Ikea. At one time, its total number of stores in China reached 63, after acquiring the defunct German OBI's China operation, but it had to close more than 20 of them after the acquisition due to poor performance and losses. At the present, B&Q also focuses on the mega urban markets (with 53 percent of the total) and Tier 1 cities (40 percent), with virtually no stores in the lower tier cities. The American Home Deport was a latecomer, whose entry was not approved by the Chinese government until 2005. Through acquisition of a domestic retailer (the Tianjin-based Homeway) in 2006, it acquired 14 store locations and turned 12 of them into Home Depot brand stores. Unfortunately, like B&Q, Home Depot had to downsize by closing five of its 12 stores between 2009 and 2012, reducing its presence from six to three urban markets and abandoning the Beijing market completely. In 2012, Home Depot announced it would close all seven remaining stores, joining a growing list of international retailers who failed in grasping the local consumer culture (Burkitt, 2012). Its closures caused 850 associates to lose their jobs.

Best Buy is another high-profile Western retailer in China. Although in legal terms it operates 277 stores in the country, the majority of them were acquired from a domestic chain—Five Star Electronics. Best Buy opened only eight stores under its own corporate banner, but all of them were shut down on the same day in 2010. The Best Buy story will be told in more detail in Chapter 7.

The fashion retailers Zara and H&M grew and expanded much faster than most other Western retailers for three reasons. First, they had the advantage of entering China after the country lifted all trade barriers to fulfill its obligations to the WTO, with Zara opening its first store in 2006 and H&M in 2007. Second, Chinese consumers' appetite for new clothes and low-cost fashion has been growing significantly, creating a culture of "rapid-fire adaption of runaway trends for mass consumption" (Fong, 2006). Indeed, Chinese consumers, especially the young and female consumers, are now much more fashion conscious than before. Third, the large number of newly developed shopping centers in many cities provided suitable business venues and retail space for their operations. While both Zara and H&M are fast fashion retailers operating with a business model that moves garments from the design table to stores quickly and focusing on trendy clothes at affordable prices, H&M is much more aggressive in expansion than Zara. It had only 64 stores in China in 2011 (Hansegard & Burkitt, 2011); on September 20, 2012, it opened its 100th store (Wang, 2012), adding 36 new stores in less than a year. By the end of 2012, H&M had 114 stores in 47 cities, and Zara had 60 stores in 31 cities. They both entered the mega urban markets and Tier 1 cities first, with a flagship store at an attention-grabbing location. While they still heavily concentrate in the large urban markets, with 70 percent of their stores in the mega urban markets and Tier 1 cities, they have begun to spread to smaller cities including Tier 4 cities (see Table 5.2), where consumers already know the brands.

Sales data are not available for H&M and Zara's China operations, but according to Swedish bank Handelsbanken, H&M is more profitable in China than in any of its other markets (Hansgard & Burkitt, 2011).

Japanese Retailers

Japanese retailers are among the earliest foreign entrants. Of the first 15 foreign retailers approved by the Chinese government in 1992 for experiment, four were Japanese (Wang & Jones, 2001). Yet their expansion has been much slower and geographically limited, compared with those from North America and Western Europe. Most Japanese retailers are department stores and supermarket operators. Jusco, which began retail operations in China in 1996, set up only four department stores in its first five years in China. However, one of them (the one in Shanghai) did not survive for long and was closed in 2000. Its expansion has accelerated only after 2005. It now has 27 outlets in 14 cities, becoming the second largest Japanese retail chain in mainland China by store locations, next only to Uniqlo. Still, it focuses on the mega urban markets (with 48 percent of all stores) and the Tier 1 cities (26 percent). Only recently has Jusco begun to explore Tier 2 urban markets.

Isetan entered China even earlier—in 1993. It once had six department stores in five cities—two in Shanghai and one each in Tianjin, Jinan, Chengdu, and Shenyang, all mega urban markets or Tier 1 cities; but three of them (those in Shanghai, Jinan, and Shenyang) were closed due to losses (Liu, 2013). Ito-Yokado, a GM retailer, is another slow starter. In the 13 years since its entry in 1997, it opened only 12 stores in only two cities: eight in Beijing and four in Chengdu. This was less than one store opening per year. Nine of them were opened after 2005. Daiei, another Japanese food retailer, once had 12 stores in a single city—Tianjin. In 2005, it sold its entire operation to the Beijing-based Wu-Mart (one of China's "national team" members), announcing that it was leaving China. Lawson, a CVS chain, suffered a similar fate. In eight years between 1996 and 2004, Lawson opened 96 stores, all in Shanghai. Unable to make a profit, Lawson conceded its controlling ownership to its local partner—Lianhua Group—in 2004. With the injection of additional capital from Lianhua, the transformed Lawson was able to expand by 100 additional stores in less than a year ("Shanghai Lawson begins to make a profit," 2004). In 2011, Lawson bought back shares from Bailian Group (now the parent of Lianhua) and regained majority ownership. It is now poised to expand on its own.

Despite being a latecomer, entering China in 2002, Uniqlo expanded much faster than all other Japanese retailers in China. By the end of 2012, it operated 170 outlets in 41 cities. Uniqlo is also a fast fashion retailer, competing with H&M and Zara head-on—not only in the mega urban markets and Tier 1 cities, but also in the lower tier cities (see Table 5.2). It now has more stores in Tier 4 cities than do H&M and Zara, and aims to move further ahead of them. China has become Uniqlo's most important overseas market.

Southeast Asian Retailers

Major players from Southeast Asia, dubbed "second tier TNCs" (transnational corporations) by Coe and Wrigley (2007), are largely in two retailing categories: hypermarkets and department stores. The former are represented by RT-Mart, Lotus, Trust-Mart, E-Mart, Lotte Mart, and PARKnSHOP; the latter include Parkson and New World (see Table 5.1). Although they are not on par with the retail superpowers of Wal-Mart, Carrefour, Tesco, and Auchan, in terms of financial capital and IT resources, the Southeast Asian retailers have been able to grab much larger market shares in China than the Japanese retailers.

Since its entry in mainland China in 1997, the Taiwan-based RT-Mart has opened 143 stores in 88 cities: not as many stores as those of Carrefour but with a much wider geographical distribution and a higher level of market penetration. Compared with Carrefour, RT-Mart has a higher proportion of stores in the lower tier cities: 13 percent in Tier 3 cities, 9 percent in Tier 4 cities, and 19 percent in other lower tier cities (see Table 5.2). The Thai-based Lotus is another early entrant and leader in setting up hypermarkets in China with impressive results. In 2010, it operated 74 stores in 23 cities. Lotus had more stores than RT-Mart until 2006, but its growth has since been stagnant and surpassed by RT-Mart. In October of 2013, Lotus announced to sell half of its China stores (36 of them) to the Beijing-based domestic Wu-Mart, retaining retail operations in two provinces only: Guangdong and Hunan (Li, 2013).

Compared with the other Southeast Asian food retailers, the Korea-based E-Mart is a much slower starter. In seven years after its first store opened in Shanghai in 1997, E-Mart was largely dormant with no expansion at all. It was not until 2004 that E-Mart began to expand by opening a second store in Shanghai. One year later, it opened two more stores in Shanghai and Tianjin respectively. By 2010, it expanded to an operation of 27 stores; but in the following year in 2011, it sold 11 stores, reducing the chain's operation to 16 locations in only four cities (with nine stores in Shanghai, five in Tianjin, and one each in Wuxi and Suzhou). It withdrew from Beijing completely.

Lotte Mart, also a South Korean-based hypermarket operator, entered China 11 years after E-Mart. Yet it expanded much more quickly and has achieved a much high level of market penetration. Its retail operation in China began only in 2008 with the acquisition of the Dutch Makro. One year later in 2009, Lotte acquired another supermarket chain—Times—which was established in Nantong of Jiangsu Province with Hong Kong investment. All 65 Times supermarkets were brought under the Lotte banner. Lotte continued to aggressively seek acquisition targets in other cities. By the end of 2010, it already had 80 stores in 33 cities, exceeding both Lotus and E-Mart.

The Taiwan-based Trust-Mart was another successful story. Since opening its first store in mainland China in 1997, it has set up more than 100 stores spread across 33 cities. In 2007, it sold 35 percent of its ownership to Wal-Mart, which was envious of many of the premium store locations that Trust-Mart had developed. Wal-Mart, through negotiation, secured the option of buying the remaining shares of Trust-Mart before February 2010, but the transaction has yet to be completed. Trust-Mart's identity and nationality are still ambiguous.

PARKnSHOP is a retail arm of Hong Kong's Hutchinson Whampoa Limited (HWL). It started expansion with an ambitious plan, but met a series of blows. Initially, it intended to focus on two affluent regions: South China centered on Guangzhou, and East China centered on Shanghai. It entered Shanghai in 1994 in a partnership with the local government, and quickly expanded to 14 supermarkets. Further expansion was, however, blocked by the state government, which at the time prohibited foreign investors to exceed 49 percent of an enterprise's ownership. Not being able to grow in Shanghai, PARKnSHOP sold all but one of its stores to the Dutch Royal Ahold in 2000. In 2006, it returned to Shanghai with a change in format: by opening a hypermarket. Sadly, the hypermarket did not survive either, and was closed in less than two years. In 2012, it closed its last store in Shanghai and shifted its focus on expansion in South China. Of its 44 stores in 2010, 40 were in the Province of Guangdong, confined to the three affluent cities of Guangzhou, Shenzhen, and Dongguan.

Both Parkson and New World also established a fair presence in China, but with a focus on the department store format. Parkson was also among the first foreign retailers approved by the Chinese government in 1992 to enter China. Since opening its first store in Beijing in 1994, it has opened 47 stores in 30 cities. New World is a subsidiary of the Hong Kong-based New World Development Company Limited. It has set up 37 stores in 17 cities, with 10 in Shanghai and six each in Beijing and Wuhan. In almost all other cities, it has only one store. The New World Department Stores are operated under two banners: Spring Paris in Shanghai, and New World in all other cities. Department stores can spread over widely because they do not depend on regional distribution centers as heavily as the food-oriented hypermarkets and supermarkets. Moreover, most of them lease floor space to brand-based retail agents or suppliers.

Performance of International Retailers

Naturally, total sales are related to the size of the retail chain and the degree of market penetration. Overall, the Western and Southeast Asian retailers sell much more than the Japanese retailers, as is shown in Table 5.1.

According to the China Chain Store Association (2011), most of them are among China's top 50 retail chains: RT-Mart (6th), Carrefour (7th), Wal-Mart (9th), Parkson (16th), New World (20th), Trust-Mart (27th), Tesco (31st), Lotte Mart (33rd), Lotus (34th), Auchan (35th), and Metro (40th). The sales of the Japanese Jusco and Ito-Yokado are only higher than those of E-Mart and PARKnSHOP.

Since number of stores varies among the foreign chains, per store annual sales are also compared. Surprisingly, the Japanese Ito-Yokado tops all others, with a whopping 588.5 million yuan per store. Auchan and RT-Mart are the second best performers with 329 and 351 million yuan per store—much higher than Metro (243.8) and Carrefour (230.8). Among the least efficient are Wal-Mart (182.6), Lotte Mart (180.6), Tesco (159.0), Trust-Mart (158.6), E-Mart (148.1), and PARKnSHOP (88.3). Of the department stores, both Parkson and New World seem to be more efficient than Jusco. The president of Auchan (China)'s Development Division is quoted as saying: "only three foreign retailers in China are making a profit, and Auchan is one of them. Expanding too fast often results in poor-performing stores. Auchan's profitable performance is attributed to its prudence in growth speed" ("Auchan expands prudently in China," 2011).

BUSINESS MODELS AND CORPORATE STRATEGIES

There is no one single formula for success for all retailers. Each corporation devises its own strategies, which makes study of organizational structures important (Wrigley & Currah, 2006). According to retail industry analysts (Koopman, 2000), every growth strategy must be built on the following pillars in order to maintain a competitive edge: (1) the retailer must offer a competitively superior product as defined by local consumers; (2) the retailer must be able to develop superior economics across the value chain that delivers the product to the local consumer; and (3) global retailers must be able to execute in the local environment. This section relates success and failure to the various business models and corporate strategies with regard to format, merchandise sourcing, acquisition of real estate, and adaptation to local market conditions.

Western Retailers

In general, the Western retailers possess more capital resources than their Japanese and Southeast Asian counterparts to invest and expand in China, but the examination here goes beyond this general factor and looks at other aspects of corporate strategies.

When choosing a retail format for expansion in a foreign market, international retailers consider its associated leverage advantages from supply chains and the need to adapt to local conditions (Goldman, 2001). Evidently, all Western retailers (except the fast fashion retailers) choose the big box format to ground their retail capital in China. This format is new in China and has allowed the Western retailers to dominate specific sectors with little competition in the local market. It seems that the hypermarket, which offers a wide assortment of consumer goods to mass consumers at competitive prices, proves to serve the local markets better than the competing formats such as the department store and the supermarket. Wal-Mart operates in China with four formats: supercenters (Wal-Mart's term for hypermarket), Sam's Club (warehouse membership clubs), neighborhood centers (mini-supermarket), and discount convenience stores (CVS). However, the majority of its outlets, 209 out of 219, are supercenters. Its other formats grew very slowly. After 16 years in China, Wal-Mart still has only six Sam's Clubs and two neighborhood centers. In March 2012, it announced that it would close all the discount convenience stores and cancel the 3-year-old experimental program completely. Carrefour, Auchan, and Tesco all also chose to expand with hypermarkets.

Metro focuses exclusively on the warehouse membership club format, open only to registered members, many of whom are corporate consumers and small retailers. Yet this format does not seem to serve the local market as successfully as does the hypermarket. While each city has numerous small retailers, it is not clear whether these membership clubs are their preferred "suppliers" and if purchasing from these clubs would leave them with a reasonable profit margin, given that there exist numerous domestic wholesalers and suppliers in the country with a loosely regulated distribution system. For individual consumers, real savings from shopping at a membership club would be achieved by purchasing in bulk. Yet due to the lack of private automobiles and shortage of living space among the ordinary Chinese consumers, few shoppers can carry multiple bags on a single shopping trip, or have space at home for a second refrigerator to store bulk groceries. There are already signs of a lack of consumer support for membership clubs, suggesting that this format may not be viable in the Chinese market, at least not yet. So far, Wal-Mart operates only six Sam's Clubs in the whole country. One of its three stores in the city of Kunming was launched as a Sam's Club, but had to be converted to a supercenter shortly thereafter. The Dutch Makro also had great difficulty expanding with this format and ended up selling its entire operation to Lotte Mart in 2008, leaving the German Metro as the only club chain that still seems to be expanding.

The supermarket does not seem to be a competitive format either. The Dutch Royal Ahold established a supermarket chain (The Tops) in 1996 in Shanghai under a joint venture with China Venturetech Investment Corp., and later expanded to 40 stores, including the supermarkets it acquired from PARKnSHOP in 2000 (Baljko, 2006). However, like PARKnSHOP, it failed miserably due to fierce competition from local supermarkets and had to withdraw from the country completely after five years of presence in Shanghai. Carrefour introduced eight supermarkets in Beijing in 2004 under a different banner—Champion Supermarket—but they were never able to make money. In June 2006, Carrefour sold them off to focus on hypermarkets (Li, 2006a).

Ikea, B&Q, and Home Depot, which specialize in furniture and home improvement products, focus on promoting high-quality and Western-style products with the DIY (do-it-yourself) concept. While China's booming housing market presents auspicious market conditions with enormous demand, products from Ikea, B&Q, and Home Depot are too expensive to most ordinary citizens—the largest segment of the consumer market. They cannot compete with the numerous domestic retailers that sell less expensive, albeit lower-quality, products. The DIY concept does not work well in China either. Most new apartments are sold with bare brick walls and concrete floors, but furnishing them with studs and drywall is not an option because they would reduce valuable living space. Few purchasers have the skills required to complete them or to renovate them. What is preferred is a DIFM (do-it-for-me) business model. Although both B&Q and Home Depot offer professional services through their own enlisted contractors, the service charges are also much higher than the other, less-qualified contractors. This is the main reason for these retailers' slow expansion and for the demise of the German OBI and the American Home Depot. This also explains why B&Q has been focusing its operations in the more affluent mega urban markets and the first-tier cities (see Table 5.2). There is insufficient demand for its products in the lower tier cities. Even in the large urban centers, B&Q is closing stores to reduce operation scales due to the market challenges. In 2008, B&Q launched a program, dubbed "Transformation," to make extensive changes in store layout, product mix, and presentation, and to adapt to consumer preference and local market conditions. However, the program brought about limited success (Zhuang, 2012). Another foreign retailer of home improvement materials, the French Leroy Merlin, opened only two stores in China (both in Beijing) since its entry in 2004. Yet one of them had to be closed in August 2012. The fate of the remaining store is not difficult to predict. Apparently, it will take a much longer time to nurture the China market for consumption of these high-quality and high-priced products, and there is a lot more for foreign retailers in this sector to learn to adapt to the local consumer markets.

Given that the large format stores introduced by the foreign retailers need to be supported by a relatively large trade area, and because the mobility of the Chinese consumers is still somewhat limited, almost all the hypermarkets provide free shuttle buses to bring in shoppers from an expansive surrounding area, including the primary trade areas of their competitors. Figure 5.3 shows how the free shuttle buses extend the trade area of a Carrefour hypermarket in Minhang District of Shanghai to compete with the nearby hypermarkets. These bus services are provided seven days a week because weekday shopping traffic in Chinese cities is high, compared with that in the Western economies (Lo & Wang, 2006).

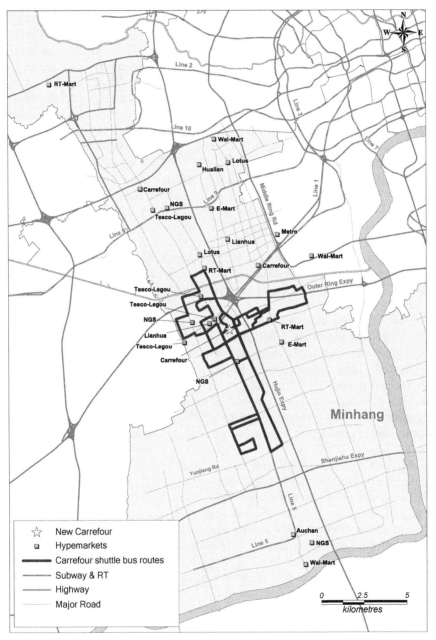

Figure 5.3   Free shuttle bus provided by a Carrefour hypermarket in Minhang District of Shanghai.

(Minhang, with a population of 2.5 million, is an exemplary battleground for foreign hypermarket operators. Many of them offer free shuttle bus services. The Carrefour store, illustrated in this figure, used to operate 15 bus routes; the number is now reduced to 10.)

A particular format must be supported not only by the right location and trade area but also by available and affordable real estate. In general, retailers employ one or both of the following approaches to acquiring business premises: constructing self-owned stores, or leasing commercial space from other developers or property owners. At home in the U.S., Wal-Mart customarily acquires land at strategically selected locations and builds its own stores (Simmons & Graff, 1998). In Canada, it works closely with a commercial property developer–Smart Centers—and leases commercial space from it. In China, Wal-Mart also chose to lease properties from domestic real estate developers to minimize sunk costs. It formed strategic alliances with two major Chinese developers: Shenzhen International Trust & Investment Corporation (SZITIC) and Wanda Group. SZITIC is Wal-Mart's longtime partner in China. Most facilities that house its supercenters in Shenzhen were constructed and are owned by SZITIC, but are leased to Wal-Mart. To facilitate Wal-Mart expanding further and faster, SZITIC in 2002 created a subsidiary named SZITIC Commercial Property Development Ltd., whose main purpose is to search for sites, obtain land use rights, and develop retail premises in different cities to meet the expansion needs of Wal-Mart. In 2004, it broke ground in Shenzhen to build a new 200,000 m² facility to house Wal-Mart's Asia and China HQ Offices and a new Sam's Club ("Wal-Mart's Asia HQ Office will have a new home in Shenzhen," 2004). To beef up its financial capability, SZITIC Commercial Property Development Ltd., in late 2004, entered a joint venture with Singapore's largest real estate corporation—CapitaLand Group. The two parties announced plans to raise new capital through the Hong Kong Stock Exchange.

Wanda Group, whose core business is in property development, is based in the city of Dalian in northeast China. In addition to commercial properties, Wanda develops large-scale housing projects and often combines the two types of development on the same tract of land. Wal-Mart entered an agreement with Wanda to lease commercial spaces in Wanda-developed properties. In 2007, 10 Wal-Mart supercenters were operated in Wanda-built shopping centers, with six more to open shortly after (Wang & Zhang, 2006).

Metro employs a different approach. To control leasing costs and reduce reliance on third-party developers, Metro created its own property development arm (Lu, 2000). Since construction of self-owned stores requires large sums of investment, it certainly affected the speed of expansion. In 2005, Metro began to lease spaces from Chinese developers and opened its first store in Shenzhen in leased space. It opened its second store in Beijing also by leasing retail spaces (Li, 2006b). As costs of leasing soared in recent years, more foreign retailers chose to acquire land use rights and develop self-owned commercial facilities. Tesco in 2007 created Tesco Property Holdings Limited as an independent company to purchase, develop, and operate property developments in China. Unlike Metro, Tesco chose to develop shopping centers, branded as Lifespace Centers, where the Tesco-Legou hypermarket sits as the anchor. The remaining space is subdivided and leased to third-party retailers to generate income to help cover the construction and maintenance costs of the shopping centers. This is also the same business model that Hymart-Hymall employed before being acquired by Tesco.

As land and commercial properties in large urban centers became scarce and expensive, most Western retailers entered a new stage of expansion through acquisition. According to Alexander (1997), international retailers sometime acquire a minor interest in a retail operation, in order to monitor the performance of that company. If things proceed as expected, minority interests may lead to outright acquisition.

Auchan and RT-Mart first formed the joint venture—Sun Holdings—in 2000, with Auchan and RT-Mart (China) holding each other's one third shares of their respective China operations. In 2011, the two moved one step further to create a joint stock company named Sun Art Retail Group Limited, and went public through an IPO at the Hong Kong Stock Exchange. While the two retailers retain their respective brands with separate operations, they now join forces in negotiating with suppliers and sharing distribution facilities. It has been widely speculated that Auchan may eventually gain control over RT-Mart's mainland China operation, as it did in 2001 when it acquired the majority ownership of RT-Mart's operation in Taiwan.

Tesco purchased 50 percent of Hymart-Hymall's ownership in 2004— another Taiwanese retail chain with 25 hypermarkets. Two years later, Tesco augmented its ownership to 90 percent and changed all the Hymart-Hymall store signs to the Tesco-Legou banner (Liu, 2006). Similarly, Wal-Mart in 2007 obtained 35 percent of Trust-Mart's total shares ("Wal-Mart aims to control Trust-Mart," 2007). At the same time, it provided 376 million yuan of loans to some other shareholders in exchange for 30 percent of the voting right, effectively controlling Trust-Mart's China operation. According to the agreement, Wal-Mart has the option to acquire the remaining shares by February 2010. Although the acquisition passed Ministry of Commerce's antitrust review, its completion has been delayed three times. Many of the Trust-Mart stores are franchised outlets without state government approval and proper land use application. This resulted in a complicated ownership structure within the Trust-Mart chain. Many franchisees want a favorable deal from Wal-Mart, but Wal-Mart demands that they clean up their own house first by obtaining proper business registration and licenses. Once the acquisition is complete, Wal-Mart plans to consolidate the two operations and bring all the Trust-Mart stores under the Wal-Mart banner, ending the dual-brand transition.

Both B&Q and Home Depot also tried to expand through acquisition, but have been much less successful. Home Depot even approached B&Q in 2005 for an outright purchase ("Home Depot is reported to enter China via acquisition of B&Q," 2005). The only Western retailers who did not resort to this route of expansion are Metro and Ikea, mainly because of the lack of appropriate acquisition targets in China. As a result, their expansion has not been as rapid as the other Western retailers.

For international retailers, another daunting task is to secure supplies of merchandise and distribute them to their local stores. For both economical and cultural reasons, foreign retailers purchase almost all the products from local suppliers. Wal-Mart focused on logistics. After moving its Global Purchasing Center from Hong Kong to Shenzhen in 2001, Wal-Mart has established three branches in Dongguan, Fuzhou, and Shanghai, respectively. Wal-Mart deals with over 15,000 Chinese suppliers (Wal-Mart China, 2007). Besides its purchasing centers, Wal-Mart has built three distribution centers, one each in Shenzhen, Tianjin, and Shanghai, to supply its stores in China. However, because the stores are spread widely in 95 cities, with many cities having only one to two stores, the distribution centers can hardly reach all constituent stores, and the *economies of places* (Amin, 2003) have not been achieved in China. Most merchandise is still shipped to its stores directly from suppliers, which contributes to higher merchandising costs. This may have contributed to Wal-Mart's low per-store sales (see Table 5.1).

This problem is not unique to Wal-Mart. All other Western retailers face the same difficulties in China, where they have not been able to replicate their efficient distribution systems developed in their home countries. To compensate for the "lost profits" in merchandise distribution, almost all foreign retailers turned to squeezing suppliers by imposing a variety of fees including store entrance fees and promotion fees. Carrefour was the most notorious. In 2006, Shanghai Commerce Information Center, together with FMCG Research Center, conducted a survey of suppliers for their experiences in dealing with retailers. Ninety-eight suppliers participated in the survey to rate 51 retailers, both foreign and domestic. The foreign retailers rated are listed in Table 5.3. Wal-Mart received the highest rating in all three categories: general satisfaction, cost of doing business with the retailer, and level of trust. Carrefour was rated as the most expensive retailer to do business with, and it did not have a good relationship with the surveyed suppliers.

Some retailers pay their suppliers after the merchandise is sold, but retain a portion of the markups as a source of income. In 2004, B&Q retained only 18 percent of the markups. This, however, increased to 32–34 percent in 2006 and further to 53 percent in 2007 (Bai, 2011). It also demanded that products from all suppliers must achieve a minimum amount of sales in the B&Q stores, and a threshold portion of the price markups be levied, even if minimum sales are not achieved. In a number of cases, suppliers not only did not receive any payment from B&Q due to low volume of sales, but were told they owed money to the retailer. In November 2007, a group of domestic manufacturers publicly denounced B&Q for its heavy-handed treatment of its suppliers, and refused to continue supplying products to

Table 5.3   Rating of Foreign Retailers by Chinese Suppliers, 2006*

Retailer	General satisfaction	Cost of doing business with	Level of trust
Wal-Mart	3.78	2.82	4.19
Metro	3.51	3.31	3.94
Lawson	3.41	3.37	3.69
E-Mart	3.23	3.32	3.54
Auchan	3.21	3.68	3.73
Carrefour	2.96	4.04	3.75
Lotus	2.96	3.44	3.13
RT-Mart	2.83	3.72	3.26
Hymart-Hymall	2.79	4.0	3.31
Trust-Mart	2.53	3.40	2.50

* scores range from 1 to 5, with 1 being the lowest and 5 being the highest.
Source: Shanghai Commerce Information Center and FMCG Research Center, 2006.

the B&Q stores. B&Q filed a lawsuit against the group for defamation and arrears (Fu, 2007). The lawsuit dragged on for four years until 2012, when the Court of Shanghai found B&Q at fault and ordered it to pay 16 million yuan to the plaintiffs. The negative publicity surely damaged the retailer-supplier relations.

At a European Day of Commerce conference in 2001, the President and CEO of the Dutch Royal Ahold stressed the importance of social reputations of companies with the following remarks:

> We see consumers and consumer groups who increasingly make their choices, positively and negatively, based on the social reputations of companies. And we see governments looking to hold companies accountable for their behaviors everywhere in the world. (Crawford, 2001)

The top brass of the Western retailers certainly know very well the importance of developing and maintaining good relations with the various levels of government in China. They have been making concerted efforts to foster a positive corporate image as *an outstanding corporate citizen*. In their survey of foreign retailers, Tacconelli and Wriglet (2009) were informed that strong relations with governments in China has been an essential prerequisite to secure prime sites and receive favorable tax treatment. After becoming Wal-Mart CEO in 2000, Lee Scott paid five visits to China to meet with high-ranking government officials including the Head of State (Che, 2002). Wal-Mart uses a corporate slogan for the same purpose: "work with the community; pay back to the community" (Wail-Mart China, 2004), Each time it opened a new store, Wal-Mart announced, at the grand opening ceremony, a donation to charitable organizations or communities to "help the neighborhood, support education of children, and protect the environment" (Wal-Mart China, 2007). Between 1996 and 2003, it donated a total of US$1.2 million to such initiatives. In November 2004, it made another donation of US$1 million to China's Tsinghua University to help establish a Center for the Study of Retailing, with Lee Scott presenting the check to the university in person (Ma, 2004). Wal-Mart even relaxed its global non-union policy in China, allowing unions to be formed in its China stores, a big concession to the demand of the Chinese government. Apparently, its public relations efforts have worked in its favor. Despite the fact that Wal-Mart had always maintained majority ownership in its joint ventures before China's admission to the WTO, it was never admonished by the Chinese government, as was Carrefour in 1998 (Wang, 2003).

As revealed in Siebers' survey of international retailers (Siebers, 2011), local policies are in many cases more important than state policies for their expansion in China. As such, Western retailers often took advantage of local government officials who pursued political credits measured by the amount of FDI that they were able attract to their cities. These officials often courted the Western retailers and offered them land and sites at premium locations with deep discounts. It was reported that the government of Hangzhou posted for public bidding a piece of land zoned for commercial use, as was required by the state government, but it attached the stringent condition that the successful bidder must bring in one of the top 100 retailers in the world (Zhou, 2006). In the end, only SZITIC Commercial Property Development Ltd.—the Wal-Mart partner—qualified for the bidding and subsequently obtained the land use right at a price even lower than residential land. Similar deals have happened in other cities.

H&M and Zara did not have to face the same challenges as the other Western retailers because they entered China after the country had relinquished all the trade barriers. Their stores are typically mall based, and are much smaller in size than the big box stores. They claim their stores can bring large numbers of shoppers to the host malls, and often use this claim as a bargaining chip for rent reduction. They also want flexible rental leases and contracts, because a new shopping center is often built nearby with a much better brand mix (Hansegard & Burkitt, 2011). They also source most of their products in China to reduce production costs and shorten the turnaround time, with new arrivals in stores every month or every few months ("H&M: Democratic style keep price flat," 2012). Focusing on mid-priced but trendy clothes, they set up a new price tier between low-end, home brands and foreign, luxury brands, and redefined the cheap chic aesthetics (Fong, 2006; Kingsbury, 2007). In the meantime, they differentiate themselves from each other to reduce competition within the same shopping center. For example, Zara mainly designs black, white, and gray garments, and generally attracts working women, whereas H&M offers a wider variety of collections in different colors. H&M occasionally teams up with luxury designers and celebrities to design co-branded lines. The Versace for H&M line was launched in 2011, and was well received in China because many Chinese consumers want more fashion clothing but can rarely afford luxury products ("Consumed by fashion: Sweden's H&M tells the story of China's rising middle class aspirations," 2012).

Japanese Retailers

The expansion of the Japanese retailers was seriously affected by a combination of three factors: the formats they adopted to penetrate the China market, the financial difficulties of their parent companies at home, and the rigidity in business decision making.

Unlike their Western counterparts, the Japanese retailers entered the China market with the conventional formats of department store (e.g., Yohan, Jusco, and Isetan), supermarket (e.g., Daiei and Ito-Yokado), and convenience stores (Lawson). They also focused on high-end consumers and targeted wealthy families. As has been mentioned previously, these formats have proven less competitive than the hypermarket format in Chinese cities. The department store was the dominant retail format in China until the mid-1990s. In the late 1980s and the early 1990s, there was massive construction of glamorous department stores in all urban centers. By the time the Japanese department stores arrived, this sector of the retail market was already saturated. Their department stores suffered further in the late 1990s when faced with competition from more specialized stores. Supermarkets encountered similar circumstances. In the late 1980s and the 1990s, numerous state-owned grocery stores were converted into supermarkets and convenience stores. In Shanghai alone, there existed 1,743 supermarkets and 4,267 convenience stores in 2005 (Shanghai Economic Commission, 2005). Besides, wet markets were abundant and are still popular among many urban consumers. The Japanese supermarkets suffered because of competition from both domestic supermarkets and local wet markets.

Shortly after their entry in the mid- and late 1990s, most Japanese retailers encountered financial crises in their home country, triggered in part by the infamous East Asian Financial Crisis. Yohan, one of the first 15 foreign retailers approved by the Chinese government in 1992, entered China in 1995 and built two large department stores in Shanghai. Sadly, because its parent company went bankrupt in 1997, its short-lived operations in Shanghai were handed over to its Chinese partner—Shanghai No. 1 Department Store Group. Daiei was the first foreign retailer to open supermarkets in China. In the 10 years after its entry in 1995, it was able to expand to 12 stores, all confined to the city of Tianjin. In 2004, its parent company, under pressure from its creditors, sought restructuring help from a state-backed corporate turnaround body—the Industrial Revitalization Corp. of

Japan ("Japan's Daiei to sell 39 outlets", 2006). Part of the restructuring plan was to sell some of its operations (including those in China) and use the proceeds to repay debts. In 2005, Daiei had to sell its entire operation in Tianjin to the Beijing-based Wu-Mart Group, and withdrew from China completely ("Beijing Wu-Mart acquires Tianjin Daiei," 2005). Jusco, Ito-Yokado, and Lawson encountered similar difficulties, and the investments needed for expansion were not forthcoming. To build up its financial muscles and increase competitiveness, Isetan merged with Japan's 4th largest department operator—Mitsukoshi—in 2008 to form Isetan Mitsukoshi Holdings Ltd. ("Japan's Isetan, Misukoshi to merge in Spring [of 2008]," 2007). The impact of the merger on Isetan's ability to expand in China has so far been minimal: it announced it would open its second store in Tianjin in the late half of 2012 and plans to open a second store in Chengdu in the distant 2016, but closed three stores in Shanghai, Tianjin, and Shenyang.

Another factor that has affected their expansion was the lack of flexibility in business decision making. To use what has become a classic example, every new store location that Lawson chose in Shanghai had to be approved by the headquarters office in Japan. As well, Lawson was permitted to open stores only in areas west of Shanghai Railway Station, but not in areas east of the station ("Shanghai Lawson begins to make a profit," 2004). While many Western and Asian retailers were aggressively seeking entry approval from local governments and bypassing the state government, the Japanese retailers were largely following the rules to the letter and patiently awaiting deregulation. While the Japanese retailers have been law-abiding corporate citizens and they never got into trouble with the Chinese government, they lost first-mover advantages to their competitors in many cities and have paid high prices in a market where regulation was far from being perfect and under-the-table deals were rampant. While forming joint ventures with local partners was necessary before 2004, as it was a firm requirement on the part of the Chinese government, the Japanese retailers were too slow to buy out their local partners and consolidate their operations and business decision making in China. Ito-Yokado has two main joint ventures in China: one in Beijing, the other in Chengdu. The former operates eight stores; the latter only four. Its third joint venture, also in Beijing, is with Wangfujing Department Store Group, focusing on fresh food-oriented supermarkets. It has opened only two stores. Not until 2012 did Ito-Yokado establish its solely-owned, unified operation—Ito-Yokado (China) Investment Limited—to consolidate its segmented operations in the country (Chong, 2012). Until recently, Jusco had four joint ventures in mainland China, in Guangzhou, Shenzhen, Qingdao, and Beijing. The first two were responsible for expansion in South China, whereas the latter two were given the task of growing in eastern and northern China. However, its stores in south China had a different name from that of the stores in the rest of the country. In February 2012, AEON Japan, the parent of Jusco, also announced the establishment of its China headquarters office in

Beijing to consolidate its China operations and investment under one unified banner—Aeon.

Despite their slow growth, the existing Japanese stores perform relatively well (see Table 5.1). Although only Lawson is included in the survey (see Table 5.3), Chinese suppliers seem to be satisfied with the way Japanese retailers do business with them. It should be noted that while the Japanese department store chains are still expanding, albeit slowly, they have recently modified the format by adding either a food department or a supermarket, usually at the sub-ground level of the department stores. Two years ago, Jusco expanded its shopping center in Qingdao by adding more floor space to the supermarket as well as to the department store. The new Jusco stores in Shenzhen and Guangzhou are all more like hypermarkets.

Uniqlo, like its European counterparts H&M and Zara, did not have the burden of having to form a joint venture with Chinese retailers. As Naoki Otoma, Chief Operating Officer of Fast Retailing that operates Uniqlo, said in an interview (Sanchanta, 2010), "In China, we will grow organically without alliances or collaborations. There are no Chinese companies that can do a better job than us." Uniqlo presents a different focus from its competitors by selling causal and affordable basics (Azuma, 2012). In more recent years, Uniqlo has been experimenting with a new business model, involving large-scale, drive-in outlets away from central-city shopping centers, to take advantage of lower rent. Its first outlet opened near Shanghai in 2012 (Staff Reporter, 2012). Similar outlets are planned for Beijing and Guangzhou.

Southeast Asian Retailers

Information about the corporate strategies of the Southeast Asian retailers is scant. As is revealed in Table 5.1, most Southeast Asian retailers mimic the Western retailers by using the hypermarket as the leading format to penetrate the China market. The fact that they are able to expand with impressive results proves once again that by far the food-oriented hypermarket competes better than other formats in China. Except Hymart-Hymall, all the Southeast Asian retailers rely on their local partners or local developers for business premises. Hymart-Hymall was the pioneer to develop a chain of community shopping centers with its hypermarket as the anchor store. Three such shopping centers were built in Shanghai (Wang et al., 2006).

The Taiwanese retailers have benefited from two major factors that were not available to other foreign retailers: preferential government policies, and their cultural and ethnic affinity with the mainland. In as early as 1988, the State Council announced the provision of major preferential policies that both encouraged and protected business investment from Taiwan. This gave Taiwanese investors a competitive edge over other Southeast Asian retailers. Trust-Mart was established by Winston Wong, the son of the founder of Formosa Plastics. Both father and son enjoy good business relations with the mainland. Further, the Taiwanese retailers are more familiar with the tastes and preferences of the mainland Chinese due to cultural similarity.

Despite these advantages, the Taiwanese retailers often played with government rules, like Carrefour did. When restrictions were still in place limiting foreign retailers to joint ventures in a handful of cities, RT-Mart aggressively opened stores in many other cities with different names to disguise its corporate identity (Gu, 2006). In 2005, after restrictions were lifted, it quickly flipped the store signs to the RT-Mart brand and the number of stores increased instantly. Trust-Mart did the same, making Wal-Mart's outright acquisition of it bumpy and difficult.

It is also widely reported that the expansion of Taiwanese retailers has been achieved at the expense of their suppliers, and delay in payment was a common occurrence (Ai, 2005). This was confirmed by the results of the survey of suppliers conducted by Shanghai Commerce Information Center and FMCG Research Center (see Table 5.3). Not surprisingly, the three major Taiwanese retailers received the lowest ratings in the survey: the least satisfied by the Chinese suppliers; the most expensive to do business with; and the least trusted by suppliers.

To overcome their limitations in capital resources and their lack of competency in management of large-scale retail/logistics operations, the Taiwanese retailers all sought for partnership with the Western retail giants. As described earlier, RT-Mart teamed up with Auchan by first exchanging one third of ownership in their respective China operations in 2000 (Gu, 2006), and then formed a new public company to raise development capital on the stock exchange. Hymart-Hymall entered a joint venture agreement with Tesco in 2004 by relinquishing 50 percent of its ownership to the resource-rich British retailer ("British supermarket giant Tesco lands in China," 2004); it later sold another 40 percent of its ownership to Tesco. Trust-Mart conceded 35 percent of its ownership to Wal-Mart in 2007 and agreed to sell the remaining shares to Wal-Mart. It seems that the Taiwanese retailers do not intend to run the hypermarket as their core business. They know they cannot compete with the Western retail heavyweights in a long battle and will eventually sell their entire operations to the global retailers.

The two South Korean retailers have business models that are distinct from each other. E-Mart sought the path of organic growth and focused on the mega urban markets and Tier 1 cities, but it grew slowly and painfully. Lotte Mart adopted the strategy of acquisition for both entry and expansion. Except in the case of Makro, Lotte Mart selected its acquisition targets in smaller urban centers. Of the 83 stores it operated in 2010, nearly 60 percent were in third- and fourth-tier cities (see Table 5.2). In other words, it has made the deepest penetration in the smaller urban markets, among all foreign retailers. Yet its per store sales are comparable with those of Wal-Mart (see Table 5.1). It is also the only Asian retailer to acquire a western retail chain in China, although it moved away from Makro's warehouse format.

The two department store operators Parson and New World both rely on leasing or subletting store spaces to individual agents who sell brand-specific merchandise, particularly apparel and shoes. They enter into agreements with certain suppliers of branded goods, known as concessionaires, who are permitted to occupy designated areas in the stores and to establish their own sales counters for their products. The department operators receive a percentage of the revenue generated from such concessions as a commission (Parkson Retail Group Limited, 2005). To do this, they do not expand through franchising, but own almost all of the department stores that they operate (Koh, 2013). This reduces the daunting task of merchandising and distribution on the part of the department store operators, and the rentals provide recurring income to the retailers, which is especially important in the years of slow sales growth.

As stated in the prospectus for its IPO in the Hong Kong Stock Exchange, Parkson's long-term goal is to be the largest department store chain in China. It aims to achieve this goal by adopting the following four key strategies (Parkson Retail Group Limited, 2005): (1) grow its department store chain through expansion and gain market share through consolidation and merger and acquisition; (2) upgrade stores to continue to move further upmarket; (3) further develop relationships with brands, in particular international brands seeking to enter the PRC market; and (4) continue to upgrade IT systems. In 2005, Parkson operated 36 department stores in China (China Chain Store Association, 2006), of which 12 were acquired stores previously owned by Chinese retailers (Parkson Retail Group Limited, 2005). In more recent years, Parkson began to enter the business of shopping center development to further leverage income growth—a trend that will be discussed in Chapter 8.

New World adopts a similar business model. Of its total revenues in 2012 (HK$3. 5 billion), 69 percent came from concessionaire sales, and only 19 percent from direct sales; the rest came from rental and management fees (New World Department Store China Limited, 2013). This "revenue tool" is also used by the Japanese department store operators to some extent, but does not seem to be used by the Western retailers in China, except Carrefour.

6 Nurturing National Champions

When China was expected to relinquish all the remaining regulatory barriers to the entry of overseas retail capital in late 2004, the array of impacts of international retailers on host countries that Dawson (2003) summarizes had either been felt by China or were imminent. The state government in 2004 devised the *National Strategies for Reform and Future Development of China's Distribution System* and handpicked 20 domestic firms to form the national team (as described in Chapter 3). This chapter examines how effective the state efforts have been in nurturing domestic champions to compete with the aggressive international retailers and to fend off foreign competition. Specifically, this chapter recounts the creation and rise (or fall) of the domestic retail giants, analyzes their business operations including the degree of market penetration, and comments on the challenges that they have been facing in the new retail economy.

BAILIAN GROUP—THE NATIONAL TEAM LEADER

Shanghai is China's wealthiest and most lucrative urban market, which has always been eyed by international retailers as a fertile ground to park their retail capital. Shanghai is also a vanguard and an entrepreneurial city in the economic reform. In the 1990s, Shanghai nurtured a number of the country's largest retail chains including Lianhua, Hualian, and NGS, which occupied the top three positions among the largest 100 chains for nearly a decade. As the retail market matured, business concentration and consolidation began to occur. Two forces were driving the process: internal urges resulting from competition-induced pressure; and government intervention and facilitation.

In 2003, the government of Shanghai created the country's largest retail conglomerate by merging four companies into one super-group, and named it Bailian Group. The four participating companies, business groups themselves, were Shanghai Yibai, Hualian (China United), Friendship, and Shanghai Materials Trading Group, all directly under the Shanghai Commission of Commerce (see Figure 6.1). The merger was dictated by

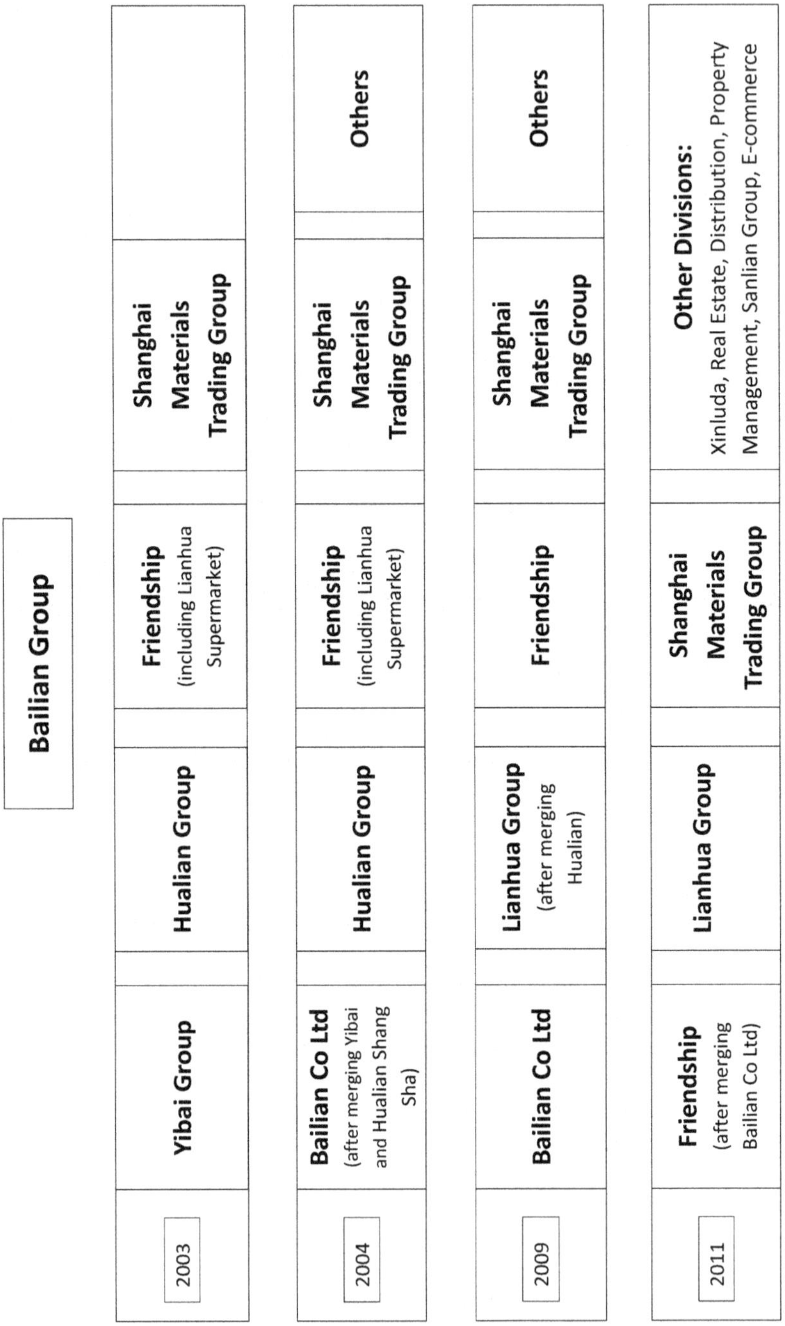

Bailian Group

2003	**Yibai Group**	**Hualian Group**	**Friendship** (including Lianhua Supermarket)	**Shanghai Materials Trading Group**	
2004	**Bailian Co Ltd** (after merging Yibai and Hualian Shang Sha)	**Hualian Group**	**Friendship** (including Lianhua Supermarket)	**Shanghai Materials Trading Group**	**Others**
2009	**Bailian Co Ltd**	**Lianhua Group** (after merging Hualian)	**Friendship**	**Shanghai Materials Trading Group**	**Others**
2011	**Friendship** (after merging Bailian Co Ltd)	**Lianhua Group**	**Shanghai Materials Trading Group**	**Other Divisions:** Xinluda, Real Estate, Distribution, Property Management, Sanlian Group, E-commerce	

Figure 6.1 The changing composition of Bailian Group, 2003–2011.

the Shanghai Commission of State-Owned Assets Supervision and Administration.[1] The new group aimed to consolidate the individual companies' resources and to streamline their business activities.

Shanghai Yibai was formed in 1995 on the foundation of Shanghai No. 1 Department Store. It later expanded to include Shanghai-Yohan Department Store, Oriental Department Store, and a number of other enterprises. Hualian was created in 1993 as a supermarket chain. By 2002, it already owned and was operating 1,200 chain stores spread in 10 provinces, but with a heavy focus on the Yangtze River Delta Region. Friendship Group was established in 2000. Among its various subsidiaries were Lianhua [United China] Supermarkets, Friendship Department Store, and Homemart (a building materials and décor retail chain). Shanghai Materials Trading Group was not a retail-specific corporation; it was included in Bailian simply because it was a poor performing state enterprise at the time, and the Government of Shanghai wanted it to be lifted by the other group members.

Apparently, the merger was made in time to prepare the city for heightened competition after China had to remove all barriers to foreign retail capital. At the time of Bailian's creation, the Government of Shanghai made it crystal clear: it would not withdraw its business interests from this new entity; instead, it aimed to maximize the value of the government assets through its control over Bailian. Other sources of capital (including foreign investment) would be introduced and accepted by the group only after Bailian firmly established itself as a national leader and a competition-resilient group. The purpose of the Government of Shanghai was to build Bailian into an *unsinkable aircraft carrier* in Shanghai and join the ranks of the world's top 500 companies. It also wanted to set itself as a model for other state-controlled corporations to restructure themselves and to maintain and increase the value of the state assets. As a result of the merger, Bailian instantly became the largest retail conglomerate in the country, with total capital assets of 28 billion yuan and more than 4,000 retail stores, with combined sales of 70 billion yuan in 2004.

Bailian's business scope is wide, ranging from supermarkets, hypermarkets, CVS, department stores, and shopping centers to materials trading, real estate development, and automobile sales and parts (see Figure 6.1). However, some of the member groups were engaged in business operations in the same formats. For example, both Yibai and Friendship operated department stores and supermarkets. The internal competition had to be reduced or even eliminated. While resources were consolidated after the merger, streamlining their business activities was never easy. Initially, Bailian attempted to reorganize the various functions into eight specialized divisions, but that did not fly. It took nearly eight years to make the necessary progress.

Shortly after the creation of Bailian, Yibai and Hualian Shang Sha (another department store chain) were merged in 2004 to form a new business group within Bailian, named Shanghai Bailian Co. Ltd. In 2009, an arrangement was made for Lianhua Supermarket (a subsidiary of Friendship) to acquire Hualian Supermarket, which had been suffering losses. In 2011, another step was taken for Friendship to merge and absorb Shanghai Bailian Co. Ltd. In the current regulatory environment of China, these mergers all required the approval of the Ministry of Commerce and the State-Owned Assets Supervision and Administration Commission of the State Council.

It must be emphasized that the mergers were never easy to materialize. The four original participating groups were all stock companies at the time of the merger with different stakeholders, though all were controlled by the government of Shanghai. Each of them had its own board of directors, and each had its own strategic plan to be implemented. The mergers also resulted in elimination of top management positions. Resentment and resistance were therefore expected. For one example, Hualian Shangsha was a profit-making department store chain at the time of the merger, but it was forced to merge with Yibai, which was performing poorly. The board chair of Bailian Group has always been appointed by the Government of Shanghai, and the top officials and senior managers of all component companies are always determined and appointed by the parent group. The subsidiaries are given no autonomy in choosing their own chair and CEO, even though they are public companies. In 2006, Xue Quanrong—a confidant of Chen Liangyu, the Party Secretary of Shanghai at the time—was appointed the new (and the second) board chair of Bailian Group. Only one year later, he was disgracefully removed and arrested, along with his party boss Chen, for his part in a series of corruptions and crimes. The third and current chair, Ma Xinsheng, was once a deputy party secretary of the Shanghai Commission of State-Owned Assets Supervision and Administration. While touted as having extensive experience in managing and restructuring assets of large state-owned enterprises, he has no previous experience in the business of retailing.

Each of the three chairs of Bailian Group tried to implement a distinct growth strategy. The first chair, Zhang Xinsheng (period of tenure 2003–2006), had many years of experience in retail management. He emphasized rapid expansion of the group into other parts of the country. The boldest move was to invest in Dashang Group (the country's second largest domestic chain of the time) in 2005 by acquiring 60 percent of Dashang International (a subsidiary of Dashang Group) for 720 million yuan. It was later augmented to 1 billion yuan (Zhou, 2007). This would allow Bailian to expand into North and Northeast China (including Beijing). However, its expansion in Beijing was extremely bumpy. Hualian Supermarket's operations in Beijing were bleeding. Lianhua was not able to penetrate in Beijing's prime urban markets, and its hypermarkets were limited to the outskirts of Beijing: in Tongzhou and Daxing only. A number of difficulties were cited by Bailian's CEO Lu Yongming (Yan & Zhang, 2008): local (including local government) resistance, inability to leverage local suppliers, and a lack of capacity by its Shanghai-based distribution centers to supply stores outside the city. In 2004, Hualian Supermarket withdrew from Beijing completely, and Lianhua had to reduce its store locations in Beijing by 30.

The second chair, Xue Quanrong (period of tenure 2006–2008), ordered to reduce the speed of expansion and even withdraw from some markets, and to focus on beefing up its market positions in the Yangtze River Delta Region. Among his major decisions was to withdraw its investment from Danshang International, which was executed quickly in 2006. In the same time period, Bailian withdrew its investment from Wushang Group in Wuhan.

After his installation, the third chair, Ma Xinsheng (2008–present), ordered to expand again, but cautiously. New strategies included selecting acquisition targets carefully and teaming up with other investors to reduce risks. In 2008, Ma entered a strategic relationship with Huishang Group (which is 100 percent owned by the government of Anhui Province) by injecting funds into the latter ("Bailian Group plans to invest in Huishang and form strategic partnership," 2008). In 2009, Bailian formed a joint venture with a Canadian shopping center developer—Ivanhoe Cambridge—to renovate and operate a large shopping mall in Changsha of Hunan Province (with Ivanhoe holding 60 percent of the total shares).

In 2005, Bailian Group owned 50.1 percent of the group's total assets (Bailian Group, 2006), and these shares were not traded on the stock market. This was to ensure that the control of the group remained in the hands of the Government of Shanghai. As a state-controlled company, its burden of footing the bills of wage, salary, and pension was high. The company had 8,011 employees on its payroll, plus another 4,825 retirees, whose pensions were, at least partially, a liability of Bailian. Of the 8,011 payees on its payroll, only 88 percent were active employees. It is not clear from its 2005 annual report what the other 12 percent of the payees were doing, but they could have been on long-term disability or maternity leave. In that same year, 70 percent of the employees were sales personnel, 13 percent were technical support staff, and 17 percent held various management positions. It reported to have business operations in six provinces (Shanghai, Jiangsu, Beijing, Zhejiang, Anhui, and Shandong), but 90 percent of its business income came from its home city of Shanghai.

In 2010, Bailian still held 44 percent of the group's total shares, slightly lower than it did in 2005. The next 9 largest shareholders, all being banks and insurance companies, collectively held another 9.4 percent, and none of them exceeded 2.5 percent. With such an ownership structure, the independent board members could hardly be influential in the group's decision making. Of its 6,879 employees in 2010, the proportion of sales personnel decreased to 60.5 percent, a 27 percent decrease from 2005; but its management personnel increased to 35.3 percent, an 18 percent increase from 2005. In its various operations, profit margins for supermarkets and other types of retailing were 12.7 percent and 20.3 percent respectively, which reflected good performance in the retail industry. In comparison, the profit margins derived from its real estate division and its catering/tourism operations were 84 and 91 percent, respectively. According to Bailian's own annual report, the number of provinces from which it drew business income was reduced from six in 2005 to four in 2010—Shanghai, Zhejiang, Liaoning, and Chongqing, with 98 percent of its business income achieved from Shanghai alone (Bailian Group, 2011).

Friendship Group now operates 28 department stores; 25 of them are confined to Shanghai. The 28 department stores still use their original names that enjoy high levels of brand recognition among local consumers. Friendship Group also operates 12 shopping centers, with eight of them located in Shanghai. (The other four are in Harbin, Shenyang, Chengdu, and Chonqing.)

Bailian's presence outside of Shanghai has been weak. Hualian once boasted to have 1,396 stores in a dozen of provinces. Yet, 1,183 of them were franchised stores ("The reasons behind the merger of Lianhua and Hualian," 2009). Outside of Shanghai, Lianhua's engagement was mainly through cooperation with local retailers. These forms of involvement point to the fact that Bailian is still largely a regional player with a strong presence in Shanghai and the Yangtze River Delta Region. In the words of Zhao Ping of the Institute of Finance and Trade, who is affiliated with Chinese Academy of Social Sciences, "many mergers in retailing end up with only having the same party secretary for all involved enterprises; everything else remains unchanged" (Wang, 2006). In the words of a foreign retailer, "mergers in China can surely increase the operation scales and scale economy, but it does not necessarily result in a significant increase in core competitiveness" (Wang, 2006). Between 2004 and 2010, Bailian expanded store locations by only 5.8 percent; its sales increased by 53 percent, slower than all other national team members (see Table 6.1). More importantly, its position in the top 100 retail chains slipped from Number 1 to Number 3, being surpassed by both Suning and Gome.

As the leader of the national team, Bailian still has a long road to tread in order to become a national player and to live up to the expectation of the state government. In 2010, total retail sales were 103.7 billion yuan (or US$16.5 billion), which was only 4 percent of that of Wal-Mart (China Chain Store Association, 2011). Under the current management and after the recent major restructuring, expansion beyond Shanghai will continue, but with a different focus. The new focus is on two formats: shopping centers and outlet malls. Its shopping centers will be anchored by its own Friendship Department Store and Lianhua Supermarket, without having to depend on the mercy of other retailers. Its first outlet mall in Shanghai was claimed to be a huge success. Two more were opened in 2011 in Wuxi and Nanjing. The fourth one is slated to open in Wuhan in 2013, with more having been planned for construction in Beijing, Shenzhen, Chengdu, and Jinan. Without exception, all the chosen host cities are either mega urban markets or first-tier cities.

Table 6.1   Members of the National Team among the Top 100 Retail Chains, 2010

Chain	Home base	Rank among top 100 chains		Number of stores			Sales (in billion yuan)		
		2004	2010	2004	2010	Change (%)	2004	2010	Change (%)
Suning	Nanjing	4	1	193	1342	595.3	22.11	156.22	606.6
Gome	Beijing	2	2	227	1364	500.9	23.88	154.90	548.7
Bailian	Shanghai	1	3	5493	5809	5.8	67.63	103.69	53.3
Dashang Group	Dalian	3	4	120	170	41.7	23.09	86.16	273.1
China Resources Vanguard	Shenzhen	15	5	476	3155	562.8	11.01	71.80	552.1
Huishang Group	Hefei	–	8	n/a	2915	n/a	n/a	40.52	n/a
Chongqing General Trading Group	Chongqing	12	10	153	319	108.5	13.11	38.22	191.5
Wu Mart	Beijing	10	11	608	2578	324.0	13.28	37.50	182.4
NGS	Shanghai	9	15	1232	3204	160.1	13.70	27.81	103.0
Wuhan Zhongbai Holdings Group	Wuhan	26	19	330	713	116.1	6.09	19.23	215.8
A-Best Supermarket	Shenzhen	17	22	58	113	94.8	8.50	17.41	104.8
Wushang	Wuhan	18	23	39	82	110.3	7.86	17.21	119.0
Beijing Wangfujing	Beijing	27	25	15	22	46.7	5.87	16.60	182.8

Source: China Chain Store Association, 2005, 2011

THE REMAINING MEMBERS OF THE NATIONAL TEAM

The national team has since lost several members, which were either merged with, or acquired by, other retail firms in the past few years. Beijing Hualian was closed due to poor performance. Suguo was acquired by China Resources Vanguard. Shandong Sanlian was acquired by Gome. Tianjin Home World was purchased by the American Home Depot. The last three members on the national team list are all materials trading companies, which, strictly speaking, are not retailers and never appeared in the list of the top 100 retail chains. The surviving members of the national team are examined in this section (with the exception of Suning and Gome, which will be dealt with in Chapter 7). Four of them—Dashang, Wushang, Huishang, and Chongqing Trading—are basically copycats of Bailian: they were created in a similar process and have been facing similar challenges.

Dashang Group

Dashang (meaning Dalian Commerce) was created in 1994 by combining four state-owned enterprises. In 1995, it entered into a joint venture with a Japanese retailer—Mycal. After that, it expanded with numerous mergers and acquisitions, as well as through formation of joint ventures. The Dalian Commission of State-Owned Assets Supervision and Administration represented the local government to exercise the right of the state shareholder.

Before 2003, Dashang's expansion focused on the three provinces in Northeast China: Liaoning, Jilin, and Heilongjiang. The main paths of expansion were organic growth and acquisition. Beginning in 2004, it expanded into other provinces mainly through acquisition: it bought out the Japanese Mycal in 2004; it acquired both Jinan People's Department Store and Qingdao New World Plaza to enter Shandong Province in 2005; it entered Henan Province by acquiring the province's largest shopping center in Zhengzhou in 2006. More recently, it began to explore markets in the interior province of Sichuan. Between 2004 and 2010, Dashang expanded by 42 percent in number of stores and 273 percent in sales (see Table 6.1). Nonetheless, its position in the list of top 100 retail chains slid down by one notch: from No. 3 to No. 4.

Rapid expansion resulted in heavy debts. In 2004, its debt rate reached 70 percent of its total assets. It was at that time that Dashang began to look for strategic partners and introduced Bailian in 2005, allowing Bailian to control 60 percent of its subsidiary—Dashang International. However, the short-lived marriage fell apart in less than a year. As mentioned earlier in this chapter, the second chair of Bailian, Xue Quanrong, quickly ordered to withdraw its partnership with, and investment in, Dashang in 2006. Then in 2008, Dashang sued Jinan government for illegally selling the shares of Jinan People's Department Store to another strategic partner. When asked by news media why the Jinan government wanted to bring in a new partner while the existing partner Dashang was eager to increase its ownership, the

Deputy Director of Jinan Commission of State-Owned Assets Supervision and Administration explained that the new partner was selected while taking into consideration such factors as geographical and cultural adjacencies (Hu, 2008), implying existence of conflicts between Jinan People's Department Store and Dashang.

Dashang's retail business is being carried out in three formats: department store, supermarket, and electronics specialty store. It boasts to be the country's largest department store chain with over 70 store locations, but 70 percent of them concentrate in the three provinces in Northeast China; the others are in Shandong, Henan, and Sichuan. Its geographical penetration is far less than that of the Malaysian Parkson and the domestic Wangfujing. Its supermarkets are also highly limited to Northeast China. In addition to the department stores, it has 33 supermarkets in Beijing under the banner of Tiankelong, of which Dashang became the majority shareholder (98 percent) through an acquisition in 2003. Its electronics division is even more geographically confined, with only one store in each of the cities where it has a presence. With such a low store density, it is not possible for Dashang to compete with the industry leaders of Suning and Gome. It is also important to note that most of Dashang's operations outside of the three Northeast provinces are in Tier 2 and Tier 3 cities. After it entered Beijing in 2003, it has never been able to expand there. Since Tiankelong held one third ownership of another supermarket chain in Beijing—Chaoshifa—Dashang automatically inherited those shares, and intended to increase its shares in Chaoshifa by acquiring the 25 percent ownership held collectively by the Chaoshifa employees. That intention, however, was blocked by the government of Haidian District (one of the 16 administrative divisions in Beijing), which owned 35 percent of Chaoshifa. The district government insisted that the employee shares must be sold bundled with the government shares, but the government shares were not for sale. In 2004, the employee shares were quietly sold to Wu-Mart—a Beijing-based supermarket chain, which was also commissioned to manage the government shares. This is another example of local government interventions in blocking outside retailers to expand in a city.

Now operating 170 stores, Dashang has firmly established itself as a regional leader in Northeast China. But like Bailian, it also has a long way to go to become a national leader. It has adopted the hierarchical approach to expansion: from the major urban centers of a province to second- and third-tier cities of the same province. This is embodied clearly in its operations in Shandong and Henan. However, it has completely avoided the mega urban markets of Shanghai, Tianjin, Guangzhou, and Shenzhen.

Wushang and Zhongbai

The Bailian Model was more faithfully mirrored in Wuhan—the capital of Hubei Province and a Tier 1 city in Central China. Two of the 20 national team members, Wushang Group and Zhongbai Holdings Group, are based in Wuhan, and both are also government controlled.

The predecessor of Wushang (meaning Wuhan Commerce) was the China-Soviet Friendship Department Store established in 1959. It was renamed Wuhan Department Store after the friendship between China and the USSR broke up in the early 1960s. It was transformed into a joint stock company in 1986, and went public in the Shenzhen Stock Exchange in 1992. For several years in the late 1990s and the early 2000s, the Wushang-owned Wuhan Department Store was one of the top sellers among its peers in the whole country.

The forerunner of Zhongbai was a branch operation of a then Shanghai-based stock company, established in Wuhan in 1946. After 1949, it was taken over by the state government and became a part of the state-owned Mid-South China Department Store Co. It was later renamed Central Wuhan Department Store. In 1989, it was re-established as a stock company and went public in 1997. Because its core business was facing fierce competition in the late 1990s, it diversified its operations to include both hypermarkets and supermarkets.

In 2007, the government of Wuhan, through its Commission of State-Owned Assets Supervision and Administration, dictated a major restructuring of the city-controlled retail enterprises by creating a super group—Wuhan Commerce United—and brought into it Wushang, Zhongbai, and Zhongshang. (Zhongshang was the third largest retail chain in Wuhan.) The super group is effectively a copycat of Bailian in Shanghai, with the sole purpose of creating the province's largest retail giant to compete with foreign retailers, while retaining state controls.

After the restructuring, the super group comprised 14 subsidiaries, ranging from retailing and wholesaling to catering, real estate development, and import/export. Its retail business is carried out in three formats: department store, discount supermarket, and shopping center. The intended division in retail functions was to have Wushang focus on operating full-line department stores and shopping centers, for Zhongbai to specialize in hypermarkets and supermarkets, and for Zhongshang to supplement Wushang in running discount department stores for a different segment of the consumer market.

This is another case of government-arranged marriage against the will of the parties involved. While Wuhan Commerce United is purely a business entity, it has a Communist Party Committee installed in parallel with, if not above, the Board of Directors. All three business groups are stock companies. Although the Wuhan government is the largest shareholder of all of them, there are other shareholders as well. The restructuring made the other shareholders very nervous, as their influence in decision making would be greatly reduced. As expected, the streamlining of business operations has been very slow and resisted by the three participating companies. Yintai Investment Group, a private investment firm and the second largest shareholder of Wushang, resisted fiercely the creation of Wuhan Commerce United. In fact, Yintai was originally invited to join Wushang by the government of Wuhan in 2004 as a strategic partner. To increase its influence in the strategic partnership, Yintai attempted to increase its shares to become the majority owner of Wushang. When that failed, it took Wushang and Wuhan Commerce United to court in 2011 (Yang, 2012). It is hard to imagine that a stock company would be able to run a successful and profitable business with ongoing fighting among its major shareholders.

It is a requirement of the China Securities Regulatory Commission that public companies of the same group minimize internal competitions by eliminating replications in business scopes, and maximize benefits for shareholders. Under this requirement, Wuhan Commerce United pushed ahead to merge Zhongbai and Zhongshang into a single group in 2011, similar to what Bailian did to combine Bailian Co. Ltd with Friendship (Xu and Duan, 2011). Wushang was left out because its dispute with Yintai is still going on. Despite its large size with 83 stores in 2010 (China Chain Store Association, 2011), all of the stores are restricted to its home province. Both Wushang and Zhongbai doubled their store locations and sales in the six year period from 2004 to 2010. However, Wushang's ranking among the top 100 chains slipped from 18th to 23rd, while Zhonbei's ranking improved from 26th to 19th (see Table 6.1).

Huishang

Huishang (meaning Anhui Commerce) was the weakest in the national team of 20, not even listed among the top 100 retail chains in 2004. The predecessor of Huishang was the Anhui Bureau of Material Trading and Distribution. It was changed into a joint stock company by the provincial government in 1995, and was merged with 12 other province-owned enterprises to form a business group in 2002. However, none of its subsidiaries was listed on the stock market until 2008.

Troubled with a shortage of capital, it went out in search of strategic partners. In 2008, Bailian, with a fresh chair at the time, agreed to invest in Huishang's subsidiary Commercial Capital to expand its department store chain and help it go public (with Bailian owning 30 percent). In the same year, it signed a memorandum of understanding (MOU) with Guangzhou General Merchandise Group (also a state-owned and local government-controlled enterprise) for strategic cooperation. One problem that often plagued state-owned enterprises, especially during enterprise transformation and restructuring, happened in Huishang Group as well: its board chair, Cai Wenlong, along with a few other high-level managers, was charged for corruption in 2008. Cai was appointed Huishang's board chair in 2000 by the government. Without board approval, he invested the group's limited capital in the volatile stock market several times and subsequently lost 335 million yuan. In addition, he was charged for embezzlement of 14 million yuan and for receiving bribes of another 3 million yuan. These were heavy blows for the cash-strapped Huishang.

In its current organization, Huishang's retail businesses are organized under three banners: Commercial Capital—a chain of general merchandise stores; Homeful—a supermarket chain; and Farmers Fortune—a retail chain of agricultural production materials (seeds and fertilizers, etc.). As of 2010, Commercial Capital operated 885 stores, but only 13 were department stores; the rest were small stores. Homeful Supermarket was established in 2003. By 2010, it had 885 stores, but less than 100 of them were directly owned stores in urban areas; all the others were franchised stores in rural areas. Farmers Fortune consisted of nearly 2,000 outlets, but they are not really retail stores selling consumer goods. In addition to retailing, Huishang's business scope includes wholesaling, real estate development, and tourism/hotels. All of its operations are limited in Anhui Province. Although its total retail sales were reported at 40.52 billion yuan in 2010 and ranked the 8th among the top 100 chains, only 25 percent were from Commercial Capital and Homeful Supermarket.

Chongqing General Trading Group

Chongqing General Trading Group is the only national team member in Western China. Established in 1996 by the local government through combining several state-owned enterprises, its business dealings ranged widely from retailing and wholesaling to trading of chemicals, automobiles, agricultural production materials, real estate, and imports/exports. As such, it was not a retail-specific company. To create the largest retail conglomerate of Western China, the government of Chongqing embarked on a journey of expansion by copying Shanghai's creation of Bailian. In 2004, the Chongqing Commission of State-Owned Assets Supervision and Administration announced, and subsequently arranged, the acquisition of C-Best Department Store—Chongqing's largest department store chain—by Chongqing General Trading Group. C-Best, established in 1950 and also a state-owned enterprise, was reluctant and even resisted the acquisition, but the government insisted and was coercive; it persuaded and manipulated the other shareholders of C-Best to transfer their stakes to Chongqing General Trading (Chen et al., 2005)

Chongqing General Trading already had its own department store chain—New Century Department Store—before the acquisition, so eliminating internal competition was necessary. In 2010, an administrative arrangement was made for C-Best to merge with New Century, so that the two chains could share the same distribution platform and warehouse facilities (Luo et al., 2010). With the merger also came senior management shuffling: the chair of New Century was promoted to the chair of the new C-Best, while the former chair of C-Best was demoted to its general manager. One year later in 2011, nine senior managers of C-Best resigned from their posts ("Top management at C-Best reshuffles," 2011). No explanations were given, but the resignations suggest the C-Best management team's discontent with the merger and acquisition.

According to the *China Chain Store Almanac* (China Chain Store Association, 2005, 2011), Chongqing General Trading expanded by 108 percent in store locations and 191 percent in sales between 2004 and 2010, and its rank among the top 100 chains improved from the 12th to the 10th position. As is revealed on its corporate website, it currently operates 286 retail stores of various formats and sizes, with 263 (or 92 percent) in the Chongqing City region; another 17 (6 percent) in its neighboring Sichuan Province. After the most recent restructuring, its new geo-strategy is to expand into the medium- and small-sized cities in Guizhou and Yunnan Provinces in southwest China.

China Resources Vanguard

The identity or "nationality" of China Resources Vanguard is somewhat ambiguous. Its predecessor was China Resources, a trading company registered in Hong Kong in 1948 by the Communist Party on the eve of the founding of the People's Republic of China. It was changed to China Resources Group in 1984 and began to open supermarkets in Hong Kong. It was not until 1992 that it started opening retail stores in mainland China. Ironically, it entered mainland China as an overseas-Chinese investment. One of the first 15 Sino-overseas joint ventures approved by the State Council in 1992 was Shanghai Runhua Ltd., with China Resources being its overseas partner. Despite being a business group wholly owned and directly controlled by the state government, it is still officially known as China Resources Vanguard (HK) Co. Ltd.

With the backup of the state government and rich capital resources, China Resources was expanding rather aggressively. In 2000, it acquired Vanguard Department Store in Shenzhen, and renamed itself China Resources Vanguard. In 2004, it acquired Suguo Supermarket—the 8th largest chain by sales with 1,345 stores in that year. (China Resources Vanguard itself was ranked only 15th in that same year.) Subsequently, it acquired Tianjin's Home World Supermarket in 2007, Wuxi Supermarket in 2009, Guangzhou Hongcheng Supermarket in 2010, and Jiangxi Hongkelong Department Store in 2011. As a result of the series of acquisitions, it expanded significantly, over 500 percent, in both number of stores and total sales between 2004 and 2010 (see Table 6.1). It moved up from the 15th position among the top 100 chains in 2004 to the 5th position in 2010. It now boasts over 3,000 retail outlets under 10 different banners, spreading across more than 100 cities in 29 provinces. Nonetheless, 60 percent of the stores are under the Suguo banner. It probably has achieved the deepest geographical penetration in the country among all domestic supermarket chains.

Wu-Mart and A-Best

Unlike the previously examined national team members, both Wu-Mart and A-Best were started with private capital. Wu-Mart was created in Beijing in 1994 by a U.S.-trained post-doctoral fellow named Zhang Wenzhong, who returned to China in 1993. While not government-created, Wu-Mart worked closely with the Beijing Government. In the earlier years, its main activity was to provide management services to the inefficient, state-owned stores. For example, in 1997, the Beijing government merged over 200 stores to form a chain, and commissioned Wu-Mart for management; it became the first modern retail chain in Beijing.

In 2001, the Government of Beijing gathered 12 government-owned retail enterprises to form the Capital City Commercial Chain Co. Ltd. Wu-Mart was invited to be a part, but only one year later, it withdrew its participation to operate as an independent retailer. In 2003, it went public and became listed in the Hong Kong Stock Exchange. Since then, it has been expanding steadily through three paths: providing management services to other retailers, leasing stores from other retailers (and retaining the stores' employees), and forming joint-venture/cooperatives with other retailers/investors by acquiring partial ownership. Wu-Mart won strong support from the Beijing government because it promised to retain as many workers as possible while managing the government-owned stores, including poor performers.

With new capital resources, the expansion of Wu-Mart accelerated and went beyond Beijing. In 2004 and 2006 respectively, it acquired the local Chaoshifa (for 25 percent of its ownership) and Meilianmei supermarket chains. Between 2004 and 2008, it acquired the defunct Japanese Daiei supermarket chain in Tianjin, 28 percent of the Yinchuan Xinhua Department Store in northwestern China, and 85 percent ownership of the largest supermarket chain in Shaoxing City of Zhejiang Province—Zhejiang Co-Op Supermarket (with 92 stores).

In the last 20 years, Wu-Mart has been involved in the mission of reforming 20 state-owned retail enterprises with over 400 stores. This alone retained 8,000 employees, who otherwise would have been unemployed. This was considered a major contribution by the Beijing Government, for which Wu-Mart received a high profile award from the State Council.

Unlike the state-controlled retail groups examined previously, Wu-Mart is retail focused, with retail operations focusing in four cities: Beijing (184 stores), Tianjin (52 stores), Yinchuan (51 stores), and Shaoxing (100 stores). Selling to institutions and *groups of purchasers* has been a strategic part of the Wu-Mart business plan. In 2009, it shrewdly signed an agreement with all the military units in Beijing to be their sole supplier of food and daily-use goods.

The examination of Wu-Mart ends on a disturbing note: in 2008, its founder Zhang Wenzhong was sentenced to 18 years in jail for bribery, fraudulence, and misuse of company capital. In China, bribery of government officials was common and even necessary for getting everything a business would need to grow and succeed. His in-camera trial left ample room for researchers and observers to guess whom Zhang bribed.

Little information is available about A-Best Supermarket. All that is known is that it was formed in 1995 in Shenzhen with private capital. In

1998, it hired foreign retail experts to advise its management. The number of stores increased modestly from 13 in 2001 to 28 in 2003. By 2010, its number of stores jumped to 106. From the beginning, A-Best was opening stores in both Shenzhen and other cities. Outside of Shenzhen, it targets mainly medium-sized and small, urban centers.

Like most other members of the national team, both Wu-Mart and A-Best have seen their position among the top 100 chains sliding down.

Beijing Wangfujing and Shanghai NGS

Wangfujing was a single-store retailer until 1996. It began to expand into a chain first by acquiring other department stores in Beijing, and then through both acquisition and greenfield development in other cities (Sun, 2002; Wang, 2011; Wang & Chan, 2007). In 2004, it entered a partnership with the Japanese retailer Ito-Yokado to raise capital for further expansion (with Ito holding 40 percent of the ownership). In 2009, it obtained a line of credit from East Asia Bank for 300 million yuan (China Chain Store Association, 2010). When it was named a member of the national team in 2004, it had 15 department stores with combined sales of 5.87 billion yuan. Six years later in 2010, its number of stores increased to 22 with total sales of 16.6 billion yuan. Its rank among the top 100 chains moved up slightly from 27th to 25th. Of the 22 stores, six are located in Beijing; the rest are spread across 14 different cities in 13 provinces. Compared with the other national team members, Wangfujing is a focused retailer committed to department store retailing, and has been building itself into a national chain, with its stores spread across more cities and provinces than those of the other domestic department store chains including Dashang Group. Except Guangzhou and Beijing, all the other host cities are interior cities in Central and Western China. Further, most of its stores in Central and Western China are located in Tier 2 and Tier 3 cities, avoiding the congested mega urban markets and Tier 1 cities.

NGS (meaning Agro Business) was created in the mid-1990s in Shanghai to operate supermarkets. It was once the country's third largest retail chain and expanded into a business group in 2004. Its core business has always been in hypermarkets and supermarkets, but it also operates CVS under two banners—Alldays and Kedi. In addition, it operates a discount junior department store chain—Wuyuan Modern Mart—with 200 outlets in the Shanghai City region. Its comparative advantage is that it owns large tracts of farm land in suburban Shanghai to grow produce and supply its supermarkets. This greatly helps to control supply-related costs.

In 2006, the Government of Shanghai arranged for NGS to be merged into Shanghai Guangming Group—a government-controlled group parallel to Bailian. NGS lost its independence thereafter. The Guangming Group was originally formed in 2004 by bringing together several brand-name food producers in Shanghai. By adding NGS to Guangming, the group extended its business operations from food production to retail distribution. In 2010, it boasted 3,200 store locations, mostly in Shanghai but also in the neighboring Suzhou, Wuxi, and Hangzhou. Despite its size, it experienced a steep slide in its rank among the top 100 chains: from 3rd place in 2000 to 9th in 2004 and to 15th in 2010.

A SYNTHESIZED DISCUSSION

The examination of the national team members in this chapter reveals a number of striking commonalities among the government-owned and controlled retail enterprises. It also points to a series of challenges that they have been facing on their way to becoming true national players.

While the state government has withdrawn from operating retail stores, the local governments, mostly municipal but also provincial, are required to retain their stakes in the formerly government-owned enterprises. Therefore, government-manipulated mergers in China are made not only to increase business efficiency, but also to increase the value of the state assets. Intervention and manipulation are made through the hands of the municipal Commissions of State-owned Assets Supervision and Administration. In most cases, mergers or acquisitions were carried out against the will of the involved parties. The joint venture between Bailian and Dashang was good for the state government, but did not necessarily benefit the companies involved and the independent shareholders. Since the super groups were created to include both high performers and profit-losing enterprises, even including non-retail enterprises, their core business often suffered.

All the members of the national team devised grand plans for rapid expansion, but they all ran into the common difficulty of not having enough working capital. Apparently, capital-raising in the stock market was not as successful as anticipated. Many stock companies have not paid dividends to independent shareholders in nearly 10 years because all the cash flow was used for fast expansion. All government-controlled groups welcomed external investment in the form of strategic partnership, but the bottom line was that the strategic partners had to be kept as minority owners who would not attempt to gain control over the group. Whenever there was a dispute between the local government and a strategic partner, the loser was always the latter with no exception. In fact, any significant changes in government shares, even local government shares, must have the approval of the State government.

For most groups, their business scope goes beyond retailing, including wholesaling, catering/tourism/hotels, imports/exports, and even real estate development. If non-retail-related sales were excluded, their market positions as retailers would be much weaker. Their involvement in retailing spans across multiple formats, including supermarkets, hypermarkets, CVS, department stores, and shopping centers. These multiple operations resulted as a legacy of the planned economy: government frequently combined several different enterprises into one group, and preserving jobs was particularly important for maintaining social stability. Decisions to close divisions could not be made lightly.

While the mergers both raised the level of consolidation and increased scale economy, the "arranged marriages" have not made the groups much stronger. None of them is as focused on retailing as are the foreign retailers in China, and none has become a true national leader in a specific retail subsector. Few of them even have a customer-friendly website with an updated list of stores or a functioning store locator. Because their market penetration (in terms of geographic distribution) is relatively low and most are limited to their home city or home province, none of them has become an effective defender of the national market.

Nonetheless, the 11 members of the national team examined in this chapter all experienced significant expansion in number of stores and significant growth in sales, though their growth rates vary, as shown in Table 6.1. Between 2004 and 2010, China Resources Vanguard's total sales quintupled. Dashang and Wuhan Zhongbai's sales more than doubled. Six of the groups saw their total sales increased between 100 and 200 percent. Relatively speaking, Bailian had the smallest growth rate, at only 53 percent, though its total sales are the largest among the 11 retail groups. It is also important to note that seven of the 11 examined national team members saw their ranks in the top 100 chains slip, with Bailian being surpassed by the two electronics retailers Suning and Gome. Only China Resources Vanguard, Wuhan Zhongbai, and Beijing Wangfujing moved up their ranks.

According to China Chain Store Association (2010), domestic retailers, large and small, are still facing the following five challenges.

First of all, access to loans from state banks is limited, as banks are wary of issuing large loans to retailers. Unlike manufacturers that usually have large fixed assets as guarantees for bank loans, retailers have fewer fixed assets. In most cases, they lease premises from other property owners and even work with negative capital. Apparently, the state supports that were promised in 2004 were inadequate.

Second, total taxes levied on retailers are high in China. The chair of Bailian repeatedly called for a reform of the state tax system for equal treatment. Currently, a retailer's operation in each city pays corporate tax to the local government. This is why Bailian's operations outside of Shanghai each have to form a separate company. However, the overseas retailers are allowed to calculate and pay corporate tax by the corporations' China headquarters. Paying taxes separately is costly because multiple accounting is required and poor performance in one city cannot reduce the amount of taxes for the profitable stores in another city. At the same time, some local governments still give preferential treatment to international retailers.

Third, retailers pay much higher prices for electricity than do manufacturers. This is a heavy burden for retailers because all large store facilities provide air conditioning for extended periods of time during the year and mainly during peak hours during the day. In 2009, the State Commission of Development and Reform (2009) issued a circular to local governments and to the electricity distribution authorities, requesting them to consider charging retailers the same hydro rate as they charge manufacturers. As well, the State Commission requested to postpone the implementation of the newly proposed time-of-use and tiered-rate pricing system in the country. This will give retailers more time to improve energy efficiency in their store facilities.

Fourth, operating costs have gone up significantly. In addition to high utility costs, both wages and rent have gone up. Retailing is notorious worldwide for its low pay to store workers. This is also the case in China. After the state government several times ordered to raise minimum pay, retailers have been pressured to increase wages, in order not to lose store workers.

Finally, accessible and affordable real estate (including raw land) became increasingly scarce, especially in the large urban centers. While all retailers face this challenge, it may affect the domestic retailers more than the international retailers, because the former are less able to raise development capital than the latter.

7 The Setback of Best Buy and Media Markt

An Analysis of China's Consumer Electronics Retailing

After nearly two decades of opening its retail sector to the outside world, China is now flooded with stores operated by international retailers, particularly in food and general merchandise retailing. Wal-Mart, Carrefour, Metro, Tesco, RT-Mart, Parkson, and Jusco are all familiar names to the Chinese consumers not only in the mega urban markets and Tier 1 cities, but also in many lower tier cities. These chains have commanded significant market shares in their respective retail sectors in China.

It is of great interest to note, however, that among the various retail sectors in China, consumer electronics has been the most resistant to foreign competition, thanks to two of the national team members—Gome and Suning. Best Buy, the first international retailer of consumer electronics (CE) to penetrate the Chinese market, did not enter China until 2006. On February 22, 2011, it suddenly announced the closure of all its China stores due to underperformance. This surprised not only the Chinese consumers, but also Best Buy's Chinese competitors. As the largest CE retailer in the world, its recent setback in China is no small matter. It raised two important research questions: Why are the Chinese CE retailers much more able to resist foreign competition than the other domestic retailers? What went wrong for Best Buy in adapting to the Chinese retail environment and to the local domestic market? This chapter explores the answers to these questions and supplements Chapters 5 and 6 to complete the unfinished stories.

THE STORY OF BEST BUY IN CHINA

Best Buy first entered China in 2006 through the acquisition of China's then-fourth-largest CE retailer—Jiangsu Five Star Appliances. The acquisition was completed in two phases: in 2006, Best Buy acquired a 75 percent ownership of Five Star (for US$180 million); two years later in 2008, it purchased the remaining 25 percent (for another US$185 million), turning Five Star into a wholly-owned subsidiary. Phonetically, the Chinese translation of Best Buy is very close to its English pronunciation, but its Chinese name (百思买) literally means "think a hundred times before (you) buy." This unlucky translation might have foretold Best Buy's subsequent misfortune in China.

As with its operation in Canada, Bust Buy adopted a dual-brand strategy in China, retaining the Five Star brand while opening Best Buy-branded stores as a separate corporate entity ("Revisiting Best Buy's acquisition of Five Star at the first anniversary," 2008). In terms of economic geography, Best Buy adopted the approach of *contiguous diffusion* (Berry, 1972) in store development, meaning that it sought to establish market dominance in one large urban center first, before opening more stores in the adjacent cities. Between 2006 and 2009, Best Buy opened six stores, all in Shanghai, where Five Star had no presence at all. It was not until 2010 that Best Buy began to expand beyond Shanghai to test the neighboring markets of Suzhou and Hangzhou—both Tier 1 cities. In 2010, it opened one store in Suzhou, where 14 Five Star stores already existed. In the same year, it opened another store in Hangzhou, where seven Five Star stores were present. The adoption of the contiguous diffusion approach was based on logistics considerations, as it would be easier for Best Buy to build an elaborate distribution center in Shanghai first, from which the stores in Suzhou and Hangzhou could be supplied.

Best Buy transferred its prevailing operational model from North America to China with little modification. All of its China stores were large format outlets. But unlike in the U.S. and Canada, where most Bust Buy stores are one-story facilities in power centers, its China stores were mostly in shopping malls. Internally, all Best Buy stores were organized by categories of products to make comparative shopping easier for consumers. Typically, each store was divided into five zones: cell phones; digital technologies; computer and office supplies; image and sound systems; and home appliances. The last zone was unique in its China stores, as its North American stores do not usually carry home appliances.

Best Buy placed great emphasis on quality service and price transparency in order to distinguish itself from its Chinese competitors. Uniquely, all Best Buy stores had a "Technical Consultation Precinct" (staffed by its "Geek Squad Taskforce") and a "Customer Experience Zone" (known as the "Magnolia home theater"). Members of the "Geek Squad Taskforce" not only advised customers on selection of networked products, but also provided them with installation service and after-sale technical support at their homes (Shi & Shang, 2010). Within the Magnolia zone, consumers could touch and try the various products before choosing a set of components for a home theater (Zhao, 2010). While prices at Best Buy stores were not the most competitive, they were all posted on the company's corporate website and were made transparent to all consumers. Best Buy did not reward its sales associates with commissions so as to provide a hassle-free shopping environment, where shoppers would feel comfortable when browsing for merchandise and making purchase decisions.

Despite its international reputation, organizational strength, and rich resources, Best Buy was unable to turn its China operation into a profitable international division after five years of effort. The total sunk cost that the closure incurred is unknown, but it cannot have been light. After the closure, Best Buy decided to focus business growth on development and expansion of the Five Star chain. The subsidiary is headquartered in the City of Nanjing. While listing 256 stores in the country (China Chain Store Association, 2010), it is in fact largely a regional player, with 60 percent of its stores confined to one province—Jiangsu Province. Another 23 percent of its stores are located in the neighboring provinces of Zhejiang and Anhui. Most of these are located in second- and third-tier cities. With no outlets in any of the five mega urban markets, Five Star lacks a strong brand image in the country. Needless to say, Bust Buy has a long way to go before it can claim a significant share of China's CE market.

WHO ARE GOME AND SUNING?

Best Buy's inroads in China were largely blocked by its nemeses Gome and Suning—the two homegrown CE retail giants. In a relatively short period of 20 years, both of these firms have established themselves as China's largest retailers of all categories. At the end of 2010, Suning was operating 1,342 stores in more than 400 cities and towns, with sales of RMB156 billion (US$25 billion). In total, it employed 120,000 workers, for which it was praised as a model enterprise by the Chinese government. In the same year, Gome was operating 1,364 stores across the country, with sales of RMB154 billion, very close to that of Suning (see Table 6.1). In 2011, Gome and Suning were ranked by Planet Retail as the 11th and 14th largest retailers of electronic/entertainment/office suppliers in the world ("Gome and Suning ranked among the top 30 EEO retailers," 2011). Table 7.1 lists the milestones in the course of their development. There are important similarities between Gome and Suning in their growth trajectories, but also notable differences.

Table 7.1 Milestones of Gome and Suning Development

Year	Milestones	
	Gome	*Suning*
1987	First store opens in Beijing operated by Huang Guangyu	
1990		Suning is established in Nanjing by Zhang Jindong, with a single store engaging in wholesaling of air conditioners
1993	The Gome chain is created	
1995		Suning enters retailing
1999	Expand beyond Beijing and begin to open stores in other cities (first in Tianjin, and then in Shanghai	

(continued)

Table 7.1   (continued)

Year	Milestones	
	Gome	*Suning*
2000		Retailing income exceeds whole-saling for the first time
2001		Being transformed into a stock company
2002		Expands beyond Nanjing into Beijing, Shanghai, Chongqing, Ningbo, and Changzhou, to become a national chain
2003	· Begin to open stores in Hong Kong · Become the largest consumer electronics retailer in the country · Ranked the 4th largest among the top 100 retail chains in China	
2004	Begin to trade in Hong Kong Stock Exchange	Begin trading in Shenzhen Stock Exchange
2005	· Begin to expand through acquisi-tion, acquiring Black Swan (Harbin); Yi-hao-jia (Shenzhen), and Zhongshang (Wuhan) · Begin to form strategic relations with commercial property developer Wanda	
2006	· Acquire the 3rd largest CE retail chain—Yolo—for RMB5.268 billion · Become the largest retail chain of the country	
2007	Acquire the 4th largest CE retail chain—Dazhong—for RMB 3.6 billion	
2008	Acquire 10% ownership of the 7th largest CE retail chain—Sanlian—for RMB537 million	
2009	Huang is removed from Board of Directors and stripped of his posi-tion of board chair; he is jailed for 14 years; Gome falls into a crisis; Chen Xiao, CEO, assumes the responsibility of board chair	· Exceeds Gome to become the largest retail chain in China · Acquires Laox of Japan and Citicall of Hong Kong
2010		Launches Suning.com
2011	Announces launch of Gome.com	

Compiled from various sources.

Similarities

Both companies were founded by an individual entrepreneur with a single store, but expanded steadily into true national chains. Gome was founded in 1987 by a self-made entrepreneur, Huang Guangyu. A middle-school dropout, Huang was born a business genius. He started with a single store in Beijing, selling radio sets and watches. Initial growth was slow: it took six years for Huang to create the Gome chain as it was in 1993 (see Table 7.1). Six years later, in 1999, Gome expanded beyond Beijing, first into Tianjin, and then into Shanghai. Suning was founded in 1990 by a state employee, Zhang Jindong, in the City of Nanjing. Initially, this one-person business focused on wholesaling of air conditioners. It was not until 1995 that Suning ventured into retailing. It took another five years for its retail income to exceed that of its wholesaling. Shortly after, Suning was transformed into a joint-stock company and expanded into a national chain.

Both Gome and Suning adopted the strategy of *hierarchical diffusion*: that is, they opened company-owned stores in provincial capitals first, before expanding into smaller cities in the surrounding regions, through a combination of organic growth and franchising.

Both companies went public in the same year to raise much needed capital for further expansion. Gome began trading in the Hong Kong Stock Exchange in 2004 via the reversed takeover of a shell company. Suning went public with an IPO in the Shenzhen Stock Exchange in the same year. With the newly raised capital from the stock markets, both companies then embarked on a period of rapid business expansion from 2004, as illustrated in Figure 7.1.

Both Suning and Gome also had strong government backing. As discussed in Chapter 4, the Ministry of Commerce in 2004 selected 20 companies to be members of the national team of retailers. The selected companies became recipients of State support in the form of tax breaks and special bank loans. The purpose of the program was to nurture a group of large domestic retailers in anticipation of heightened competition upon China's accession to the WTO. Both Suning and Gome were among the companies selected. The special support from the State government was equally significant in driving their later success.

More importantly, both companies do business in unconventional ways. Due to their enormous purchasing powers, both Gome and Suning have been able to develop and dictate a unique form of agreement with their suppliers. In this relationship, suppliers (i.e. producers) contribute to each new store in exchange for their products being sold in the new store. Suppliers must: pay for the cost of decorating the area of the store where their products are to be displayed; provide free demos for store display and for showing to customers; and send their own sales representatives to the store to promote their products and explain the

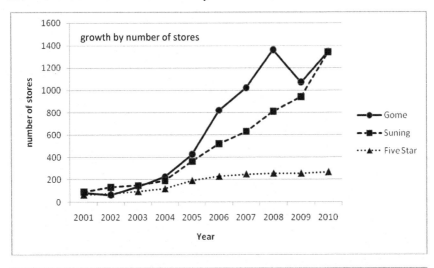

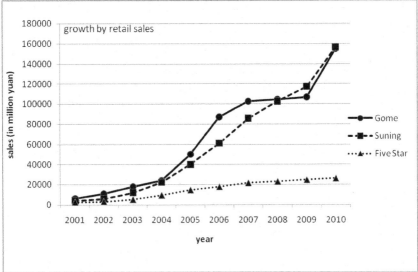

Figure 7.1   Growth of Gome, Suning, and Five Star, 2001–2010.
(The growth of Gome and Suning took off after 2004 when both companies became listed on stock market.)

features of their offerings to consumers (Gu, 2010; Shi & Shang, 2010). In some cases, these sales representatives are recruited and trained by a local marketing firm on behalf of the producer but also at the latter's expense.[1] The sales reps are paid with commissions tied to their sales performance, which is based on both number of units sold and the total amount of sales. Accordingly, merchandise in Gome and Suning stores is organized and displayed by brand, rather than by category.

This represents a fundamentally different way of premeditating the configuration of retail space in their stores than in a typical Best Buy store. While other foreign retailers (such as Carrefour and B&Q) also use supplier-dispatched and paid employees to work in stores, it is not to this extent, nor on such a scale.

Gome has been known to its suppliers as a ruthless price chopper. In the early 2000s, an eminent producer of air conditioners in China, Gree, had a protocol with its distributors to maintain a minimum retail price in order to avoid undue competition in the market and also to maintain a certain level of profit for both the producer and the retailers. In 2004, Gome unilaterally slashed the retail price of the Gree air conditioners below the agreed minimum, igniting a fierce price war in the CE retail sector. When asked by Gree to respect the protocol and issue an apology for its unilateral action, Gome refused. Consequently, Gree stopped supplying Gome with its products, and Gome retaliated by boycotting Gree air conditioners throughout its entire chain (Sun, 2005). In the end, Gree had to develop its own retail channels in the country, mostly through franchising. This is one example of the power shift from suppliers to retailers in China. Since then, Gome and Suning have gradually taken the power of price setting away from the domestic producers, and both retailing and production of CE products entered an era of thin profit margins. Gome and Suning also led the way to bypass wholesalers and deal directly with manufacturers, short-circuiting the distribution channel significantly.

Gome and Suning are also notorious for charging non-cost-related fees and obtaining discounts from their suppliers. These include store entrance fees, grand opening sponsorships, and "corporate commissions" calculated on the number of units sold. In addition, they are able to negotiate for longer grace periods for credit payment (typically between 30 and 45 days), effectively using suppliers' capital to finance their own expansion.

Both Gome and Suning invested heavily in building an efficient distribution network to support their nationwide expansion. As of 2010, Suning owns one national-level distribution center, seven regional distribution centers, and 50 localized distribution centers. Gome has built a similarly extensive infrastructure.

Finally, the recent expansion of the two retail chains was boosted greatly by two government-subsidized programs. The first one, effective between September 2009 and May 2010, provided incentives to consumers for trading in their old home appliances including television sets, refrigerators, washers, air conditioners, and computers (Ministry of Finance & Ministry of Commerce, 2009; "How much do you know about the trade-in program?", 2010). The second program, which started in 2008 and ended in 2013, provided rebates to customers in rural areas for purchasing CE products (Ministry of Finance & Ministry of Commerce, 2008). Gome and Suning benefited much more than did Best Buy and Five Star due to their extensive store networks.

Dissimilarities

Gome expanded aggressively through a series of high-profile acquisitions, while Suning expanded mainly through organic growth and franchising. In 2005, Gome acquired three local chains—Black Swan, Yi-hao-jia, and Zhongshang—to enter Harbin, Shenzhen, and Wuhan respectively. In 2006, it acquired China's third largest CE retail chain, Yolo, to become the country's largest retailer. Yolo was created in 1996 by Chen Xiao in Shanghai. It was a regional player until 2003, when it began to expand into the provinces of Jiangsu, Zhejiang, Fujian, Henan, and Guangdong. In 2005, Yolo operated 193 retail outlets with annual sales of RMB15.2 billion (Sun, 2006).

In 2007, Gome acquired China's fourth-largest CE retail chain, Dazhong. The first store under the name of Dazhong opened in Beijing in 1989 by Zhang Dazhong. It was a tiny store of 10 square meters. Dazhong expanded into a chain in 1999. By the end of 2006, it operated 97 stores with annual sales of RMB8.7 billion (Sun, 2007). In 2008, Gome purchased a 10 percent ownership of the Shandong-based Sanlian Commerce, the country's seventh largest CE retail chain, becoming Sanlian's largest shareholder (See Figure 7.2).

Although Gome retained the brands of the acquired companies for their market recognition, these acquisitions cemented Gome's position as the country's top CE retailer. Unlike Gome, Suning sought for expansion mainly through organic growth and franchising. On May 1, 2006, it opened 22 new stores; on May 1, 2007, 26 new stores were opened. As Figure 7.3 shows, Suning's model brought with it improved store performance, while Gome's rapid expansion came at the expense of store performance.

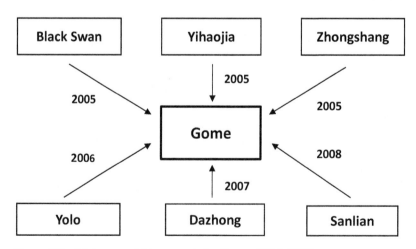

Figure 7.2   Major acquisitions made by Gome, 2005–2008.

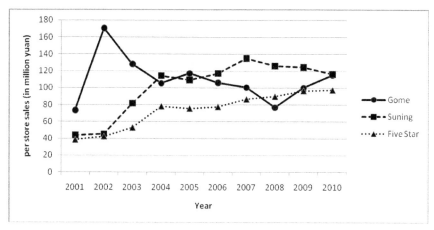

Figure 7.3 Comparison of Gome, Suning, and Five Star by per-store retail sales, 2001–2010. (Gome's expansion was achieved at the expense of store performance.)

Both Gome and Suning emerged as industry leaders during the height of China's economic reform, when the government was promoting private companies to help shoulder the burden of creating jobs. Relevant regulations were largely absent during this time, and the situation created fertile ground for unethical or even illegal business conduct and practice. In November 2008, Huang, the founder of Gome, was detained by police for suspected crimes (Barboza, 2008). In May 2010, he was charged with illegal business conduct, insider trading, and bribery of government officials, for which he was sentenced to 14 years in jail.

The government officials that Huang bribed included Guo Jingyi and Sun Haiting. Guo was Deputy Director of the Treaty and Law Department in the Ministry of Commerce. He allegedly helped Huang to bring about two very important business deals. In 2004, Gome was working toward listing itself in the Hong Kong Stock Exchange through a shell company. This involved a series of secretive and complicated maneuvers, including Huang setting up an offshore company with registration in the British Virgin Islands, and selling 65 percent stakes of the shell company to this offshore company, in order to allow Gome to buy in. However, this would exceed the maximum foreign ownership allowed by Chinese law at the time. Guo presided over the revision of the relevant foreign investment law to facilitate the Gome transaction. In 2006, when Gome was about to complete the acquisition of Yolo, a public hearing was required and held at the Ministry of Commerce's Office of Anti-Trust Investigation, of which Guo was a deputy director. Although all CE retailers present at the meeting voiced strong concerns about the possible monopoly of Gome and were against the proposed acquisition, the Ministry of Commerce approved the deal with no explanation. For his assistance, Guo received 1.1 million yuan from Gome ("Guo Jingyi receives death sentence," 2010; Goldkorn, 2010). Sun was former director of the Tax Evasion Investigation Agency under the State Administration of Tax and Revenue. He reportedly provided false inspection reports to help cover Gome's significant tax evasions. These scandals should not be interpreted as the only factors in Gome's rise to the top of China's retail sector. Rather, they show that the playing field was never level, with certain domestic retailers enjoying cozy relationships with regulators, giving them an advantage over their foreign counterparts.

Despite becoming a publicly traded enterprise in the Hong Kong Stock Exchange in 2004, Gome was still largely a family-controlled business, and Huang had been treating the company as his own private empire, with several key positions being held by Huang family members. In addition to Huang being board chair, his wife, Du Juan, heads Gome (Hong Kong); his sister, Huang Xiuhong, is general manager of Gome East China Division; and his brother-in-law, Zhang Zhiming, was in charge of several important divisions. This has caused resentment and even animosity among its top managers, who were not given company stocks as incentives. After Huang was imprisoned, Gome temporarily fell into a financial crisis: the Hong Kong Stock Exchange halted trading of Gome's stocks; shareholders panicked about the uncertainty of Gome; suppliers worried about Gome's ability to pay for the already delivered goods, and thus did not want to support the opening of new stores.

Chen Xiao, the founder of Yolo and the CEO of Gome, succeeded Huang to become board chair. Chen took three steps to save the company from turmoil. First, he insisted on closing bleeding stores, slowing down the pace of opening new stores, and focusing on improving sales performance of the existing stores (i.e., to raise per store sales; see Figure 7.3). Second, he convinced the board of directors to introduce Bain Capital, a Boston-based private equity firm, as a new partner to raise fresh capital. The deal allowed Bain Capital to become the second largest shareholder in Gome with a 14 percent stake. But Bain's purchase came with a condition: it demanded the right to nominate three directors to Gome's board. If Bain did not see its representatives appointed to Gome's board in a timely fashion, it would have the right to rescind the contract and collect 2.4 billion yuan (about US$350 million) from Gome as "compensation" (Li, V., 2010). In other words, in exchange for Bain's investment, Gome had to concede part of the corporate decision-making power to Bain. Third, in July 2009, the board launched an option motivation plan for 105 management-level employees, encouraging them to make more concerted contributions to the company ("China's Gome still haunted by recent scandal," 2010).

The new shares that were issued to Bain Capital effectively diluted the stakes owned by Huang, and the ability of Bain Capital to nominate executive directors reduced the decision-making powers held by the Huang family. These changes undoubtedly met strong opposition from the Huang family. After several months of internal fighting, Chen was pushed out of Gome by the Huang family. The key factor in the power reversal was the release of Huang's wife, Du Juan, who was initially sentenced to three years in jail for her part in the crimes, but was quickly released without justification to resume her role as an executive board member. China simply did not want to see the downfall of the country's largest homemade retailer, despite the crimes that its founder committed.

At Suning, founder and chair Zhang Jindong also owns a 30 percent stake of the company, as does Huang at Gome, but no members of his family have been reported to hold important positions in the organization. In addition, Suning offers company shares to its high-level managers to motivate them to work hard. In another positive note, there has been no report that Suning was caught for illegal business conduct and bribery.

WHAT WENT WRONG WITH BEST BUY?

As stated by Borgström et al. (2008, p.4), "Any firm entering a new market will face some degree of disadvantage compared with the local firms. Therefore, as a precondition to expand into international markets, a firm would have to possess a competitive advantage in order to offset the disadvantages associated with being an entrant in the host country." Best Buy has certain competitive advantages in terms of its brand, image, and capital. Yet despite these advantages, the company failed in its attempt to conquer the China market. So what went wrong?

1. *Best Buy put too much emphasis on standardization, failing to adapt adequately to the local retail environment and its customs.*

A major issue in internationalization of retailing is one of **standardization** versus **adaptation** (Sternquist, 2007). In a foreign market, the company is placed in the middle of culturally different surroundings, where the regulatory environment, the retailer-supplier relationship, and consumer behaviors can be vastly different from those in the retailer's home country. This is so even if the retailer sells universally standard products (such as consumer electronics). It would appear with hindsight that the Chinese suppliers and consumers did not respond well to Best Buy's prevailing North American business model in China. Best Buy insisted on organizing merchandise by category, consistent with its standard big box format in North America. In order to provide a hassle-free shopping environment, the company did not reward its sales associates with commissions. It is reported that the suppliers in particular did not like the way Best Buy conducted business in China. They were concerned that their products might be disadvantaged by mixing them with other brands and without the presence of their own sales representative on site to promote them. Moreover, they did not like Best Buy selling its own private label products, such as Insignia and Dynex ("Setbacks of Best Buy in China," 2010).

As with its North American stores, Best Buy in China was committed to price transparency, with all of its prices posted on its corporate website. This also meant that prices were fixed across the chain and were not negotiable. The domestic CE retailers, however, do not post prices on their websites (except promotions), and it is common practice for consumers to engage in some amount of price negotiation with the manufacturers' sales representatives. The latter system seems to work better for the price-conscious Chinese consumers. As a result, Best Buy was often used as a showroom for consumers to view and experience the products, due to its friendly customer service. However, consumers did not always buy the product at a Best Buy store, and often turned to other retailers to make a purchase, where they could bargain for a lower price.

2. The effectiveness of its dual brand strategy was questionable.

An international retailer often acquires local companies as a convenient mode of entry or as an effective means to eliminate local competition (Douglas, 2001). In most cases, the acquired brand ceases to exist and is converted to the banner of the new owner. However, if the acquired brand has already gained strong national recognition, the international retailer may want to preserve it, at least for a certain period of time, in order to retain the large number of loyal customers, while introducing its own brand.

Researchers have different views on the benefits and effectiveness of using dual (or multiple) brands to maximize market shares. When describing the benefits of dual brands, Mitchell (1993) states that two strong brands can accomplish more than each brand separately. Similarly, Saunders and Guogun (1996) assert that a combination of two brands is almost always assessed as better than the use of merely one brand as a stand-alone. Other researchers, however, see that intrinsically, the presence of multiple brands in the same market could lead to cannibalization, though the risk may be reduced by clearly delimiting the "territory" of each brand. In addition, there would be duplication of staff at the corporate headquarters, and marketing dollars would have to be split, thus reducing the intensity of advertisement for each brand (Chandrasekhar, 2006)

While the strategy of operating dual brands in the same foreign market has some merits, its execution requires carefully defined differentiations between the two brands. If not sufficiently differentiated, the two brands may cannibalize each other, resulting in waste of corporate resources. Although geographical differentiation between the Best Buy and the Five Star brands was clear in the first four years (with the first six Best Buy stores all in Shanghai, where Five Star had no presence), Best Buy faced difficulty when it was ready to expand into the neighboring markets. In 2010, when Best Buy began opening stores in Suzhou and Hangzhou (Zhao, 2010), there were already 14 Five Star stores in the former and seven in the latter. It seems to the author of this book that the dual-brand strategy should not be a preferred strategy in the long run. Running two brands in the same market inevitably means fewer Best Buy stores than if there were the Best Buy brand alone. This reduces the visibility of Best Buy in the local market as a stand-alone chain. What is more, maintaining two headquarters, one in Nanjing and the other in Shanghai, was no doubt costly.

3. *Best Buy came to China too late, losing first-mover advantages.*

At the time of Best Buy's entry, Shanghai had already been populated by the stores of Gome and Suning. Thus, from the beginning, Best Buy was facing stiff competition from the established domestic CE retailers, and was fighting an uphill battle with the two retail giants. Gome completed the acquisition of Yolo, Dazhong, and Sanlian before Best Buy was ready to expand beyond Shanghai. In particular, Yolo is a Shanghai-based retail chain with 60 stores in Shanghai, and Dazhong is a Beijing-based chain with 70 outlets in the country's capital. Best Buy was preempted by Gome and Suning in the rest of the country (see Figure 7.4). The failure of Best Buy in China simply means that it could not compete with Gome and Suning in Shanghai, and that it lacked confidence when competing with them in other large urban markets.

In fact, Best Buy's business model has many merits: its relationship with suppliers is fairer than that imposed by its domestic rivals, and its transparent pricing system is more ethical than the prevailing business model in China. Yet despite these positives, the brand failed before it was able to achieve the necessary scale economy. Some commentators aver that the Best Buy model is simply too "advanced" in China, where competition is still unhealthy and consumers are too bargain conscious. Ironically, both Gome and Suning are now making changes along the lines of the Best Buy model; both are experimenting with organizing merchandise by category in their new stores and introducing consumer experience zones similar to Best Buy's Magnolia "Home Theater." Suning has

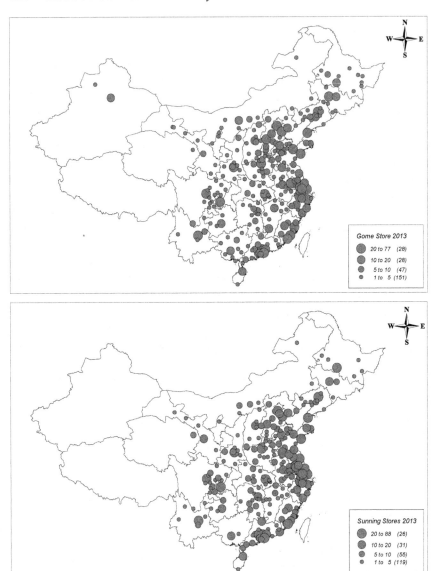

Figure 7.4   Distribution of Gome and Suning stores in 2013.
(The map on the top shows the distribution of Gome stores; the map at the bottom shows the distribution of Suning stores.)

even recently announced the introduction of a transparent pricing system and has disallowed bargaining.

Best Buy has since focused on expansion in China through the growth of Five Star. Limited expansion has been achieved (see Figure 7.5), but its expansion will be no easier. The national market is already dominated by

Gome and Suning, with the former holding 8.9 percent of the national market share, and the latter 8.7 percent; Five Star holds only 2 percent (China Chain Store Association, 2010). Both Gome and Suning continue to expand aggressively, with Suning recently announcing to open its first store in the Tibetan city of Lhasa on May 25, 2013 ("Chinese electronics store opens outlet on roof of the world," 2013). This makes Five Star's strategy of organic growth difficult to achieve, particularly given the high cost of leasing commercial properties.

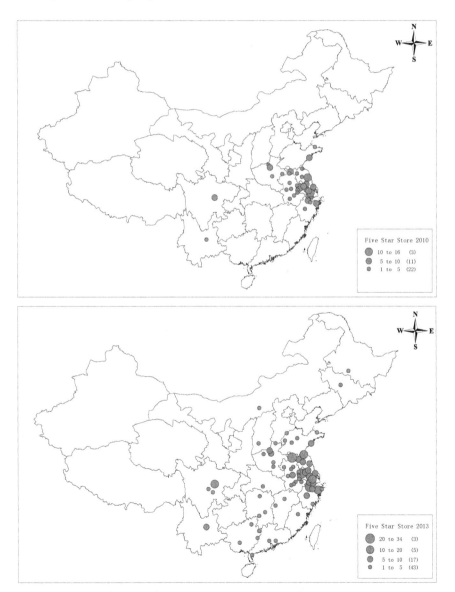

Figure 7.5   Distribution of Five Star stores in 2010 and 2013.

THE SETBACK OF MEDIA MARKT AND
THE SLOW GROWTH OF YAMADA

China is an enormous market of consumer electronics. Even though the ownership of such appliances as TVs, refrigerators, washers, air conditioners, computers, digital cameras, and cell phones is already high across the country (see Table 2.2), consumers replace them from time to time with new models. The China market is too tempting for foreign retailers to neglect, and the setbacks of Best Buy did not discourage other international retailers to try their luck. Unfortunately, they did not do any better than Best Buy and have suffered the same fate.

The German Metro, in partnership with the Taiwanese Foxconn, invested to bring the Germany-based Media Markt to China in 2010 (with Metro owning 75 percent of the joint venture and Foxconn 25 percent). It has since opened seven stores in Shanghai. As Europe's leading CE products retailer, Media Markt forecast that it could open 100 stores across China by 2015 (Lang, 2010; Chang, 2011). Its spatial strategy seemed to be too similar to that of Best Buy: use Shanghai as its stronghold and spread to other cities from there. Its business model was also similar to that of Best Buy: procure products and goods from suppliers with cash (for lower prices); organize merchandise in stores by categories, instead of brands; staff stores with retailer-paid employees only (instead of manufacturer-dispatched sales associates) to avoid internal competition; and focus on customer experience and service.

Media Markt made a high pitch when it landed in Shanghai in November 2011: "They [referring to Best Buy] are gone; we are here to meet all your needs" (Wang, Q., 2011). It also distinguished itself from Best buy with two characteristics: (1) empower store managers with a high level of autonomy in business decision making, combined with stock options as incentives for their high performance; and (2) count on Foxconn (one of the largest electronics assembly plants in the world) to supply the Media Markt stores with CE products at controlled prices. Despite the merits of its business model, the Metro-Foxconn joint venture could not sustain the steady injection of capital required to expand the chain to achieve scale economy. On March 11, 2013, after less than three years, the joint venture announced it would close all seven Media Markt stores in Shanghai due to the underperformance of the subsidiary chain, making it "the German version of the Best Buy story" (Torsten Stocker, Partner at Monitor Group; quoted in Wilson & Waldmeir, 2013). In the words of Olaf Koch, Metro's Chief Executive, the German retailer now wants to "concentrate resources where returns will be greatest, principally in Metro's cash-and-carry warehouses" (Dauer, 2013; Wilson & Waldmeir, 2013).

Another latecomer of foreign CE retailers is Japan's Yamada Denki, which also entered China in 2010. As the Japanese appliance market matured, Yamada, the largest CE retailer in Japan and the second largest in the world, had also begun expanding to overseas markets, with its entry in China as the first step of an aggressive globalization effort. Avoiding Shanghai—the place where Best Buy and Media Markt each met their waterloo, Yamada chose to open its first China outlet in Shenyang—a Tier 1 city in Northeast China ("Yamada Denki: China bound," 2010). Without further expansion in Shenyang, it jumped to Tianjin and opened its second China store there in 2011—a city 660 km away from Shenyang ("Yamada Denki to open new store in China," 2011). One year later in 2012, it opened its third store in Nanjing—the home turf of Five Star ("Japan's Yamada Denki opens third store in China", 2012). Its Nanjing store is located in the city's largest retail node—Xinjiekou, where two Suning stores, one Gome store, and one Five Star outlet already exist. Apparently, Yamada takes a different spatial approach in rolling out stores in China than did both Best Buy and Media Markt. However, in every aspect, its business model is similar to those of Best Buy and Media Markt, except that the Yamada stores carry general merchandise as well as electronic appliances. They also include restaurants and children's amusement areas, "inviting families to stay long in the stores for a delightful shopping experience" (Yamada Denki, 2013).

Typical of Japanese retailers, Yamada is much more prudent than were its counterparts Best Buy and Media Markt, with a much less ambitious expansion plan in China. It has been opening only one store per year since its entry. It did have a plan to open two new outlets in 2013, but the company announced in November 2012 to reassess its China strategy and temporarily suspended the plan (Lang, 2013). On the surface, the delay was caused by the recent territorial dispute between China and Japan on sovereignty over the Pinnacle Islands (known as Diaoyu Islands to the Chinese, but Senkaku Islands to the Japanese). The deep reason is Yamada's inability to expand and to make a profit. It is also reported that Yamada is now exploring the feasibility of entering Vietnam, Indonesia, and other emerging markets in Southeast Asia (Lang, 2013).

8 Development of Shopping Centers as New Consumption Space

Another wave of global flow of retail capital and production of consumption space in China is represented by the boom of shopping center development. China did not have shopping centers until the mid-1990s. Since then, there has been considerable development and construction in many urban centers. The boom has led to competition among the large cities of Beijing, Shanghai, Tianjin, Guangzhou, and Shenzhen to build the country's, or even Asia's, largest shopping mall (Li, 2004; "China's largest shopping mall to be completed in Beijing," 2004). Many other municipal governments enthusiastically welcome investment, especially FDI, in large shopping centers to raise their city's profile.

The shopping center in China is an exclusively urban phenomenon. New shopping centers have played a key role in attracting brand name international retailers to the Chinese cities in the last two decades. There are more shopping centers in Shanghai and Beijing than in any other city in China. By the end of 2010, 74 shopping centers were in operation in Shanghai with a total of 9 million m^2 of consumption space (Shanghai Shopping Center Association, 2011). Known as the business capital of China and the national center of consumption, Shanghai has developed a robust and sophisticated retail sector in the last 20 years. It now leads all of China in shopping center development. While Beijing has a smaller number of shopping centers, with about 40 in total, it has one of the country's largest shopping malls—New Yansha Mall. In more recent years, many other cities are in favour of building large shopping centers. According to the recent report by CB Richard Ellis (Moss & Chan, 2012), seven of the 22 most active shopping-center-development urban markets in the world in 2011, as measured by square meters completed, are in China. These are Shenyang (1st), Wuhan (2nd), Chengdu (3rd), Guangzhou (4th), Chongqing (9th), Tianjin (19th), and Beijing (19th)—all are mega urban markets and Tier 1 cities. Of the top 20 urban centers measured by square meters of shopping centers under construction, 12 are in Chinese cities. Heading the list are Tianjin (where 2.4 million m^2 were under construction), Shenyang (2.2 million), and Chengdu (1.9 million).

Despite the large number of shopping centers now existing in China, no shopping center directory of any kind ever existed. Even the president of China's Chain Store Association under the auspices of the Ministry of Commerce lamented the lack of official statistics on the number and nationwide distribution of shopping centers. Without the benefit of systematic data, this chapter focuses on the major sources of retail capital, the emergence of domestic developers, development patterns, and the lessons to be learned.

BACKGROUND AND CONTEXT

The shopping center was the most successful land use, real estate, and retail business concept of the 20th century (Beyard & O'Mara, 1999). It dominated the retail landscape in the North American and European cities for nearly 40 years from the 1950s to the late 1980s. Shopping centers were so pervasive that they served the entire metropolitan city in a hierarchical system, consisting of neighborhood, community, regional, and super-regional centers. By the count of the International Council of Shopping Centers (2011), there now exist more than 100,000 shopping centers of various sizes in the U.S. The large centers not only serve as shopping destinations, but also offer a wide range of dining, entertainment, and recreation experiences. The booming development, at the same time, has created an industry of shopping center developers and real estate investment trusts (REITs), responsible for developing and managing most of the large shopping centers.

By the early 1990s, major technological innovations in the distribution system led to the emergence of another retail revolution—the creation of the "big box store." In less than ten years, the big box store has become the leading retail format in the Western retail system, and the associated "power centers" have become the prevailing form of big box store conglomerations because they offer lower rent and result in lower operating expenses for their retail tenants than their counterparts in an enclosed mall environment. At the same time, they are seen as the cause of the 'graying' of regional and super-regional shopping centers and the demise of the department stores that were the most important mall anchors in North American shopping malls (Kmitta & Ball, 2001; Doucet, 2001; Kim, 2004).

Not all industry leaders admit that graying of shopping centers has occurred, but shopping center development has slowed down considerably since the 1990s in both the U.S. and Canada. Many shopping centers have experienced loss or change of anchors, a phenomenon described as "re-tenanting" of shopping centers (Christopherson, 1996). The result is a decline in investment opportunities and suppressed investment for many shopping center developers and REITs (Wrigley & Lowe, 1996; "Traditional mall now a hard sell," 2004). Wary developers are seeking overseas opportunities in which to park their surplus capital.

In contrast to its declining popularity in the U.S. and Canada, the shopping center was introduced in China in the late 1990s as a retail innovation and a new platform for retailing. The high demand for shopping centers in Chinese cities presented golden opportunities for both developers and investors, as well as for retailers. Recognizing the investment potentials and business opportunities for its corporate members, the International Council of Shopping Centres (ICSC) held its 12th annual Asia-Pacific Conference and Exhibition in Shanghai in 2004. Eight years later, ICSC returned to Shanghai to hold its 2012 Retail Real Estate World Summit to tackle the issues ranging from the latest development trends to investment opportunities in emerging markets. For the participants, China is an ideal venue for such a conference because it is the most explosive market and by far the dominant country when it comes to development activity driven largely by its large population and growing middle class (Mattson-Teig, 2012). According to a recent report by CB Richard Ellis, a commercial real estate firm, "more than half of the shopping malls being built on the planet today are being built in China" (Rapoza, 2012, p. 1). Demand for shopping centers has been propelled further by the proliferation of international retailers in China. Shopping centers provide international retailers, especially fashion retailers (such as Zara, H&M, and Uniqlo) and luxury retailers, locational advantages over retail strips.

Alongside the opportunities were challenges for shopping center development in Chinese cities. Shopping centers were being developed simultaneously with big box stores. This means that the Chinese cities skipped the era of shopping center dominance that lasted for four decades in North America. Therefore, from the beginning, the Chinese shopping centers have been facing strong competition from the big box retailers. While shopping centers provide a comfortable shopping environment, merchandise prices are typically higher than in the discount big box stores. In addition, because private automobile ownership is still relatively low (compared with that in the North American cities), even the large urban markets may not be able to support the super-regional shopping malls that usually require suburban locations and extensive spatial markets.

SOURCES OF CAPITAL AND NEW CONFIGURATIONS
OF REAL ESTATE OWNERSHIP

In the early years of shopping center development, the participating investors were almost exclusively from Southeast Asia, particularly Hong Kong, Taiwan, Thailand, and Singapore. Many Western investors were watching the trend closely, but were cautious about committing a significant amount of capital to commercial property development in the still precarious China market. They feared the risk of heavy losses in the form of sunk costs—costs that are committed by a firm to a particular use (in this case, grounded in the shopping center) and are not recoverable in the case of exit (Mata, 1991). The lack of knowledge of the Chinese market, and of a clear understanding of how to manage the risks involved, was the major barrier that Western investors needed to overcome.

Two important new trends have emerged since the beginning of the new millennium. First, domestic shopping center developers (such as Wanda) have emerged to play an important role in building shopping centers in Chinese cities. Second, Western investors, including both professional REITs and retailers, have begun to be engaged in development of new shopping malls or management of existing centers. In the wake of the global real estate recession, the lack of expansion opportunities in the mature markets has prompted more Western developers and investors to look beyond their own national borders for growth opportunities and to invest in shopping centers in China.

Asian Capitals

Asian capitals played an important role in the early period of shopping center development in Chinese cities. Of the 37 existing centers in Shanghai in 2005, 24 (65 percent) were developed with overseas capital from Southeast Asia, particularly Hong Kong (16 centers), Taiwan (5), Singapore (2), and Thailand (1) (Wang et al., 2006). Participation from North American and European investors and developers was absent, a very different pattern of investment from that of hypermarket development (see Chapter 5). Furthermore, almost all the Asian investors/developers were ethnic Chinese, well-connected to Mainland China with good political and business relations with state or local governments, which made negotiation for favorable land use rights easier.

For instance, Hutchinson Whampoa Real Estate Ltd., the developer of Westgate Mall in Shanghai,[1] is owned and controlled by Hong Kong billionaire Lee Ka-Shing, who is known to be a friend of such state leaders as Deng Xiaoping and Jiang Zemin. CITIC Pacific Ltd., the developer of CITIC Square[2] on Nangjing Road West, is a subsidiary of CITIC Hong Kong (Holdings) Ltd., chaired by the son of late Chinese Vice President Rong Yiren. The Rong family was historically rooted in Shanghai and enjoyed close relations with the Shanghai municipal government ("The red capitalist Rong Yiren passed away," 2005).[3] Hang Lung Properties is another Hong Kong-based investor that enjoys extensive connections in Mainland China. The developer entered China in the early 1990s when real estate prices were at rather low levels and opportunities were abundant, and was granted favourable land use rights by the Shanghai Municipal Government in late 1993 to construct two luxury shopping centers: Grand Gateway Plaza (140,000 m²) and Plaza 66 (52,000 m²). Even the Thai-based developer of Super Brand Mall (240,000 m²), Chai Tai Group, is a business conglomerate owned by an overseas Chinese family. Many of these Asian investors and developers are also known to be generous donors to local governments (in exchange for favorable relations). For instance, the Chairman of Hong Kong's Shimao Group, a Mainland Chinese emigrant and the developer of Bailian-Shimao International Plaza (58,000 m²), donated US$2 million to help Shanghai with its bid for the 2010 World Expo.

Similarly, property investors from Hong Kong played an important role in the early stages of shopping center development in Beijing. They include Cheung Kong Holdings Ltd. (which developed The Mall at Oriental Plaza at the intersection of Wangfujing and Chang'an Boulevards); Sun Hung Kai Properties (which developed Sun Dong'an Plaza on Wangfujing Boulevard); New World Group (which developed New World Shopping Mall); and Henderson Land Development Company Ltd. (which developed Henderson Shopping Center).

CapitaLand, a Singapore-based REIT, is a more active participant. Compared with the other Asian investors, CapitaLand is a professional developer, more dedicated to the shopping center business. In 2004, it formed a joint venture with the domestic SZITIC Commercial Property Development Ltd. to develop shopping centers in China ("CapitaLand moves closer to China REIT," 2005). By 2006, it already had 25 shopping malls in China, with 21 of them being anchored by Wal-Mart supercenters (Jennings, 2006). As of 2012, it has 59 projects in 36 cities, with 47 in operation. Its shopping centers are operated under three different banners: CapitaLand Plaza, CapitaLand Mall, and Raffles City. Its flagship shopping center—Raffles City, an 8-story vertical mall with 40,000 m² of retail space—opened in 2004 in the heart of Shanghai (between Nanjing Road East and People's Square). In 2008, it acquired 50 percent of ownership of Summit Mall from a troubled domestic developer and took over its management (Shanghai Shopping Center Association, 2010).

The Japanese Aeon is one of the earliest Asian retailers to build shopping centers in China. Its first enclosed mall was a community shopping center built in the late 1990s in the City of Qingdao, and anchored by a Jusco Department Store and a Jusco Supermarket. However, it did not resume building more shopping centers until very recently, when Aeon announced that it would develop regional shopping centers under the banner of Aeon Mall. Three are scheduled to open for business between 2014 and 2015, in Tianjin, Suzhou, and Guangzhou ("Japanese retailer plans to open three new Aeon Malls in China," 2012).

Similar to Aeon, the Malaysian Parkson also waded into shopping center development. In 2012, it acquired a shopping mall in the city of Tianjin for 700 million yuan (US$117 million). In 2013, it acquired land use right in Qingdao for 1.57 billion yuan (US$260 million) to build a brand new shopping center (Koh, 2013). The shopping center will be part of an integrated development called Beer City Project. Parkson will operate a department store in the center and lease space to tenants. The mall is expected to begin operation in 2015 while the land rights expire in 2050.

Western Capitals

The first western REIT to invest in shopping centers in China is the U.S. Simon Property Group. Based in Indianapolis, Simon boasts to be the largest real estate company in the world, engaged in the ownership, development, and management of retail properties, primarily regional malls, Premium Outlet centers, and community/lifestyle centers. It owns, or has interests in, more than 300 retail real estate properties in North America and Asia (Simon Property Group, 2012). In July 2006, Simon Property Group signed a cooperation agreement with the Morgan Stanley Real Estate Funds (MSREF) and SZITIC Commercial Property Co. Ltd (SZITIC CP)[4] to develop shopping center projects in China. Simon and MSREF would each own 32.5 percent of the enterprise, with SZITIC CP owning 35 percent ("Simon, SZITIC CP and MSREF join forces to develop retail in China," 2006.) More than 12 potential projects were revealed in the agreement. Each project was to be a multi-level retail destination of 40,000–70,000 m², and would be anchored by a Wal-Mart store. In some of the malls, Warner Theaters would also be an anchor tenant. Their first shopping center project was a 46,000 m² mall in Hangzhou, completed in 2007. In March 2012, Simon Property Group signed a memorandum of understanding (MOU) with the Shanghai-based Bailian Group to jointly develop a Premium Outlet Center in Pudong District of Shanghai ("Simon Property Group and Bailian Group agree to jointly develop a premium outlet center in China," 2012). The outlet center will be built adjacent to the Shanghai Disney Resort as part of a larger entertainment and retail destination.

Another source of capital from the U.S. is Taubman Center. A mall REIT headquartered in Bloomfield, Michigan, Taubman's core business is in the development, leasing, and management of regional and super-regional shopping centers, with a portfolio of 27 leased and/or managed properties in the U.S. In 2005, it founded a subsidiary—Taubman Asia, headquartered in Hong Kong—to tap the development potentials in the major growth markets of China and South Korea. To target the mainland China market specifically, it formed Taubman TCBL in 2011 as a subsidiary of Taubman Asia. TCBL was a Beijing-based consulting firm formed in 2005 with offices also in Shanghai, Shenzhen, Chengdu, Chongqing, and Shenyang. Its core business was to provide retail-focused real estate consulting services to property developers, retailers, and institutional investors in China. Taubman acquired TCBL for its extensive China market knowledge. The acquisition was to speed up Taubman's engagement in shopping center development in the hot China market.

Like most other foreign investors, Taubman takes the path of joint venture in its business endeavors in China to lower investment risks. Shortly after its creation, Taubman TCBL announced a joint venture with the Beijing Wangfujing Department Store (one of the 20 National Team members, see Chapter 6) to invest and manage a 90,000 m² shopping center in the city of Xi'an. It should be pointed out that the joint venture did not build the shopping center by itself. The center was built by a domestic developer—Shaanxi Fuli Real Estate Development Co. Ltd.—as part of a large-scale mixed-use complex. The Taubman-Wangfujing joint venture simply acquired the majority ownership of the shopping center (to be anchored by a Wangfujing Department Store) and will manage the operation of the center after it opens for business in 2015 (Finkelstein, 2012).

As mentioned earlier, China had no professional shopping center developers until the mid-2000s. Most domestic developers lacked the required capital and expertise in shopping center development and management. They often relied on bank loans to finance the development and, as such, were vulnerable to fiscal policy changes imposed by the state government. In order to make a quick profit, some domestic developers leased only the anchor retail spaces, and sold the smaller units to independent retailers or to individual investors, turning the center into a condominium complex (Cheng, 2004; Wang et al., 2006). Consequently, the management's ability to control the desired tenant mix was lost, which led to undue competition within the center, poor performance, and high vacancy rates. Unable to hold the properties even for an initial period of loss, some domestic developers were eager to find buyers, particularly international buyers, to bail them out, presenting opportunities for foreign investors.[5] Macquarie Bank Ltd. of Australia seized such opportunities and joined other investors to buy nine shopping malls in China for a 24 percent stake (Liu, 2005; Jennings, 2006). In June 2005, Morgan Stanley purchased the loss-incurring Shanghai Square for US$100 million ("International REITS purchase 30 shopping centres," 2005). Later, it completed negotiations with a local developer to purchase a proposed (and municipal government-approved) suburban shopping center project—Air Modern Mall—for US$25 million ("Morgan Stanley is in negotiation," 2006).[6] In 2008, Blackstone Group, a U.S.-based investment and asset-management firm listed on the NYSE, invested in four shopping centers in Shanghai to provide management and leasing services (Shanghai Shopping Center Association, 2010).

In China, where land is owned exclusively by the state, it is extremely important for the international REITs to negotiate and secure long-term land use rights, to minimize the risk associated with high sunk costs. Some international REITs find it much easier to enter the market through acquisition of completed properties or approved projects, rather than attempting to obtain raw land for new construction. This saves them the trouble of going through land use rights negotiation and the public hearing process. Some domestic developers insist on retaining joint ownership. Considering that the political and business environments in China are still precarious, it may not be a poor investment option for the resource-rich international REITs to have a Chinese partner, as many international retailers do in China. In 2009, the Canada-based Ivanhoé Cambridge, one of the world's 10 largest real estate companies, acquired a 60 percent ownership of a shopping center developed by Shanghai's Bailian Group in the City of Changsha, and renamed it as La Nova (Zhan & Pan, 2009). It should be pointed out that not all foreign investors or REITs intend to hold the properties for a long period of time. Their intent is often to improve the value of a center by reducing vacancy rates and then sell the center to other investors for a one-time return. For example, Blackstone purchased 95 percent of ownership of Channel 1 in Shanghai in 2008 for one billion yuan, and sold its shares to the Hong Kong-based New World Group for 1.4 billion yuan in 2011, a 40 percent return in three years ("Blackstone divests in China," 2011).

A number of Western retailers also entered the business of shopping center development in China, abandoning a decade-long strategy of leasing, mainly because suitable commercial real estate has become increasingly difficult or costly to obtain. According to Cushman & Wakefield Inc., a New York-based real estate service firm (Bloomberg News, 2011), retail rents in Beijing's downtown Wangfujing district almost doubled between 2007 and 2011; in Shanghai's Nanjing Road W. retail strip, they jumped more than 50 percent in the same period. Many leases that foreign retailers signed 10–15 years ago are due, or will be due shortly, for renewal. In addition to building a shopping center to house their own stores and to control leasing costs, the Western retailers intend to generate revenue by leasing the remaining spaces to other retailers to help service the financing of the center. These foreign retailers often establish a subsidiary as their own development arm for this purpose.

As a latecomer in China, Tesco found its expansion hindered by the high cost of renting retail space. It therefore switched from relying on leasing retail space from others to developing and owning properties by itself. In 2007, it set up a wholly-owned subsidiary named Tesco Property Holding Ltd. to "purchase, develop and operate shopping center development in China" (Waller, 2010). The Tesco shopping centers are branded as Lifespace Malls. A typical Lifespace Mall ranges between 40,000 m^2 and 60,000 m^2 in floor space, and is anchored by a Tesco-Legou hypermarket. The first Lifespace Mall opened for business in the City of Qingdao in 2010 with 76,000 m^2 of floor area. It took four years and cost one billion yuan (US$160 million) to complete. Five more Lifespace Malls have since been developed in Qinhuangdao, Fushun, Anshan, Fuzhou, and Xiamen—all Tier 2 or Tier 3 cities ("Tesco is to build a second Lifespace Mall in Xiamen," 2012).

Auchan's involvement in shopping center development is through Immochan—a commercial real estate company originated in 1976 and owned by Auchan itself. Its first shopping center in China, named Sun Art, was built in Ningbo (a Tier 1 city), with 150,000 m^2 of floor space, anchored by an Auchan hypermarket ("Auchan recruits tenants for its shopping center project in Ningbo," 2012). More centers are planned for Wuxi (Tier 1), Jiaxing (Tier 3), Hangzhou (Tier 1), and Nanjing (Tier 1), all in the two neighboring provinces of Jiangsu and Zhejiang. Auchan and

Leroy Meilin jointly developed a plaza in Beijing's Fentai District, but that plaza is more of a prototype power center than a shopping center, because the only tenants are two big box stores operated by Auchan and Leroy Meilin themselves.

For similar reasons, the Swedish Ikea entered shopping center development for its own expansion in China. This was to be achieved through its shopping center development arm: Inter Ikea Center Group (IICG). IICG was established 2001 and is based in Denmark.[7] It announced in 2011 that it would invest US$1.2 billion in the next five years to build three regional shopping centers in Wuxi, Beijing, and Wuhan ("Ikea is to expand its China mall development plan," 2012). Each of them will be anchored by a typical Ikea furniture store in big box format, along with Auchan, Suning, and Jin Yi International Cinema (a domestic movie theater chain) as co-anchors. This will increase the number of Ikea stores in China to 14 when these centers open for business. IICG looks for locations that (1) are next to metro and bus stations, or well connected with the arterial roads and regional highways; (2) are large enough to accommodate a full-size Ikea and a well-planned mall circulation; (3) have a sufficient nearby population to support a hypermarket anchor and food-beverage outlets; (4) have a reasonable level of competition; and (5) have vacant adjacent land for future expansion (Burstedt, 2011). The IICG center in Wuxi, slated to open in 2013, boasts 140,000 m² of floor area, with 400 shops and 5,800 parking spaces (Chen, 2011). The centers in Beijing and Wuhan will open in 2014 and 2015 respectively. Recently, IICG has approved an investment plan to develop a shopping center in Shanghai, where local market survey, site selection, and land acquisition are under way simultaneously. In the highly competitive Shanghai market, IICG is projecting its image as that of city builder. In the words of Ding Hui, Managing Director of IICG China, "our strategy is to work with local governments and be a partner of the development not only of the shopping center, but also [of] the city" (Chen, 2011); this is a strategy to appeal for government support and approval.

EMERGENCE OF DOMESTIC DEVELOPERS

Domestic capital began to flow into shopping centers in the early 2000s from two types of sources: state-owned (or controlled) enterprises, and non-state-owned companies (including both stock companies and private companies). Both sources include real estate developers and retailers.

The largest and the most professional domestic developer of shopping centers is Wanda Group—a non-state-owned, joint-stock company. Founded in 1988 with an early focus on residential property development, Wanda did not enter into the shopping center realm until 2002. Soon after, it expanded to engage in five major areas of business: commercial properties, luxury hotels, tourism, movie theaters, and department stores. The company now operates 60 Wanda Plazas (shopping centers), 34 five-star hotels, 814 cinema screens, and 50 department stores, in more than 40 cities (Wanda Group, 2012).

Wanda has clearly stated strategies for shopping center development ("Wang Jianlin discloses Wanda's business secrets," 2012). In site selection, it considers all accessible sites with 300,000 people living in a 5-km-radius trade area and no competitors within 2–3 km from the site. In addition to retail stores, its shopping centers have a high percentage of restaurants, entertainment, and recreation, to create attractive shopping destinations. All Wanda shopping centers were developed through Wanda Commercial Properties Co. Ltd. and managed by Wanda Commercial Properties Management Co. Ltd.—both being subsidiaries of Wanda Group. Most Wanda Plazas are anchored by a Wanda Department Store (created in 2007 and known as Wanqian Department Store until being renamed in July 2012), and almost all of them also have a multi-screen Wanda International Film City theater.

Before 2005, the majority of the Wanda Plazas were co-anchored by a Wal-Mart Supercenter. The more recent ones are co-anchored by either a Carrefour hypermarket or a Tesco hypermarket. In 2012, Wanda acquired the American AMC for US$2.6 billion to both diversify investment and enrich the content of its Wanda International Film City theaters, therefore to enhance the overall attractiveness of the Wanda Plazas.

Wanda continues to develop shopping centers in the country, with another 50 plazas under construction and more in the pipeline. To keep its lead position in China, Wanda established both an Institute of Commercial Real Estate Research and a School of Commercial Real Estate Management. The former is responsible for planning and design of the Wanda Plazas. The latter provides training to its senior and mid-level managers (Wanda Group, 2012).

A typical source of state capital is COFCO (China National Cereal, Oil, and Foodstuff Corporation)—a state-controlled corporation with its core business in production, import and export of food, cooking oil, and other agricultural products. It owns a real estate development arm—COFCO Property (Group) Co. Ltd. The predecessor of this real estate arm was a local property development firm based in the City of Shenzhen—Baoheng (Group) Co. Ltd. Baoheng was acquired by COFCO in 2004 and was renamed COFCO Property in 2006. It develops shopping centers under the banner of Joy City. The first Joy City opened at Beijing's Xidan commercial node in 2007 (one of the three largest retail nodes in Central Beijing). Its second mall in Beijing is located in Chaoyang District, opened in 2010. A third one is currently under construction at Andingmen. Outside of Beijing, COFCO has built, and is building, shopping centers in such cities as Shenyang (2009), Shanghai (2010), Tianjin (2011), Chengdu (2013), and Yantai (2013). Except Yantai (a Tier 2 city), all the other host cities are either mega urban markets or Tier 1 cities.

A number of domestic retailers have also entered the business of shopping center development for the same reasons: both investment opportunities and high cost of renting retail spaces from third parties. The largest such retailer is Bailian Group. In 1999, one of its component corporations, Shanghai Friendship (Group) Ltd., purchased a defunct department store from the Japanese Yaohan and retrofitted the five-story building into a shopping center (named Nanfang Friendship Shopping Center). Shortly after its creation, Bailian Group established a subsidiary responsible for shopping center development and management. By the end of 2012, Bailian has developed and owns 14 shopping centers and three outlet malls. Unlike the Wanda plazas that are spread out in 40 or so cities across the country, the Bailian shopping centers are all confined to Shanghai. In its 12th Five-Year Plan (2010–2015), Bailian plans to add another 10 shopping centers to Shanghai's retail landscape (Le and Yan, 2012). New developments will focus on the suburbs to keep pace with residential development. Suburban shopping centers will also serve as intervening opportunities, intercepting shoppers from going into the already congested central city.

In addition to shopping center development, Bailian was the first in the country to build outlet malls. The first outlet mall opened in Shanghai's suburban Qingpu District in 2006—26 km away from the city center. The outlet mall was composed of 250 outlets, including such international brands as Armani, Zegna, Burberry, Bally, Hugo Boss, Dunhill, Aquascutum, Ferragamo, Max Mara, Trussadi, Nike, Adidas, ESPRIT, I.T, MIZUNO, GH, D'urban, LACOSTE, ecco, Clarks, and GEOX. Since then, Bailian has built two more outlet malls, both outside of Shanghai to avoid cannibalization: one in Hangzhou, the other in Wuhan. As was mentioned earlier, Bailian signed a MOU with the American Simon Property Group in 2012 to jointly develop a Premium Outlet Center in Pudong of Shanghai, adjacent to the Shanghai Disney Resort.

Two other members of the National Team also waded into shopping center development: China Resources Vanguard and Zhongbai Group. Vanguard is developing shopping centers under different banners in different cities. Its first center opened in Shenzhen in October 2010, named Fun2. Its second center in Shenzhen is named The Mixc, to create a sense of differentiation in the same urban market. Outside of Shenzhen (such as in Beijing and Hefei), China Resources Vanguard has been building shopping centers under the banner of Living Mall. A new Living Mall of 67,000 m^2 is under construction in Weinan of Shaanxi Province (a Tier 4 city). In Wuhan, Zhongbai is building a 180,000 m^2 mall (named Zhongxiang Shopping Center), costing 600 million yuan ("Zhongbai Group builds large shopping center in Wuhan," 2012).

Typical private investors are Wenfeng Group and Shanghai Summit Property Development Corporation. The former invested US$42.5 million to develop the 84,000 m^2 Wenfeng Mall in Shanghai's Pudong District in 2003; the latter built the 290,000 m^2 Summit Mall, also in

Shanghai. It should be pointed out that domestic developers often had little experience in shopping center development and management. The lack of expertise has subsequently led to many problems, from which many lessons can be learned.

DEVELOPMENT PATTERNS AND LESSONS

Shopping centers in China not only are geographically more spread out, but also become progressively larger in order to cover the breadth in merchandise variety and range. In 2005, 37 shopping centers were operating in Shanghai, with an average size of 65,000 m² in floor space (Wang et al., 2006). In 2010, the average size of the 74 shopping centers nearly doubled, at 121,000 m² (Shanghai Shopping Center Association, 2011), with 33 of them being larger than 100,000 m², readily qualifying them as super-regional shopping centers by Western standards.

In the first 10 years of shopping center development, the majority of the malls were built in the densely populated central areas. In addition, the central city malls were concentrated in the traditional commercial nodes (i.e., the high streets). This was the case in both Shanghai and Beijing (Wang & Guo, 2007). However, there were clear differences in shopping center development patterns between the foreign and domestic investors, and among the foreign investors themselves. Investors from Hong Kong and Singapore favored construction of ancillary malls as podiums of office towers, while other overseas investors and most domestic developers tended to engage in development of free-standing malls. For example, both Grand Gateway Plaza and Plaza 66, developed by the Hong Kong-based Hang Lung Properties in Shanghai, have twin office towers soaring above them. Westgate Mall and Raffles City are also attached to an office tower hosting many well-known multinational corporations. Similarly, the Mall at Oriental Plaza, Sun Dong'an Plaza, New World Shopping Mall, and Henderson Shopping Center, all developed with Hong Kong investments in Beijing, were built as podiums of office towers in the city center. These investors favored this form of development for three strategic reasons. First, land cost for building a shopping center was greatly reduced, because the same land was also used for high-rise office buildings and the rent generated by leasing office spaces constituted a significant portion of the investment returns. Second, each tower housed thousands of office employees, mostly white-collar professionals, who themselves are frequent and affluent shoppers. Third, as Shanghai and Beijing became international economic, financial, and trade centers, there would be even greater demand for quality office space in the city. As office towers at strategic locations have great potential for property-value appreciation, many of the developers have the intention to sell these commercial properties to interested international REITs to make a one-time profit.

The Taiwanese developers seemed to focus on development of free-standing and community-oriented shopping centers outside of the central city, which could be the result of their inability to obtain favorable land use rights in the central area. In general, investors from Taiwan did not have the same monetary and political capital as did their counterparts from Hong Kong. Accordingly, they lacked bargaining powers. In fact, three of the four shopping centers that were built with Taiwanese investment in Shanghai were developed by the same investor—Ting Hsin International Group—which was also the parent company of Hymart. It was the only overseas investor that intended to develop a chain of community shopping centers with a distinct brand—Hymall (meaning Happy Shopping Mall).

With the exceptions of Beethoven Plaza and Summit Mall, all of the centers that were built by domestic developers in Shanghai before 2005 were free-standing malls; except for New World City, all the free-standing malls were located in suburban districts (Wang et al., 2006). They ranged from flea-market style centers with no anchors to full-sized regional malls. The country's largest shopping center in Beijing—New Yansha Mall, built with private investment—is also a free-standing retail destination.

In more recent years, it is no longer economically viable, even outside of the city center, for a developer or investor to acquire a block of land and build only a shopping mall on it. As a result, many new shopping centers have been built as an integral part of a multi-purpose complex occupying one or more city blocks. Typically, a shopping mall is constructed with not only office or apartment towers above them, but often also hotels, resorts, recreation, and even conference facilities, known as a HOPSCA (short for hotel, office, park, shopping, conference and apartment). These high-density developments not only create a live-work-play-shopping environment, but also maximize the floor-to-land ratios, thus becoming a more efficient, complex form of income-producing real estate (DeSwart, 2006). Of the seven Joy City Malls (five existing and two under construction), all are part of a multi-purpose and mixed-use complex including luxury apartments, suite hotels, and premium offices. Local governments support this type of development because they often act as a catalyst for non-retail development and re-generation of the surrounding area. The mixed-use developments bring new shapes to both the physical and legal structure of shopping center development, spawning new configurations for real estate ownership (Frost Brown Todd ALP, 2007). They often include multiple developers, with one owning the retail component and the others owning the other components, such as the case of the Taubman-Wangfujing joint venture in the City of Xi'an.

Unlike most of the regional and super-regional malls in North American cities, which are expansive in footprint with only one to two stories, shopping centers in China are typically vertical malls with at least 4–5 stories. It is not uncommon to see 8–10 story vertical malls in city centers. Even the 550,000 m^2 New Yansha Mall outside of central Beijing has five floors above ground and two floors below. Such a mall layout requires the support of elevators and long-range escalators, posing a challenge to shoppers strolling around to visit different stores.

A parallel trend is the construction of open-air, lifestyle centers. Examples are Sanlitun Village (completed in 2009 by Hong Kong-based Swire Property Limited) and Solana Lifestyle Shopping Park (completed in 2008 by private investment) in Beijing, and Thumbs-Up Plaza in Shanghai.

In the late 1990s and the first half of the 2000s, shopping centers were developed in the background of a booming economy and rapid urbanization. But due to the relatively low automobile ownership (by western standards), road congestion, and lack of free parking, many shoppers still rely on public transit, especially rapid transit, for access to high-order shopping malls. As a result, many regional and super-regional malls are developed in close proximity to subway/LRT stations, especially interchange stations. Most of the shopping centers that are not on or adjacent to rapid transit lines needed to provide free shuttle buses, at their own cost, to bring in shoppers.

In Shanghai, subway and LRT lines are laid out in such a way that they pass through most of the municipal-level commercial nodes. As such, many shopping centers are located both in a commercial node and at a subway station. The seven-story Grand Gateway Plaza is right above Shanghai's largest subway station—the Xujiahui Station (the interchange of Line 1 and Line 9). The nine-story Summit Mall is located above the Sun Yisen Park Station (the interchange of Line 2 and Line 3). Super Brand Mall (10 stories above ground plus two floors below) is only a two-minute walk from the Lujiazui Station, and the Join Buy City Plaza (also nine stories above ground) is connected to Jing'an Station via an underground path. In fact, 48 (or 65 percent) of the 74 existing shopping centers in Shanghai are located within 500 meters of an interchange station (Shanghai Shopping Center Association, 2011). Close proximity to subway/LRT stations not only brings in high volumes of shopping traffic for retailers but also enhances property values. During the 12th Five-Year Plan period, Shanghai plans to add another 200 kilometers of LRT lines, which will create more accessible and prime locations for future shopping centers.

Rapid expansion of international retailers, especially the mall-based fashion and footwear retailers, creates a high demand for modern and high-quality retail spaces. Developers and real estate investors, who place high expectations on the spending power of the Chinese consumer, have been active in building shopping centers in Chinese cities. More domestic capital is expected to flow into shopping center development to become retail capital, as the recent state efforts to ease housing prices reduce interest among developers in building apartment complexes (Flannery, 2011). There are different views on whether Chinese cities are "over-malled," as has occurred in many North American cities. As Sebastian Skiff, Executive Director of CBRE Asia, commented: at first glance, the nationwide number appears to be a scary symptom of overbuilding; a deeper look shows that the situation is more of a catch-up story after a long period of underdevelopment (Oliver, 2012). Either way, there have been lessons that should be learned by both developers and local governments, as development has been fueled by a lax planning regime and a lack of understanding among some local developers regarding how much space is required to satisfy consumer demand (Moss & Chan, 2012).

While many municipal governments enthusiastically courted investment in shopping centers and made many lucrative land offers to developers, few have instituted an effective planning process and approval mechanism. In other words, the shopping center is in a state of free competition, with inadequate regulations. The planning process and the approval mechanism are often inconsistent and are not as transparent as they should be. In Shanghai, for example, a two-tiered approval mechanism existed, where the district governments were permitted to approve smaller projects, but larger projects needed to be approved by the municipal government. Although the Shanghai government announced in November 2001 the introduction of public hearings into its approval process, public hearings were applied only to development of hypermarkets, not to shopping center construction. Lack of effective planning has inevitably led to irrational development patterns, leading to over-concentration of shopping centers in some local markets. Four large shopping centers were allowed to be constructed within a one-kilometer stretch of Nanjing Road West,[8] with three of them within 50 meters from each other. Similarly, there is a cluster of six shopping centers on Nanjing Road East—the city's most visited high street.[9] Certain degrees of differentiation have been attempted among the six centers. Raffle City has a large fitness club occupying the entire top floor; New World City has a Madame Tussauds Museum and an indoor skating rink; and Henderson Metropolitan Center is anchored by an Apple flagship store. Other than that, there is a high degree of similarity in their remaining stores, especially fashion stores. Even if all the six shopping centers eventually become successful, they draw shoppers from the pedestrian street with negative effects on the street-level retailers outside the shopping centers, including the two free-standing department stores. Wujiaochang (meaning Star Square) in Yangpu District has been upgraded from a district-level commercial node to a municipal-level node, with two super-regional shopping centers across the street from each other: the Wanda Plaza (260,000 m^2) and the Bailian Youyicheng (120,000 m^2).

Another challenge that shopping center developers, especially domestic developers, faced was a lack of expertise and experience in feasibility studies, trade area analysis, and recruitment of desired tenants. Without robust location analyses or market surveys prior to construction, developers often rushed to build and open a center even before tenants were properly recruited and secured. In North American cities, super-regional shopping centers were often built in phases. For instance, Canada's West Edmonton

Mall, once the largest shopping center in the world, was completed in three phases to test the market response and control investment risks. In China, however, even the largest malls were completed in one phase, which contributed to high vacancy rates and revenue losses from the very beginning.

A domestic developer—Aika Investment (Group) Ltd.—built a 160,000 m² mall in Beijing in 2005, but the project went terribly wrong due to the inexperience of the developer in managing and operating the mall. To begin with, it was never able to fill the retail spaces with enough tenants. Only nine months into business, it had to cancel all the existing leases and vacate the occupying tenants, and turned the building into a wholesale market (Hong, 2005; Yang, 2005; "Beijing Aika Shopping Center undergoes transformation," 2006).

The 550,000 m² New Yansha Mall in Beijing was developed by a domestic real estate developer—Century Golden Resources Group—and is managed by Beijing New Yansha Causeway Bay Company Ltd.[10] From conception to completion, the mammoth mall was built in one year, costing 3.8 billion yuan ("The future of the world's largest mall is uncertain," 2005). But when the mall rushed to open on the occasion of the National Day (October 1) in 2004, large areas of the mall were vacant. In addition to the two large anchors—the 43,000 m² Yansha Friendship Department Store, and the 12,000 m² Guiyou Department Store, the mall had only 165 tenants (Beijing New Yansha Causeway Bay Company Limited, 2007, 79–82), compared with 480 retail stores and service outlets in the same building today. Within its first year of operation, 45 percent of the tenants left the mall and 19 percent could not pay their rent (Beijing New Yansha Causeway Bay Company Limited, 2007), suggesting a lack of either experience or prudence on the part of the mall developer and management. Although tenant replacement rate declined to 20 percent three years later, the mall could not get the shopping traffic it expected because it is too large to be efficient. Besides, its two large anchors overemphasize top-notch, upscale retailing. To attract more local visitors, the mall management has increased spaces for recreation, entertainment, and dining. The entire 5th floor (120m x 600m) is configured as a "boulevard of (sit-in) restaurants" (Beijing New Yansha Causeway Bay Company Limited, 2006), instead of the usual food court.

The South China Mall is another disaster. The mall was built in Dongguan City of Guangdong Province by a domestic developer–Alex Hu–who became a billionaire from making instant noodles. Designed as a retail destination and trumpeted as the world's largest retail center, the 660,000 m² enclosed mall features seven zones modeled on international cities, nations, and regions, including Amsterdam, Paris, Rome, Venice, Egypt, the Caribbean, and California. Features include a 25-meter replica of the Arc de Triomphe, a replica of Venice's St. Mike's bell tower, a 2.1-km canal with gondolas, and a 555-meter indoor-outdoor roller coaster. A "jumble of Disneyland and Las Vegas wrapped in one," the South China Mall is nearly three times the size of the massive Mall of America in Minnesota (Barboza, 2005). When the mall opened to the public in 2005, more than 90 percent of the shops remained un-leased and were vacant. The mall is still pretty much empty today. Why has it become a story of "(you) built it, they DON'T come"? A number of fundamental flaws contributed to the failure of the mammoth project. The developer did not have the required expertise and experience in recruiting and packaging willing tenants, although Hu had sent a team of designers traveling around the world for inspiration and in search of ideas. Although Dongguan has a population of 8 million within its administrative region, a high proportion of them are factory workers. The mall was therefore conceived to rely on an average of 70,000 visitors a day from outside of the city region. However, Dongguan does not have an airport; nor are there highways adjacent to the mall. These locational deficiencies render the mall unreachable to a large number of outside visitors that are required to support it. Consequently, the developer sold the controlling interest in the mall to a business entity of Peking University, the Founders Group, and suffered from a devastatingly high sunk cost ("New South China Mall," 2012). Dick Groves, a Hong Kong-based retail consultant, summarizes succinctly: "when it's easy to get financing without having to convince someone of the project's feasibility, and without having to show pre-lease commitment, you can start to get into trouble" ("The not-so-great mall of China," 2009).

Similar problems occurred in Shanghai. Built underground and integrated with the subway station at Shanghai Science and Technology Museum and Century Park, Asia Pacific Square was intended to be a shopping paradise for tourists and visitors. The underground mall consisted of 450 small units, ranging from 10 to 20 m² in floor space. Three years after its completion in 2002, about 80 percent of the units were still empty (Wang et al., 2006). Its developer, lacking experience in shopping center development and management, was desperately looking for investors to buy it out (Gong, 2004). It was revived only after Xiangyang Market, an infamous paradise for fake brand retailers, was eliminated from the central city in 2006 and the merchants relocated to Asia Pacific Square.

Even the larger shopping centers in Shanghai had difficulty filling their retail spaces. CEPA Mall consists of more than 180 store units, but only 70 were occupied by retailers on the day of grand opening in January 2005 ("The opening of CEPA Mall," 2005). When Summit Mall opened in December 2005, more than one hundred units on the upper floors had no tenants (Jiang, 2005). Super Brand Mall, even after four years in operation, still suffered from a high vacancy rate in 2005, with only eight units having a business presence on the top three floors and the rest of these floors not even partitioned, because the mall management did not know who the tenants would be (observed in the field by this author, 2005). This created a very negative image for the 240,000 m² super-regional mall located in the heart of Pudong District. Without adequate tenants to fill the planned facilities, the mall's ability to lure customers and hold them captive in shopping bliss—the so-called Gruen effect—is lost.

In five to ten years from now, many existing shopping centers will be due for periodic renovations, necessary for preserving the value of the assets, but many mall owners may not have the required capital to carry out such renovations.

9 Luxury Retailing

Despite having made deep inroads into China and capturing significant market shares in such sectors of retailing as supermarkets and general merchandise, foreign retailers have increasingly felt that they can no longer compete with their Chinese counterparts on price. Instead, many of them turned to selling quality, instead of quantity (Donadio, 2010), leading to a new wave of retail internationalization characterized by luxury-goods retailing.

A recent study by global management consulting firm Bain & Co. reports that Chinese consumers have become the top buyers responsible for 25 percent of global purchases of luxury goods (The Associated Press, 2012). Associated with this new wave of retail internationalization is a series of new issues and concerns. The Chinese government is concerned with a high-end "wallet drain" to the coffers of the foreign retailers. The international retailers complain about the high government taxes and duties that constitute barriers to their business expansion in China; they are also fighting a seemingly unwinnable war against counterfeiting. The general public on the other hand worries about the social impacts of the world's leading brand retailers, who aggressively promote luxury goods in a country where the average income is still much lower than in the advanced economies. Impacts on the young generation of consumers are a particular concern. This chapter explores these issues and the challenges in managing the growth of luxury-goods retailing in China.

THE NATURE OF LUXURY GOODS AND THE CHINA MARKET

Consumer products, brands, attitudes, and preferences act as signals of identity. Particular brands are sought for what they represent in social environments (Cordell et al., 1996; Cova, 1997; Elliott & Wattanasuwan, 1998). The scarcer the goods of a brand, the more valuable they are. In the luxury brand industry, rarity expresses exclusivity and self-image.

Therefore, volume of production and rarity of the product are in conflict (Giacalone, 2006).

In general terms, luxury goods are those products that are made in premium quality and unique style, supplied in limited quantity and sold at high prices. They are also known as "status commodities," as possessing them is perceived to be associated with a prestige image of high social status. While they are highly desirable and characterized with exclusivity, they are inessential and do not necessarily command clear functional advantages over their counterparts (Australian Center for Retail Studies and TNS, 2007). Luxury retailers are often classified into different categories by their merchandise specialty: made-to-measure or ready-to-wear fashion, fashion accessories, jewelry and watches, perfume and cosmetics, wines and spirits, and luxury automobiles (Chevalier & Lu, 2010). They often require different distribution channels or even promotion tools.

In China, luxury retailing is represented in all of the categories, and luxury goods have become a symbol of success and a badge of wealth. World Luxury Association's *2009–2010 Global Report* highlights three distinct characteristics of the China market. First, Chinese consumers of luxury goods are much younger than the world average, with 73 percent of them under the age of 45. Forty-five percent of the Chinese consumers are between 18 to 34 years old, compared with 37 percent in Japan and 28 percent in Britain in the same age group ("China's luxury consumers younger than world average", 2011). Second, while most international luxury brands choose Beijing or Shanghai as launch pads and focal points, they have begun to open stores in China's second-tier cities. Third, Chinese shoppers spend four times more on luxury goods overseas than at home ("Chinese shoppers spent 400% more on luxury goods overseas than at home", 2011).

Foreign brands are sought after by Chinese consumers enthusiastically for a variety of reasons. Benefiting from the economic reform in the past 30 years, a class of social elites and celebrities with considerable wealth and spending power has emerged; they are fond of flaunting their wealth by wearing brand-name clothes and watches, and carrying luxury bags. They became rich by running businesses (including real estate development) or working for foreign-owned companies as senior managers. Many of them were born in the late 1970s and the 1980s as the cosseted only child of the family. Unlike their parents who grew up in an era of scarcity and are used to living a thrifty life with the die-hard habit of saving for retirement, the young elites spend lavishly to enjoy life. As well, it is embedded in Chinese culture that consumers worship foreign brands. They attach importance and high social value to foreign products, and perceive foreign brands as superior to national labels. This attitude, while not new in China, runs much higher among the young consumers than among their parents and grandparents. The booming luxury retailing is also supported by the widespread social and business gifting for relation building, which is often linked to bribery of officials in exchange for business and personal favors. Luxury goods of obvious high value flatter both the gift giver and the receiver (Barboza, 2009).

There are no reliable statistics on the total consumption of luxury goods in China. According to the World Luxury Association's 2009–2010 Global Report, total sales in the mainland China market reached US$10.7 billion in 2010 ("Chinese luxury goods consumption reached US$10.7 Billion," 2011). However, the accuracy of the report has been challenged and questioned. Another report by McKinsey predicts that expenditure on luxury goods will increase by 18 percent annually, and reach US$27 billion by 2015 (Atsmon et al., 2011). The Chinese government is concerned with the "leakage" of revenue, and levies three taxes on luxury goods imports in order to protect and nurture national brands: a custom duty of 6.5–18 percent; a sales tax of 30 percent; and a value-added tax of 17 percent ("Luxury goods and the China price," 2011). Depending on the type of luxury goods, total tax can be as high as 60 percent. This has resulted in significant price differentials in China and abroad. According to a study by the Ministry of Commerce, the average price of 20 luxury goods is 45 percent higher in mainland China than in Hong Kong, 51 percent higher than in the U.S., and 72 percent higher than in France ("Lower tax on luxury goods should be the trend," 2011), though it is not clear if the differences can be entirely attributed to government taxes. Due to the price differentials, a large number of Chinese consumers buy luxury products abroad ("Chinese shoppers spent 400% more on luxury goods overseas than at home," 2011). In addition to price differentials, limited selection in China and the fear of buying counterfeits are reasons for shopping abroad. It is reported that some of the top-spending consumers do virtually all of their high-end shopping in Europe, Hong Kong, and the U.S. as tourist-shoppers. Even some airline crew members, airport workers, and group tour guides were engaged in the smuggling of luxury goods into China (Li, 2012a).

MARKET PENETRATION AND STRATEGIES OF INTERNATIONAL RETAILERS

Almost all luxury brands in the world are now selling products in China. Some of them entered China in the early and mid-1990s, when they operated within a small number of tourist-oriented hotels. It was not until 2004 that they began to open flagship stores in high-profile cities and large retail shops in other urban centers. Table 9.1 lists the geographical distribution of seven of the brands in China.

Table 9.1   Major Luxury Goods Retailers in China—Store Distribution by City, 2012

City name	City Tier	Prada	LV	Hermès	Gucci	Fendi	Tiffany	Miu Miu	Total stores by city
Shanghai	mega	3	3	3	4	1	5	2	21
Beijing	mega	3	3	3	4	3	3		19
Shenyang	1	2	2	1	1	2	2	1	11
Hangzhou	1	2	1	2	1	2	1	1	10
Guangzhou	Mega	1	1	2		2	1	1	8
Shenzhen	Mega	1	2	1	1	1	1	1	8
Chengdu	1	1	1	1	1	1	1		6
Dalian	1	1	1	1	1	1			5
Harbin	1	1	1	1	1		1		5
Tianjin	Mega	1	1		1	1	1		5
Kunming	2		1	1	1		1		4
Nanjing	1		1	1		1	1		4
Qingdao	1	1	1	1			1		4
Suzhou	1		1	1	1	1			4
Wuxi	1		1	1	1	1			4
Xian	1	1	1		1	1			4
Wuhan	1		1		1		1		3
Changchun	1		1			1			2
Changsha	1		1		1				2
Fuzhou	2		1		1				2
Ningbo	1		1		1				2
Sanya	4		1				1		2
Taiyuan	2	1	1						2
Wenzhou	2	1	1						2
Xiamen	2		1		1				2
Changzhou	2				1				1
Chongqing	1						1		1
Hohhot	2		1						1
Jinan	1				1				1
Shijiazhuang	2				1				1
Urumqi	2		1						1
Zhengzhou	2				1				1
Total stores by chain		20	33	20	28	19	22	6	148
No. of host cities		14	27	14	22	14	15	5	

Source: Retailers corporate websites.

Louis Vuitton (LV) has made the deepest market penetration in China, with 33 outlets in 27 cities (Table 9.1). This is followed by Gucci with 28 stores in 22 cities. Prada, Hermès, Fendi, and Tiffany exhibit similar levels of market penetration, each with 20–22 stores in 14–15 cities. Miu Miu, owned by the parent company of Prada, is still in the early stage of expansion, with only 6 outlets in 5 cities.

To maintain their brand image and high retail prices, the luxury retailers deploy their store networks strategically, avoiding having too many locations in the same city and making them too commonplace. Table 9.1 reveals that luxury retailers concentrate heavily in six cities: Shanghai, Beijing, Shenyang, Hangzhou, Guangzhou, and Shenzhen, with four of them being mega urban markets, and the other two being Tier 1 cities. A regional strategy is also obvious. In Northeast China, all the listed retailers are present in the city of Shenyang, with some also in Dalian and Harbin—two tourist cities in the region. In Southwest China, they chose to operate from Chengdu and Kunming (only Tiffany is present in Chongqing). In East China between Tianjin and Nanjing, there are more luxury stores in Qingdao than in Jinan, even though the latter is a provincial capital. Of the ten Tier 2 cities with a presence of foreign luxury retailers, seven are provincial capitals. Wenzhou, also a Tier 2 city, is chosen by both LV and Prada for being an exceptionally wealthy urban market. That city, dubbed as the birthplace of China's private economy, is full of vibrant business activities and has nurtured a large number of wealthy entrepreneurs with high spending powers. LV has also taken the lead to set up stores in Northwest China: one in Xianjiang's Urumqi, and another in Inner Mongolia's Hohhot. There are virtually no luxury stores in Tier 3 and Tier 4 cities, with the exception of Sanya—a popular resort city in South China's Hainan Province. Some foreign brands expanded with franchised outlets, in addition to opening wholly-owned stores. In the words of Tim King, Dunhill's Managing Director—North Asia, "the franchisees are very useful in the tertiary cities, where . . . they are our eyes and ears" (Cafolla, 2007).

Foreign luxury retailers resort to a variety of strategies to penetrate the China market. Many of them have shifted production, or at least part of their production, to China, in order to reduce production cost and raise the levels of profit. An investigation by a Hong Kong-based news daily—*Ming Pao*—revealed that a factory in Zhongshan City of Guangdong Province (named W. K. Maxy Industries Ltd., with investment from Hong Kong) makes products for such European brands as Hugo Boss, Versus Versace, Aigner, and Prada ("Factory in Zhongshan City makes luxury handbags for Prada," 2011). According to Prada's IPO Prospectus submitted to the Hong Kong Stock Exchange, about 20 percent of Prada's collections are made in China (Passariello, 2011). Another investigation found that the production of a GUCCI handbag in a factory (named Huaxia Shan No. 2 Factory) in Dongguan City in Guangdong Province costs about 500–600 yuan, or at most 1,000 yuan if highest grade leather is used. Yet, the bag is sold in a

GUCCI boutique store in Xiamen for over 10,000 yuan ("The journey of luxury goods," 2011). Subtracting taxes and transportation costs, the level of profit should still be very high.

In order to conceal the fact that the products are made in China (because "made-in-China" conjures up an image of low or poor quality among consumers, leading to distrust in the product), the CEO of Prada reportedly contemplated replacing the "made-in-China" label with one of "made-by-Prada" ("Prada contracts production to Dongguan of China," 2011). Some other foreign companies have Chinese factories do most of the production, but ship the "semi-finished" products back to their home country for final touches, so that the products can be legally labeled as "made in the retailer's home country" to maintain the brand image.

More leading brands are tailoring their goods and services to suit the needs of Chinese consumers. For example, Hermès markets limited editions of mini Birkin bags, designed specifically for Chinese women (Shen, 2011). They also spend heavily on establishing a luxury culture in the China market. Their brand-building efforts are not only through print and television advertising, but also through luxury events and customized lifestyle publications (Australian Center for Retail Studies and TNS, 2007). Since February 2011, seven world-class luxury brands have opened exclusive branded video channels through China's leading internet television site **Youku.com** ("Luxury brands step up online video marketing efforts with Youku," 2011). These are: Louis Vuitton, Dior, Burberry, Gucci, Omega, Mido, and Cartier. Youku.com is considered an attractive choice for online marketing in China because the largest group of Youku.com viewers is composed of young, educated, urban professionals, who match the luxury brands' targeted demographics. In another example, Emporio Armani officially opened its online store in mainland China in December of 2010 (Shen, 2011). Burberry is now on four Chinese social media sites (Kuo, 2013).

Another strategy is to **raise capital in Asia to make money in Asia**. Prada began to trade shares on the Hong Kong Stock Exchange on June 24, 2011, amid much fanfare (Wassener, 2011), and its shares gained 70 percent in one year (Master & Ciancio, 2012). It is reported that Coach, in preparation for an IPO, has also extended its reach to the international capital markets via the Hong Kong Stock Exchange. The high demand for luxury goods in China and the prospect of further growth in the near future attracted many deep-pocketed investors in Asia to become stock holders. For foreign retailers, listing in the Hong Kong Stock Exchange also means being closer to the major markets (Wassener, 2011). In the words of Aaron Fisher, CLSA Global Markets Analyst, "It makes perfect sense for luxury retailers to list in Hong Kong because of the proximity it provides to end-users" (Qin, 2011).

On a negative note, the international retailers of luxury goods are facing two roadblocks in their further expansion in China. First, taxes are high, which translates into high business costs and high prices, and high prices negatively affect sales volume. Second, rampant counterfeiting activities threaten the market penetration of the authentic products.

ETHICS OF LUXURY RETAILING

Unfortunately, but not surprisingly, the high profit margins of luxury retailing have encouraged the adventure of mimicry and counterfeiting, which take place in different forms (Teah & Phau, 2010). In most cases, mimic brands copy the style and design of the original brands, using colors and shapes, which affect the evaluation of the attributes of the products (Zaichkowsky & Simpson, 1996). A mimic brand may also have a similar name as the original brand, making it perceived to be from the same family of the original brand (Boush et al., 1987). In other cases, it is not necessary to copy the established product's presentation; instead, the mimic brand uses cue patterns, similar enough to evoke the imagery of the brand-name product.

Counterfeits are low-priced, often lower-quality, and illegal replicas of products that typically possess high-brand values (Lai & Zaichkowsky, 1999). It is said that they cost the Western luxury goods manufacturers billions of dollars in lost revenue each year, though some argue differently: that is, the people who buy counterfeits would never buy the genuine products because they cannot afford to pay anyway. China is often singled out as a major country where counterfeiting activities take place widely. The counterfeits are not only sold in China but exported to other countries, even including the U.S. The U.S. and EU both assert that the majority of fakes seized at their borders are made in China (Australian Center for Retail Studies and TNS, 2007).The high profit margins obtained through selling fake copies make counterfeiting a very attractive business for organized crime.

Consumers' desire for counterfeit luxury brands hinges on the social motivations underlying their luxury brand preferences: to express themselves and/or to "fit in" (Bloch et al., 1993; Teah & Phau, 2010). Many consumers knowingly buy counterfeits for two reasons: they cannot afford the authentic products, or they do not believe the authentic is worth the selling price. Twenty years ago, the made-in-China counterfeits were dubbed as *fake and inferior stuff* (假冒伪劣). The two famous venues that used to harbor a full range of counterfeit products were Xiangyang Market in Shanghai and Silk Market in Beijing. They were frequented not only by Chinese nationals but also foreigners, including diplomats. Nowadays, production of counterfeits has become a sophisticated industry using high technologies. Even the vendors themselves now use such language to promote the counterfeits that they sell: "earnestly, our products are fake, but they are by no means of poor quality" (假冒不伪劣) (author was told of this by venders in Shanghai). Indeed, some counterfeiters are able to make "genuine fakes" or "super copies," nearly identical in quality to the originals. Even though some counterfeits do not last as long as the authentic items, it does not matter to the buyers because the price is much lower, and few consumers expect to use the same product for a long time, as the luxury goods producers constantly issue and sell new "editions," which make the previous year's editions appear dated.

Luxury retailers have long waged a battle against counterfeit goods in China. In September 2011, Louis Vuitton sued several shopping malls and hotels in the City of Dalian for selling counterfeit LV brand products. At one hotel, an undercover agent working for LV purchased a shirt, a belt, a wallet, and a bag for only 1,110 yuan (less than US$200), with an invoice issued by the hotel. A notary public, who accompanied the agent during the undercover purchase, testified at the local court that both the products and the invoice were obtained at the hotel. The hotel, however, disputed that the retailer was only a tenant renting space from it. Although the invoice was issued by the hotel, it was issued for room charges and not for LV merchandise (a common form a corruption in China), so it should not be held responsible (Yan, 2011).

There is no question that counterfeiting is a serious crime in retailing because such activity infringes on the intellectual property rights of the luxury goods designers and producers. Rightfully, luxury goods makers have joined forces to fight the crime, including lobbying and pressuring the government of the country where counterfeiting activities take place. It is also reported that the government of the home country of some luxury brand makers goes so far as to confiscate the fake products that are worn and carried by tourists when they enter the country, and fine the tourists for buying and using the fake products.

While so much attention and effort have been directed toward fighting the counterfeiters and to penalize the consumers, little concern has been voiced about the ethics of promoting luxury goods aggressively by the retailers themselves. There are two types of circumstances in which profit itself is subjected to ethical criticism: one is when profits are excessively large; the other is when profit is gained unjustly (MacDonald, 2011). Several industries are commonly singled out as having unjustly large profits, particularly the banking industry and the pharmaceutical industry. Yet no study has ever questioned whether or not the profits of the luxury retailers are excessively large or are obtained unjustly.

It is widely acknowledged that the prices of luxury goods are much higher in China than outside of China (such as in Paris, New York, London, and Hong Kong). For example, a Chanel Timeless Classic Flap handbag sells for €3,100 (US$3,839) in France, but for 37,000 yuan (US$5,850) in China—a 34 percent difference; a LV Speedy 30 handbag sells for €500 (US$619) in Europe, but for 6,100 yuan (US$964) in China (Zhou, 2012b). As posted on the website of Yoka.com (retrieved on August 17, 2011), the prices of LV handbags in China ranged from 10,000 yuan to 36,000 yuan (equivalent to

US$1,500–5,500). The Western retailers claim that the high prices in China are the result of high taxes imposed by the Chinese government. Assuming an average tax rate of 50 percent, the prices of these LV handbags would be 6,600—24,000 yuan (US$1,000—3,700) minus government taxes. These prices are still excessively high relative to the levels of income even for the middle class Chinese consumers. It should be pointed out that Yoka.com is not an official distributor of LV bags, and it is reasonable to believe that the advertised prices on unofficial web sites are lower than the selling prices at the LV authentic stores; otherwise, who would buy luxury goods from an unofficial source?

The fundamental ethical question with regard to large profits is also what philosophers would call a question of "distributive justice" (MacDonald, 2011). High initial investment costs, especially in store design and fitting, have often made human resources investment a lesser priority (Petcu, 2011). While the Western luxury goods makers and retailers maintain that the prices in China (before government taxes) should be the same as elsewhere in the world, it is a well-known fact that they do not pay the same wage or salary to the Chinese sales associates as they pay the store workers in their home country. Besides, they do not lower prices even though they have moved production or part of the production to China to take advantage of cheap labor. For example, Prada's "made-in-China" items are not priced any differently than products made in Italy (Passariello, 2011). This begs the question of whether or not the profits made in China are excessively high and are gained through exploitation.

The pharmaceutical industry is often criticized for making large profits, but the society is often tolerant of that fact because pharmaceutical companies make products that many people think are worth paying for. Moreover, the prices of drugs in most countries are regulated by the government. In free market economies, luxury retailing is largely unregulated. The luxury retailers tend to maximize prices and profits with whatever means available to them.

The social impacts of luxury goods, especially the destructive side effects of an addiction to high-end Western brands, cannot be ignored and must also be discussed and debated publicly. Luxury goods reinforce and perpetuate social classes, leading to looking down on the less-affluent and to resentment of the rich. On the surface, the luxury retailers target the ultra-wealthy and super-rich social elites in China; but what they really try to achieve is to entice more middle-class consumers to become new entrants and tenured consumers, and convert brand awareness into loyalty (Atsmon et al., 2012a), because of the large and swelling size of this class. Yet with the average wage in China still fairly low, compared with that in the advanced economies, purchase of luxury goods is out of proportion to most buyers' actual income. The only way the vast majority of consumers (especially the youth consumers) can get their hands on such items is to buy fake copies in street markets or on the Internet.

The desire to own luxury goods always exists, which is a part of human nature that cannot be stopped by law or by regulations. However, luxury retailers should exercise their moral responsibility, as ethics and profits should go hand in hand (Caulkin, 2003; Moore, 2009).

MANAGING LUXURY RETAILING

In his book titled *Profit with Honor*, Yankelovich (2006) proposed a concept that he described as "stewardship ethics." Located between the two popular approaches of laissez-faire and social responsibility, the concept emphasizes the conscious efforts required to reconcile profitability with social good. In order to address the various aforementioned challenges and impacts in this chapter, efforts need to be made by all players toward managing luxury retailing in China—the government, producers, and distributors:

1. *Tax is necessary but should be reduced.*

In China, the Ministry of Commerce and the Ministry of Finance are at odds with regard to taxing luxuries. The former is inclined to lowering taxes: by lowering taxes, more varieties of imports will be brought into China to satisfy the needs of the Chinese consumers. As well, more expenditure on luxury goods will be retained in China, thus reducing high-end wallet drains. More imports also mean more competition, which exerts pressure on domestic producers to improve product quality and become more innovative.

The opposite viewpoint held by the Ministry of Finance is that high taxes should be maintained at the current level, because lowering taxes will benefit only the very rich, but not the average consumers, most of whom cannot afford luxury goods anyway. Taxes collected can be redistributed in ways that benefit the lower-income consumers. High taxes will also serve as barriers to rapid expansion of foreign retailers, who increasingly dominate the luxury markets in China. This can also provide breathing time for the domestic producers to develop and grow. Ultimately, high taxes discourage consumption of luxury goods in the country, much of which is still in poverty.

In present China, taxes on luxury goods are necessary as long as they are imposed within the bounds of the WTO rules. Such taxes should not affect the average consumers because most luxury goods are inessential items. China still does not have a personal tax filing system, as most Western countries do. As a result, income tax evasion by the rich is widely spread. Luxury taxes can be used as a means of income redistribution. At the same time, import duties should be lowered to reduce both the business costs for the foreign retailers and the price differentials between the China market and the overseas markets. This would encourage more consumers to purchase luxury goods within China, instead of buying them from foreign countries.

In Malaysia, luxury goods are also heavily taxed, where duties can be 60 percent on some goods (Malaysia Industrial Development Authority, 2011). However, the Malaysian government has recently begun to lower these taxes. In June 2011, the Legislature of Taiwan passed laws imposing luxury taxes to equalize income distribution (Sui, 2011; Wang, T., 2011; Zeldin, 2011).

In a recent move, China set up a duty-free zone in the city of Sanya in Hainan Province as an experiment (where both LV and Tiffany have set up a store, see Table 9.1). The policy, which was passed on March 24, 2011 by the Minister of Finance and the General Administration of Customs, applies to all tourists, domestic as well as foreign, who leave Sanya by air and spend up to 5,000 yuan (US$750) on imported goods, including perfumes, electronics, watches, fashion, and leather goods. Shoppers could save at least 30 percent on their purchases ("Hainan now the world's fourth Duty Free zone," 2011). Yet, the 5,000 yuan limit, which is less than the price of a low-end LV handbag, does not provide enough incentive for the heavy spenders to make most of their purchases of luxury goods in China.

2. *More stringent measures are needed to crack down and punish the crime of counterfeiting.*

The Chinese government already has laws in place as legal tools to clamp down on counterfeiting activities. In a number of landmark cases, the Chinese authorities prosecuted the violators and handed down hefty fines (Pitman, 2006). Recently, China announced that it has suspended 1,745 business licenses since it began a campaign in October, 2010 against copyright and trademark infringement. The government also sent 757 cases of forgery to court (Lu, 2011) and closed 36 illegal production facilities (Zhao, 2012b). While the authorities in China are making significant progress in keeping tighter reins on the vast counterfeiting industry, more resources and efforts need to be put into monitoring and detecting illegal activities, and tougher penalties need to be applied to enforce the law effectively.

3. *China should lend more support to, and speed up, nurturing of home-grown brands to provide alternatives.*

So far, the luxury market in China is monopolized by foreign brands, with virtually no home-grown competitors. There is a good reason for the Chinese government to be concerned about this high-end market being dominated by foreign retailers because, as a result of a lack of local competition, foreign luxury brands may engage in "unreasonable and discriminatory pricing" in the China market vis-à-vis their home markets

("Government pushing support of local brands to compete with international giants," 2011).

In its *12th Five-Year Plan*, the government of China prominently advocates the nurturing of domestic Chinese brands that can compete on a global level and move up the value chain ("Government pushing support of local brands to compete with international giants," 2011). While the road to establishing a brand as a status symbol is not a short and smooth path, breakthroughs may well be made first in fashion and accessories (including handbags). As profiled by *Jing Daily* ("Chinese creativity: Who are the emerging designers?" 2011), a new generation of independent designers (some are trained in Paris and New York) is now active in Beijing and Shanghai, pumping out a steady supply of avant-garde-leaning collections. The luxury brand Shangxia, now owned by LV, was actually created by Chinese designers. If the Chinese factories can make products for LV and Prada, they can surely manufacture quality products designed by the creative Chinese artists. More importantly, homemade quality products will not only provide alternatives to domestic consumers, but also help develop a strong sense of pride among the Chinese nationals and boost the country's self-confidence.

4. *The World Luxury Association should facilitate development of codes of ethics, and make sure that the members actually live by the codes.*

The World Luxury Association suggested five steps to mitigate the issues that impede expansion of luxury retailing in China ("Chinese shoppers spent 400% more on luxury goods overseas than at home," 2011): (1) adjust the luxury tax and refine China's duty-free policy; (2) reduce trade frictions and raise China's luxury market to global standards; (3) develop standardized regulatory policies regarding luxury pricing and sales; (4) take greater action against the counterfeit market and strengthen IP protection; and (5) increase the cultivation of a luxury consumer culture. Apparently, all the proposed steps aim to put pressure on the Chinese government to make concessions and lower barriers in favor of the international retailers. Nothing is said about business ethics and corporate social responsibilities. It is true that profit motive plays an essential role in modern corporate governance and business decision making because many corporations are public companies owned collectively by shareholders, to whom the corporate managers and directors owe a fiduciary duty (MacDonald, 2011). Nonetheless, retailers are urged to adopt certain ethical standards that guide decision making when confronting situations that may not be covered by law (Sarma, 2007). This is important because ethics functions as a form of social control, and ethical decisions ensure society's sense of justice. Specifically, both luxury producers and retailers should revisit their pricing system to ensure that their pricing and marketing practices are fair to the Chinese consumers that they target, and that the level of profit is not excessive and is justified. They should assume corporate social responsibility not only in their home country but also in the foreign countries where they sell products. The World Luxury Association should facilitate development of codes of ethics, reinforce in-house social auditing, and make sure that the member retailers actually live by the codes.

10 Conclusions

After three decades of economic reform in China, a new retail economy has evolved accordingly. In general, the retail sector has been transformed from a simple and inefficient circulation system to a much more complex and highly competitive market-oriented economy.

The retail transformation in post-reform China is a clear testimony of the Economic Transition Model (Bradshaw, 1996): all four dimensions of the transition process, as described in Chapter 1, took place in shaping the new retail economy. Retail liberalization began as early as the late 1970s by permitting entry of individual retailers into the distribution system. However, major reforms were not implemented until the early 1990s—almost 10 years after the extensive reform in agriculture and manufacturing. According to the Economic Transition Model, the delay in retail reform was due to the need for a period of economic stabilization, during which the supply of consumer goods could be greatly enriched through improved agricultural and industrial production, and inflation could be controlled effectively.

While the improved consumer market and the increased levels of consumption nurtured by the three decades of economic reform constituted the necessary conditions for sustained retail growth, it was retail deregulation that has been the fundamental driving force for the structural changes in China's retail economy. At the core of the retail deregulation was ownership reform: the abandonment of state monopoly and the mobilization of different sources of retail capital including private funds, capital raised on the stock market, and FDI. This not only resulted in a proliferation of retail enterprises and stores, which vastly expanded the distribution system, but also led to the introduction of more efficient retail formats, such as supermarkets, hypermarkets, retail chains, and shopping centers. Most impressively, some non-state-owned new companies, such as Suning and Gome, rose to become domestic retail giants and true national chains. Without the burden of an inefficient labor force inherited from the planned economy, these private companies have more freedom and flexibility in business decision making and are better able to respond to market changes. During the retail reform, the role of the government has shifted from commanding commodity supply and business operations to regulating the retail industry by legal means.

Few retail innovations originated in China, but the Chinese retailers learned fast from their international partners and counterparts. China's new retail economy is in many ways converging toward the contemporary capitalist retail economy in the Western countries. At the same time, it exhibits important differences which have Chinese characteristics. Although both the state and local governments gradually withdrew from monopolizing the retail sector, they still want to maintain certain business interests, as is revealed in Chapter 6. Many of the large domestic chains and most of the national team members are still effectively controlled by the state via local governments. This is out of the strategic consideration to prevent the national retail market from being dominated by the powerful international retailers. Even though most of the transformed domestic corporations and business groups are of joint-stock ownership, the governments insist on being major shareholders with voting powers. This means that as China's new retail economy converges further toward a market-oriented economy, public ownership, a Chinese characteristic, will not disappear completely.

Retail businesses in China have been consolidating into the hands of a smaller number of large retailers—a typical characteristic of retail structure in many advanced market economies. High concentration has been achieved in such sub-sectors as food, general merchandise, and consumer electronics. Domestic retailers have become strong market contenders in these formats. While the volume of small, individually-owned businesses is expected to shrink further, they will not disappear rapidly yet, because they offer shopping convenience and value to the mass consumers. Nonetheless, the overall degree of retail concentration in China is still low. In 2012, the top 100 chains account for only 10 percent of the total retail sales in the country (Li, 2013; Le, 2013), compared with 40 percent in the U.S. (YCharts, 2013; Schulz, 2013) and 49 percent in Canada (Daniel & Hernandez, 2012). This indicates that there is still plenty of room for further consolidation for the resourceful retailers—both domestic and foreign.

International retailers have been "the movers and shapers" of the global economy (Dicken, 2003), and they often facilitate changes in market structures. Many international retailers that have entered China are among the top 100 companies in the world. Their entry and expansion represent an integral part of the transformation of China's retail economy, and they made significant contributions to its modernization through capital investment, introduction of new formats, technology transfer, and diffusion of management know-how. With sustained growth of the consumer market and the removal of the unconventional trade barriers, their expansion has accelerated steadily. They also have had strong influences in shaping a new consumer culture in China, where shopping behaviors and consumption patterns are converging towards those in the foreign retailers' home countries—a phenomenon of "homogenization of consumers" (Levitt, 1999).

In a balanced note, a few foreign retailers also brought about problematic business practices and worrying social impacts, which prompted the Chinese government to respond with new regulations and policy interventions to limit the competitive power and social influence of foreign retailers. For example, forcing suppliers to pay store entrance fees, sponsor store openings and promotion days, and provide their own sales personnel was all introduced by foreign retailers to China. Domestic retailers had no choice but copy these practices in order to maintain competitive. The social impacts of luxury retailing are also made chiefly by foreign retailers.

Retail structure and its spatial manifestation do not result from a simple interplay of demand and supply. Corporate strategies are always an important consideration in explaining a particular retail structure and the spatial distribution of retail facilities. As Jones and Simmons (1993) demonstrate, each corporate strategy leaves a distinct spatial imprint. While all the major international retail corporations had their own geo-strategy in China, their geo-strategies have largely been dictated by the state spatial strategies of the Chinese government. As discussed in Chapters 3 and 5, expansion into interior and lower tier cities did not happen until the Chinese government revised its state spatial strategy after its admission to the WTO. The presence and expansion of foreign retailers in the form of retail chains has helped consolidate the long-fragmented local markets. An integrated national market is in the making.

In retrospect, local governments played an important, albeit "informal," role in attracting international retailers to their cities, as confirmed by Siebers (2011). After China entered the WTO, the state government had to 'legalize' most of the overseas-invested retail enterprises that were brought in by local governments. Indeed, when China opened its borders to international retail capital, virtually no rules or laws existed. Rules and laws were written, revised, and expanded constantly as foreign retailers moved in and expanded their operations. This signifies that in the early stages of economic transition, when new national policies and corresponding governing institutions were incomplete, those local governments that had the courage to take bold initiatives, despite political risks, could emerge as clear winners. Shanghai is just such an entrepreneurial city.

While none of the foreign retailers in China has passed through the complete model described by Dawson (2003), their varying levels of market penetration and performance indicate that they are in different phases of the model. Clearly, the Western retailers are taking the lead in penetrating the Chinese market, particularly in the food and general merchandise market. Wal-Mart and Carrefour can both be said to have completed the consolidation (the second) phase. They just began to exert control over vertical and horizontal channel relationships. Western retailers are also moving from organic growth, defined as new store development, towards acquisition. The Southeast Asian retailers, which mimic the Western retailers by copying the hypermarket format, have also expanded their operations with impressive results, but their staying power is unclear. Instead of committing themselves to gaining market dominance by exerting control over vertical and horizontal channel relationships, they began to relinquish a significant part of their business interests to Western retail superpowers, as did the Taiwanese Trust Mart and Hymart-Hymall (i.e., Legou). Although the Japanese retailers received the least negative publicity, they have made the least inroads in penetrating the Chinese market due mainly to the economic difficulties of their parent companies and the less competitive formats that they adopted to expand in China. They are only in early stages of consolidation. Consolidation of separate divisions under a single corporate identity will allow them to reduce the risks associated with any one location by centralized control of geographically dispersed stores (Christopherson, 1996). Over time, as China's regulatory environment improves further, the law-abiding Japanese retailers should do much better. Most importantly, the contrasts between the Western retailers and the Asian retailers suggest that cultural proximity is much less important than corporate strengths of the transnational corporations (TNCs) in resource availability, commitment, and differential advantages.

The battle among foreign retailers for a share of the China market has intensified over the last few years, as revealed in Chapter 5. Most major international retailers have relocated their resources from other parts of Southeast Asia to focus on their expansion in China. As well, a number of them have moved towards "independence" in an effort to consolidate their power in business decision making with a high level of control, even though this means high business cost. Given that the current level of retail capital concentration is still low, it is anticipated that a new wave of merger- and acquisition-driven consolidation in the retail industry will take place in China in the next 5 to 10 years—a phenomenon that happened in the late 1990s in other parts of the world (Currah & Wrigley, 2004). Foreign retailers, especially the Western retailers, will continue to be major players in reshaping the corporate and physical landscape of retailing in China.

While China is embracing global liberalism, future expansion of foreign retailers is not without new roadblocks. The entry threshold for foreign retailers is now much higher than a decade ago. The preferential tax policies that the state government used in the past to entice foreign retailers have all been phased out, leaving the foreign retailers with nearly none of the competitive edge that was enjoyed by the early entrants. As the process of retail internationalization deepens in China, its regulatory system strives to balance the needs of securing national economic sovereignty. The Chinese government will not allow the state-controlled companies to become foreign acquisition targets. The success of the foreign retailers is said to hinge on two core factors: low procurement cost and scale economy. Yet they increasingly have difficulties achieving either. Purchasing merchandise with cash did not bring down procurement costs to the level of their expectations. Often, the Chinese suppliers could not agree to the bargaining conditions because they were threatened by the large domestic retailers with a boycott. Procurement with cash also locks up large sums of capital, which hinders their expansion to achieve scale economy in China, as was the case with Best Buy. In the meantime, China is nurturing its own retail heavyweights to combat foreign competition and defend the national market. Some of them (dubbed by Chinese commentators as "native alligators") have become strong market contenders, making further expansion of foreign retailers difficult. This is especially true in the CE sector, where Suning and Gome have become strong enough to fend off foreign competition from Best Buy, Media Markt, and Yamada. Although most other domestic retailers are still largely regional players, they are strong competitors in their respective regional market. The strengthening of the national team, along with new leading retailers, will force the foreign retailers to turn to the smaller urban markets.

China at large has been referred to as the largest emerging market in the world. In literature, the term "emerging market" is broadly defined as a country with five distinctive characteristics (Khanna & Palepu, 2010; "What is an emerging market economy?" 2009; Pearson Education, n.d.; Nakata & Sivakumar, 1997). First, the country has begun to embark on an economic reform program moving from a closed economy to an open market economy, therefore "emerging" onto the global scene. Second, it is considered to be a fast-growing economy, where the GDP growth rate is dramatically outpacing those of the more developed economies, creating new middle classes and new markets for consumer products and services. Third, there is an increase in both local and foreign investments. Fourth, an emerging market is also an emerging competitor, but competition is relatively weak and has not reached a mature stage of development. Lastly, the risk of investment in an emerging market is higher than in a developed market because the emerging market is in transition, lacking internationally accepted rules and regulations and hence not stable. Often, international retailers want to take the opportunities afforded by emerging markets to quickly establish predominance before domestic competitors become strong and mature.

While China has all of the above characteristics, market conditions vary significantly within the country, as illustrated in Chapter 2. Neither an individual store, nor a shopping center, can be successful solely based on the national potential, of course. Regional differences in consumer preference are huge, and so is the competitive retail landscape (Burstedt, 2011). In China, many of its large urban centers have actually become mature markets. The mega markets of Beijing, Shanghai, Tianjin, Guangzhou, and Shenzhen are no less mature than the typical urban markets in the Western economies, and they are already saturated with retailers of all formats and calibers. In the early stage of expansion, large retailers were invariably interested in the large and affluent urban markets. In sequence of development and in consideration of scale economies, it made sense for the large retailers to set up multiple stores (especially large format stores) in a few large urban centers with high population density, so that these stores could be supported by a limited number of regional distribution centers. After a solid market leader position was established, they began to spread to cities of lower tiers. The 2nd and 3rd tier cities should be considered "emerging markets" within China, where demand is sufficient to support a large number of retail outlets; yet, competition is much less and weaker, property cost is still low, and local government is more willing to make concessions to international retailers. The fact that RT-Mart has achieved much higher sales with fewer stores than Carrefour is attributed to its deeper market penetration in the Tier 2 and Tier 3 cities (see Tables 5.1 and 5.2). A new phase of spatial switching of retail capital has already begun from the large and mature urban markets to the emerging markets. Not all emerging markets have equal opportunities for all retailers, of course. Those that are part of the "hub-and-spoke city clusters" and are around the mega urban markets and Tier 1 cities have more potential than the others, and make more economic sense in terms of logistics and merchandise supply. A more dispersed pattern of retail internationalization within China will be seen in the near future.

It is predicated that China will transition in the next 10 to 15 years from an investment-led economy into a consumption-driven and service-driven economy (Woetzel et al., 2012; Atsmon et al., 2012b). Further increase in personal income will result in more "mass consumers" to become "mainstream consumers," accompanied with higher levels of consumer literacy and more discretionary spending on consumer goods. Continued retail growth will lead to more commercial property development as well.

Retailers all know the importance of location, location, location. Store sites and locations are vital competitive assets, but a good location must be affordable. In large urban centers, property rent has soared and affordable properties at good locations have become scarce. Most foreign retailers had their current property leases signed 15–20 years ago, when rents were very low. These leases are due, or will be due shortly, for renewal. According to China Chain Store Association (Shao, 2011), the average rate of rent increase for the leases renewed in 2010 among the top 100 chains was 30 per cent. As well, capital requirements for both site acquisition and store construction are much higher now than 10 years ago. This will pose a new challenge for future expansion of foreign retailers and for them to sustain earning growth. More retail capital will be injected in commercial property development. Foreign capitals have already begun to shift from operating retail stores to building and acquiring commercial properties in the form of shopping centers. Although construction of shopping centers involves high levels of sunk cost, the investors (either international REITs or retailers) believe they can recover the cost over time through leasing spaces to third party retailers. This is another indication that China is no longer an inexpensive environment for doing business and has more characteristics of a mature market.

Traditionally, retailing is geographically tied and retailers must have a physical presence in the market (Sternquist, 2007). But this has also been changing: the emergence and growth of e-commerce or e-tailing has been destabilizing the store-based form of retailing because of its ability to lower market entry barriers and to short-circuit existing distribution channels (Wrigley, 2000). E-tailing has not had a significant impact in China yet, which is why this book does not have a separate chapter for it. In 2012, 62 of the top 100 chains were engaged in e-tailing, 10 more than in the previous year. Together, they only sold 30 billion yuan (US$5 billion), with only nine having achieved sales of 100 million yuan (Le, 2013). Still, e-commerce has been growing with attention-catching pace. Several specialized e-tailers are worth watching, particularly JD.com, Taobao.com, and Dangdang.com.

JD.com was founded in 2004 by an individual entrepreneur—Liu Qiangdong—and was the first specialized online retailer in China. It claims to offer in its virtual store 18 categories of merchandise with over one million products of more than 10,000 brands, but most of its sales are achieved through selling consumer electronics. It now owns six regional logistics centers and operates local distribution centers in over 300 cities (Baike, 2013).

Taobao.com was established in 2003 by Ma Yun—also an individual entrepreneur. Before that, Ma founded China's famous Alibaba as a B2B e-commerce platform. Unlike Alibaba, Taobao is a B2C platform, much like eBay in retail function. To support the growth of Taobao, Ma and his Alibaba created Alipay in 2004 to serve as an intermediary between retailers and consumers by securing payment from consumers and delivery of goods on the part of retailers. Alipay to Taobao is much like PayPal to eBay. By the end of 2010, Alipay had recorded 550 million transactions (Baidu Baike, 2013a). Linking 50,000 businesses with millions of consumers, Taobao is now the most popular internet retail platform in China.

Dangdang.com was established by a Chinese couple in 1999 as an online retailer of books. Its business later expanded to include selling music CDs, movie DVDs, clothes, cosmetics, and electronics. It went public in December 2010 via an IPO on the New York Stock Exchange, becoming China's first online retailer to be listed in the U.S. As of 2013, Dangdang operates 20 warehouses in the country, with the capacity of same-day delivery in 21 cities and next-day delivery in 158 cities (Baidu Baike, 2013b).

More and more consumers in China are joining their Western counterparts in social shopping—viewing editorial comments from other users on product availability, utility, quality, and price—and make purchases online. Brick-and-mortar stores of consumer electronics and books are most vulnerable to competition from e-tailers. Most electronic gadgets and appliances are standard products and are securely packaged. They are suitable merchandise to be sold in virtual stores, as long as warranty service is guaranteed. More and more Chinese consumers are buying such products online because prices are often lower than in retail stores and delivery is often free. Not wanting to lose the first-mover advantages to JD.com by too much, Suning launched its own online store—Suning.com.cn—on January 1, 2010. Gome first acquired a third-party online B2C retailer Kuba Technology—Coo8.com—in November 2010 to enter e-commerce, and then announced its corporate-branded virtual store, "Gome.com.cn," in April 2011. In addition, the U.S.-based Amazon and Newegg have both gone online in China for a share of the market.

The success of e-tailing depends on two critical factors: an intelligent and secure order- and payment-processing system, and an efficient distribution network. While the foreign retailers may possess superior processing systems, they may face more challenges than do the domestic retailers in building land-consuming warehouses and distribution centers across the country. Currently, e-tailing in China remains at a low level of competition in the form of price wars. Nonetheless, this will be a new area of development that researchers may want to monitor closely.

Retail internationalization is inevitably accompanied by periods of retrenchment and strategic readjustment, including divestment (Wrigley & Currah, 2003). Market divestment can take a range of forms, from simply altering the formats involved to store closure and complete withdrawal (Alexander & Quinn, 2002; Coe, 2004). According to Burt et al. (2003), divestment is not always a failure; it could be a proactive strategy, or even a desired outcome and financial success for shareholders. Different forms of international retail divestment have also occurred in China. Those with desired outcomes are represented by the Taiwanese Trust Mart and Hymart-Hymall, which sold their majority interests to Wal-Mart and Tesco, respectively (Chapter 5). Another example is Blackstone, which sold shopping centers after it improved the centers' value (Chapter 8). Those representing failures include Royal Ahold, Makro, Home Depot, Best Buy, and Media Markt. For these international retailers, the reason was not market failure (because the China market is huge and strong), but were organizational failure (in term of degree of adaptation to local market conditions) and competitive failure (as defined in Burt et al., 2003). It should also be pointed out that failure-caused divestment does not always lead to exit from the market. Best Buy's new route of expansion is to open "Best Buy Mobile" stores within the Five Star stores and introduce its own version of an online B2C platform, in addition to opening more Five Star stores ("China still poses retail challenge for U.S.-based Best Buy," 2012). More divestments in various forms are expected as China's retail economy evolves further and the leading retailers reshuffle among themselves. In a true market economy, it is through fair competition that weaker players are weeded out and strong ones emerge. The end results will be a healthy and mature retail sector that benefits consumers.

Appendix 1
Cluster Analysis of the Chinese Cities

There are two types of cluster analysis: hierarchical and k-means. The former is used when the number of cases in the given set of data is not excessively large and when it is not clear to the researcher how many possible clusters exist in the data set. The latter is used when the researcher already has hypotheses concerning the number of clusters in the cases or variables (Griffith & Amrhein, 1997; Norusis, 2011).

In data mining, k-means clustering aims to partition n observations into k clusters, with each observation belonging to the cluster with the nearest mean (i.e., cluster center). The procedure follows a simple and easy way to classify a given data set through a certain number of clusters (assuming k clusters). The main idea is to define k centroids, one for each cluster. The algorithm is deemed to have converged when the assignments no longer change.

Although it can be proven that the procedure will always terminate, there is no guarantee that it will converge to the global optimum, and the algorithm is significantly sensitive to the initial randomly selected cluster centers. One solution to this limitation is to run the algorithm multiple times to reduce this effect. It should also be pointed out that there is no general theoretical solution to find the optimal number of clusters for any given data set. A simple approach is to compare the results of multiple runs with different k classes and choose the best one according to a given criterion. In other words, it is helpful to re-run the program using the same as well as different k values, to compare the results achieved.

In the classification of the Chinese cities, the k-means cluster analysis is run twice. All nine variables are used. Initially, an attempt is made to group the 287 cases into three clusters (i.e., k=3, in correspondence to popular notions of Tier 1, Tier 2, and Tier 3 cities). This resulted in two small clusters and one extremely large cluster containing 89 percent of all the cities (as suggested by Figure 2.2). Progressive values of k are then experimented. At k=8, the largest cluster (Cluster 7) still contains 224 cities (see Table A-1). It is then decided to break up this large group with a separate run of cluster analysis, this time with k=2 (see Table A-2).

Of the nine groups resulting from the two runs, three are single-case clusters (Beijing, Shanghai, and Tianjin), and one consists of two cases only (Guangzhou and Shenzhen). With reference to the cluster centers (Tables A-1 and A-2) and the distances between cluster centers (Table A-3), it is decided to re-group the nine natural clusters into five city tiers (see Table A-4).

Fifteen cities could not be classified due to missing data in at least one of the nine variables, including the provincial capitals of Harbin, Wuhan, Chongqing, Xian, and Lasa. They are assigned to the closest cluster by visually inspecting three key attributes, for which data are available: population size, GDP, and total retail sales.

Table A.1 Cluster Centers, from the First Run with K=8

Variable	Cluster								ANOVA	
	1 (1 city)	2 (1 city)	3 (2 cities)	4 (1 city)	5 (8 cities)	6 (30 cities)	7 (224 cities)	8 (5 cities)	F	Sig.
Total population (10,000)	1,175	803	450	1,332	279	204	86	437	192.0	.000
Population density (person/km^2)	964	1,085	1,469	2,583	1,592	1,333	884	1,872	3.0	.004
GDP	119,720,000	70,302,455	83,055,331	148,758,036	26,134,134	13,041,030	2,604,761	36,933,251	1997.3	.000
Retail sales	52,119,941	22,786,973	29,990,663	51,337,084	10,131,269	5,224,725	983,032	15,049,837	1081.3	.000
Total wage	31,826,169	7,867,212	10,309,266	20,041,674	2,583,155	1,415,469	318,137	3,987,734	1655.1	.000
Average wage	58,805	45,248	48,768	63,546	39,449	35,177	27,722	41,458	30.6	.000
Cell phone subscribers	1,777	993	1,911	2,106	453	281	68	866	587.9	.000
Internet subscribers	4,963,373	5,333,900	2,564,050	12,500,000	1,003,519	544,028	106,176	1,251,878	1066.9	.000
Number of buses	21,716	7,897	17,063	16,272	3,816	2,136	481	5,638	234.9	.000

Table A.2   Cluster Centers, from the Second Run with K = 2 (This Run Is to Break Up Cluster 7 from the First Run)

	Cluster		ANOVA	
	1 *(168 cities)*	*2* *(56 cities)*	*F*	*Sig.*
Total population (10,000)	75.26	119.54	45.9	.000
Population density (person/km2)	814.99	1092.51	4.7	.031
GDP	1785152	5063590	519.7	.000
Retail sales	718131	1777735	166.9	.000
Total wage	230429	581260	176.0	.000
Average wage	26501.88	31382.25	38.2	.000
Cell phone subscribers	54.35	109.36	96.9	.000
Internet subscribers	82549.58	177056.20	92.8	.000
Number of buses	367	821	77.7	.000

Table A.3   Distances between Cluster Centers, from the First Run with K = 8 (Number of Cases = 287)

Cluster	1	2	3	4	5	6	7	8
1		62,263,039	47,986,841	32,241,208	106,734,240	120,515,170	131,709,197	94,955,739
2	62,263,039		15,105,124	84,675,604	46,450,845	60,430,715	71,712,674	34,714,266
3	47,986,841	15,105,124		70,469,555	60,799,231	74,823,355	86,137,108	48,909,694
4	32,241,208	84,675,604	70,469,555		131,040,109	145,035,641	156,329,577	119,188,072
5	106,734,240	46,450,845	60,799,231	131,040,109		14,038,454	25,362,517	11,951,895
6	120,515,170	60,430,715	74,823,355	145,035,641	14,038,454		11,327,117	25,970,921
7	131,709,197	71,712,674	86,137,108	156,329,577	25,362,517	11,327,117		37,297,441
8	94,955,739	34,714,266	48,909,694	119,188,072	11,951,895	25,970,921	37,297,441	

Table A.4 Natural Clusters and City Tiers

City tiers	Natural clusters	Member cities
Mega urban market (5 cities)	1	Beijing[1]
	2	Tianjin[1]
	3	Guangzhou[2,3]; Shenzhen[3,4]
	4	Shanghai[1]
Tier 1 (18 cities)	8	Chongqing[1,*]; Chengdu[2,3]; Dongguan; Foshan[*]; Hangzhou[2,3]; Nanjing[2,3]; Shenyang[2,3]; Wuhan[2,3,*];
	5	Changchun[2,3]; Changsha[2]; Dalian[3]; Harbin[2,3,*]; Jinan[2,3]; Ningbo[3]; Qingdao[3]; Suzhou; Wuxi; Xian[2,3,*]
Tier 2 (30 cities)	6	Anshan; Baotou; Changzhou; Daqing; Dongying; Fuzhou[2]; Hefei[2]; Hohot[2]; Huizhou; Jilin; Kunming[2]; Lanzhou2; Linyi; Nanchang[2]; Nanning[2]; Nantong; Shantou4; Shijiazhuang[2]; Taiyuan[2]; Tangshan; Urumqi[2]; Wenzhou; Xiamen[3,4]; Xuzhou; Yangzhou; Yantai; Zibo; Zhengzhou[2]; Zhongshan; Zhuhai[4];
Tier 3 (59 cities)	7	Guiyang[2]; Haikou[2]; Yinchuan[2] (See Appendix 2 for others)
Tier 4 (175 cities)	9	Guilin; Lhasa[2]; Lijiang; Sanya; Zhangjiajie (See Appendix 2 for others)

[1]. provincial-level city; [2]. provincial capital; [3]. sub-provincial city; [4]. Special Economic Zone; * with missing data

Appendix 2

The Hierarchy of China's Urban
Markets by City Tier, 2010
(with Data for City Proper)

Province	City	Population (10,000)	Population density (persons/ km²)	GDP (billion yuan)	Retail sales (billion yuan)	Total wage (billion yuan)	Average wage (yuan)	Cell phones (million)	Internet (million)	Buses (1,000)
Mega urban markets										
Beijing	Beijing	1174.6	964	1,197.2	521.2	318.3	58.8	17.8	5.0	21.7
Guangdong	Guangzhou	654.7	1703	841.0	343.0	105.9	50.8	19.7	2.7	8.8
Guangdong	Shenzhen	246.0	1235	820.1	256.8	100.3	46.7	18.6	2.5	25.3
Shanghai	Shanghai	1331.7	2583	1,487.6	513.4	200.4	63.5	21.1	12.5	16.3
Tianjin	Tianjin	802.9	1085	703.0	227.9	78.7	45.2	9.9	5.3	7.9
Tier 1 Cities										
Chongqing	Chongqing	1542.8	592	489.2	196.9	-	-	11.6	1.6	6.4
Guangdong	Foshan	367.6	955	482.1	140.9	-	-	9.4	1.1	3.3
Guangdong	Dongguan	178.7	725	376.4	95.9	9.4	42.6	14.1	1.2	1.4
Heilongjiang	Harbin	474.7	670	227.2	122.5	35.0	31.5	-	-	5.0
Hubei	Wuhan	515.0	1895	388.9	191.2	-	-	8.7	1.5	7.2
Hunan	Changsha	241.0	2523	225.0	118.1	22.4	36.5	3.9	0.6	3.6
Jiangsu	Nanjing	546.0	1156	382.6	179.3	45.6	44.3	7.4	1.4	6.1
Jiangsu	Wuxi	238.1	1467	274.1	98.4	16.7	44.6	4.0	0.8	3.0
Jiangsu	Suzhou	240.2	1796	299.2	89.0	23.4	42.9	4.7	0.8	3.0
Jilin	Changchun	362.3	757	205.3	85.7	23.8	33.0	3.5	2.0	4.4
Liaoning	Shenyang	512.2	1476	366.7	163.0	36.2	39.2	6.8	1.2	5.1
Liaoning	Dalian	302.0	1251	302.0	114.7	29.1	40.1	5.4	1.0	4.7
Shaanxi	Xian	561.6	1568	231.5	125.0	-	-	10.0	1.1	7.0

Shandong	Jinan	348.2	2486	251.3	129.2	34.3	38.5	5.2	1.0	4.4
Shandong	Qingdao	275.5	1373	278.9	99.2	26.6	38.4	5.3	1.0	4.3
Sichuan	Chengdu	520.9	2398	314.0	159.2	41.5	36.0	7.0	1.0	7.6
Zhejiang	Hangzhou	429.4	3606	407.0	155.0	66.7	45.1	8.1	1.5	8.1
Zhejiang	Ningbo	221.8	1083	254.9	76.2	30.3	41.6	4.4	0.8	3.2
Tier 2 Cities										
Anhui	Hefei	208.6	1063	159.1	61.8	16.2	35.5	2.3	0.3	2.7
Fujian	Fuzhou	187.3	1456	132.8	97.1	18.2	33.7	3.0	0.6	2.7
Fujian	Xiamen	177.0	1391	173.7	56.6	27.2	36.5	3.5	0.6	3.1
Gansu	Lanzhou	210.5	1290	80.5	44.8	13.2	29.3	0.3	0.4	2.1
Guangdong	Zhuhai	102.7	603	103.9	40.4	18.1	31.8	2.1	0.3	1.3
Guangdong	Shantou	503.4	2574	102.8	65.2	7.7	25.5	4.4	0.6	0.8
Guangdong	Huizhou	129.0	483	88.8	30.3	14.5	26.8	2.8	0.4	1.1
Guangdong	Zhongshan	147.9	821	156.6	55.0	9.1	36.2	4.4	0.5	1.1
Guangxi	Nanning	267.1	414	110.4	62.0	14.3	29.1	2.8	0.6	2.7
Hebei	Shijiazhuang	242.8	5324	108.2	30.4	15.5	30.6	4.3	0.7	4.1
Hebei	Tangshan	307.0	2496	191.9	45.7	17.9	36.6	3.1	0.3	1.9
Heilongjiang	Daqing	132.5	260	192.9	46.5	19.7	44.3	1.5	0.4	2.1
Henan	Zhengzhou	285.0	2822	143.2	89.4	21.6	32.7	5.2	1.0	4.4
Inner Mongolia	Huhehaote	118.8	578	118.1	56.5	10.4	42.6	1.9	0.3	2.0
Inner Mongolia	Baotou	141.5	546	180.6	57.7	10.4	37.2	2.0	0.2	1.3
Jiangsu	Xuzhou	186.2	1605	114.3	44.2	11.8	39.4	2.0	0.4	2.0

(continued)

Province	City	Population (10,000)	Population density (persons/ km²)	GDP (billion yuan)	Retail sales (billion yuan)	Total wage (billion yuan)	Average wage (yuan)	Cell phones (million)	Internet (million)	Buses (1,000)
Jiangsu	Changzhou	226.7	636	191.9	67.5	10.9	42.3	3.3	0.7	2.5
Jiangsu	Nantong	211.5	1125	114.5	39.5	10.4	38.8	2.0	0.3	0.8
Jiangsu	Yangzhou	122.0	1372	83.1	27.7	5.1	35.2	1.4	0.3	1.0
Jiangxi	Nanchang	222.5	1400	124.6	51.7	15.7	33.3	4.0	0.8	2.6
Jilin	Jilin	185.1	509	83.2	39.7	6.8	34.6	2.6	0.3	0.9
Liaoning	Anshan	147.2	2360	107.8	23.6	9.7	33.1	1.6	0.3	1.5
Shandong	Zibo	278.8	1539	188.8	68.4	14.2	31.3	2.3	0.4	2.2
Shandong	Dongying	83.3	1871	137.7	20.7	10.9	39.9	1.8	0.2	0.6
Shandong	Yantai	179.2	1434	155.3	48.4	15.8	35.0	2.6	0.3	1.7
Shandong	Linyi	199.5	436	76.9	40.6	6.9	32.3	4.4	0.2	2.0
Shanxi	Taiyuan	285.2	1953	142.2	67.0	25.2	33.6	3.8	0.8	1.9
Xinjiang	Urumqi	231.9	243	107.9	46.7	17.1	36.5	2.4	0.4	3.9
Yunan	Kunming	250.2	610	134.8	74.1	16.1	42.3	2.9	2.0	5.3
Zhejiang	Wenzhou	144.8	787	105.4	68.4	14.2	39.3	3.4	1.9	1.9
Tier 3 Cities										
Anhui	Wuhu	104.9	1961	65.2	17.2	5.7	31.8	0.8	0.2	1.4
Anhui	Huainan	180.8	716	36.3	13.1	9.7	41.7	0.8	0.1	1.0
Anhui	Maanshan	63.6	253	52.1	9.6	5.0	38.8	0.6	0.1	0.5

Fujian	Putian	213.0	767	57.2	20.5	5.6	24.8	1.3	0.2	0.7
Fujian	Quanzhou	102.9	873	70.4	28.1	8.6	26.5	1.1	0.4	0.8
Guangdong	Jiangmen	137.6	770	76.8	24.1	6.3	-	2.1	-	0.7
Guangdong	Zhanjiang	151.8	1040	62.4	3.1	5.5	33.7	3.1	0.2	0.7
Guangdong	Maoming	130.7	1495	44.5	22.6	3.3	35.1	1.0	0.1	0.2
Guangxi	Liuzhou	103.8	1578	70.9	32.0	8.5	36.2	1.1	0.4	-
Guizhou	Guiyang	218.8	910	72.6	36.6	15.5	27.4	3.1	0.4	2.5
Hainan	Haikou	158.2	687	49.0	27.7	9.4	30.6	1.9	0.3	1.0
Hebei	Qinhuangdao	82.6	2276	46.7	19.3	6.7	36.0	1.0	0.3	1.0
Hebei	Handan	147.4	3396	48.4	18.2	9.0	32.7	1.4	0.5	2.4
Hebei	Baoding	106.3	3405	48.1	11.3	6.1	28.1	2.3	0.3	2.1
Henan	Luoyang	160.1	2942	66.6	30.6	8.2	25.8	1.5	0.3	1.2
Henan	Pingdingshan	101.9	2219	40.8	13.5	8.8	31.6	0.8	0.2	0.7
Henan	Nanyang	185.3	935	38.3	20.9	7.2	24.6	1.2	0.1	0.4
Hubei	Yichang	124.8	294	65.0	25.4	4.7	22.2	1.0	0.1	1.0
Hubei	Xiangfan	221.8	604	71.2	27.9	4.0	23.6	1.3	0.2	1.3
Hunan	Zhuzhou	100.2	1866	52.1	18.3	6.2	32.4	0.8	0.1	1.0
Hunan	Xiangtan	87.8	3145	43.0	13.8	4.0	26.6	0.8	0.1	0.9
Hunan	Yueyang	87.5	702	55.0	24.9	4.2	25.1	0.8	0.1	0.9
Hunan	Changde	140.6	560	56.0	16.0	3.9	29.6	0.7	0.1	0.5
Inner Mongolia	Chifeng	121.4	172	37.8	15.1	4.0	33.7	1.0	0.1	0.4
Inner Mongolia	Eerduosi	25.3	100	50.7	15.8	2.3	47.0	0.9	<0.1	0.2
Jiangsu	Lianyungang	88.7	932	37.0	14.8	5.3	34.3	0.9	0.3	0.6

(continued)

Province	City	Population (10,000)	Population density (persons/ km²)	GDP (billion yuan)	Retail sales (billion yuan)	Total wage (billion yuan)	Average wage (yuan)	Cell phones (million)	Internet (million)	Buses (1,000)
Jiangsu	Huaian	274.5	241	68.6	25.4	6.4	31.2	1.0	0.2	0.8
Jiangsu	Yancheng	162.6	1211	52.9	21.1	4.6	31.5	0.2	0.1	0.4
Jiangsu	Zhenjiang	103.5	185	74.1	23.1	6.9	38.4	0.9	0.2	1.0
Jiangsu	Taizhou	82.1	179	45.9	13.8	3.5	33.5	0.7	0.1	0.3
Jiangxi	Jiujiang	63.8	859	39.0	10.8	2.9	27.5	0.9	0.1	0.4
Jiangxi	Xinyu	92.2	693	40.4	7.5	2.2	27.5	0.6	0.1	0.4
Liaoning	Fushun	139.1	1947	51.7	29.7	7.0	31.6	1.4	0.2	1.2
Liaoning	Benxi	95.5	629	50.8	12.2	5.8	29.5	1.0	0.2	0.7
Liaoning	Jinzhou	93.4	2142	36.1	16.0	4.5	30.2	1.2	0.2	0.7
Liaoning	Yingkou	89.3	1272	45.1	12.1	3.9	27.9	0.9	0.2	0.7
Liaoning	Panjin	60.6	2279	43.1	12.1	9.5	38.0	0.7	0.2	0.4
Ningxia	Yinchuan	91.4	396	44.0	14.7	9.3	39.3	0.1	0.1	1.3
Qinghai	Xining	114.1	3003	35.5	18.6	5.7	29.2	1.2	0.1	1.7
Shaanxi	Baoji	141.4	396	46.8	12.0	4.6	26.5	1.5	0.3	0.8
Shandong	Zaozhuang	219.6	1069	65.4	19.1	6.5	27.0	1.0	0.2	0.8
Shandong	Weifang	181.3	1284	69.0	31.6	7.7	30.0	2.0	0.3	1.0
Shandong	Jining	119.6	901	53.9	24.7	5.6	28.6	1.3	0.2	1.0
Shandong	Taian	159.3	199	58.7	19.7	4.0	24.0	1.3	0.2	0.7
Shandong	Weihai	64.5	379	50.3	19.9	5.3	26.9	0.7	0.2	0.9
Shandong	Rizhao	122.8	1108	67.0	1.7	4.0	33.3	1.0	0.2	0.4

Shandong	Laiwu	126.4	641	47.1	16.1	4.3	31.6	0.9	0.1	0.3
Shanxi	Suzhou	64.1	142	39.1	5.5	2.9	32.2	0.4	<0.1	0.2
Shanxi	Jinzhong	58.9	449	12.2	6.6	2.0	20.9	0.5	0.1	0.5
Sichuan	Zigong	150.6	1047	35.2	13.4	3.7	25.9	0.7	0.1	0.8
Sichuan	Mianyang	122.3	779	38.7	13.0	5.3	28.8	1.4	0.2	1.0
Xinjiang	Kalamayi	39.4	41	48.0	3.0	4.9	37.5	0.3	0.1	0.5
Yunan	Yuxi	42.1	419	38.2	5.3	2.0	32.0	0.5	0.1	0.1
Zhejiang	Jiaxing	83.1	1067	48.2	19.7	7.0	34.5	1.3	0.2	0.9
Zhejiang	Huzhou	108.6	516	50.6	22.6	5.2	34.3	1.2	0.2	0.7
Zhejiang	Shaoxing	64.9	1623	40.8	18.9	8.2	31.1	1.0	0.2	0.8
Zhejiang	Jinhua	92.7	1348	34.1	18.9	5.4	37.7	1.0	0.2	0.8
Zhejiang	Zhoushan	69.7	412	37.9	14.1	4.7	40.8	0.8	0.2	0.6
Zhejiang	Taizhou	153.8	524	72.9	34.7	9.2	35.5	2.0	0.3	0.5
Tier 4 Cities										
Anhui	Bengbu	92.5	939	26.7	14.1	2.9	28.0	0.6	0.1	0.7
Anhui	Huaibei	109.0	658	28.2	7.7	6.6	37.1	0.5	0.1	1.0
Anhui	Tongling	45.0	684	28.6	7.2	2.8	30.5	0.4	0.1	0.3
Anhui	Anqing	74.0	1147	19.2	11.7	2.1	23.6	0.4	0.1	0.3
Anhui	Huanshan	46.7	763	12.3	5.6	1.4	27.4	0.3	0.1	0.3
Anhui	Chuzhou	53.2	831	13.7	4.4	1.5	27.1	0.4	<0.1	0.3
Anhui	Fuyang	204.2	641	18.9	10.3	2.5	21.4	0.8	<0.1	0.6
Anhui	Xuzhou	183.9	563	21.5	4.5	0.6	18.3	0.6	0.1	0.5

(continued)

Province	City	Population (10,000)	Population density (persons/km²)	GDP (billion yuan)	Retail sales (billion yuan)	Total wage (billion yuan)	Average wage (yuan)	Cell phones (million)	Internet (million)	Buses (1,000)
Anhui	Chaohu	88.6	1133	14.1	4.5	1.2	25.8	0.4	0.1	0.2
Anhui	Luan	185.2	1127	12.7	6.4	1.9	24.6	0.5	0.1	0.3
Anhui	Haozhou	159.5	837	16.0	7.9	1.1	24.2	0.5	<0.1	0.3
Anhui	Chizhou	65.8	607	12.7	4.2	0.9	28.9	0.2	<0.1	0.1
Anhui	Xuancheng	85.8	1057	13.1	6.5	0.4	27.3	0.3	<0.1	0.1
Fujian	Sanming	28.4	273	18.7	5.8	2.1	30.5	0.3	0.1	0.3
Fujian	Zhangzhou	55.0	1191	30.0	13.0	2.7	28.7	0.9	0.1	0.2
Fujian	Nanping	49.3	956	15.3	5.8	1.8	27.2	0.4	0.1	0.2
Fujian	Longyan	47.8	1282	34.2	11.1	3.5	30.9	0.6	0.1	0.4
Fujian	Ningde	43.3	757	10.8	4.4	1.3	30.7	0.4	<0.1	0.2
Gansu	Jiayuguan	20.9	71	16.0	2.0	1.8	39.4	0.3	<0.1	0.1
Gansu	Jinchang	21.5	71	16.0	2.2	2.2	41.7	0.2	<0.1	0.1
Gansu	Baiyin	49.7	143	17.6	4.7	3.3	33.0	0.4	<0.1	0.2
Gansu	Tianshui	126.1	215	15.3	5.6	2.2	20.3	0.5	<0.1	0.3
Gansu	Wuwei	103.6	204	12.8	3.8	1.2	18.4	0.3	<0.1	0.2
Gansu	Zhangye	51.9	122	8.5	3.5	0.8	18.9	0.3	<0.1	0.2
Gansu	Pingliang	50.0	258	6.6	3.2	0.8	18.8	0.3	<0.1	0.1
Gansu	Jiuquan	40.1	118	9.3	3.2	1.0	27.0	0.3	<0.1	0.3
Gansu	Qingyang	35.6	357	7.4	2.5	0.7	27.4	0.2	<0.1	0.3

Gansu	Dingxi	46.7	111	2.7	1.5	0.7	25.8	0.1	<0.1	0.1
Gansu	Longnan	55.2	118	4.0	1.2	0.5	26.2	0.2	<0.1	0.0
Guangdong	Shaoguan	92.1	321	29.3	17.6	4.9	33.7	0.9	0.1	0.4
Guangdong	Zhaoqing	53.2	699	32.5	9.9	3.5	27.8	1.1	0.1	0.3
Guangdong	Meizhou	31.5	1057	-	4.5	1.8	35.6	0.4	0.1	0.2
Guangdong	Shanwei	52.5	1264	11.7	5.6	1.5	30.4	-	-	0.0
Guangdong	Heyuan	29.8	824	12.8	4.7	2.9	26.4	0.5	<0.1	0.1
Guangdong	Yangjiang	66.8	884	20.4	13.1	1.6	22.5	0.5	0.1	0.1
Guangdong	Qingyuan	64.4	497	31.4	11.0	2.7	31.7	0.7	0.3	0.5
Guangdong	Chaozhou	35.0	2256	10.8	5.8	1.5	28.3	0.6	0.1	0.2
Guangdong	Jieyang	69.5	3839	18.6	10.1	1.3	25.6	1.0	0.1	0.1
Guangdong	Yunfu	29.6	389	-	2.6	1.2	30.5	0.2	0.1	0.1
Guangxi	Guilin	75.8	1341	30.4	18.4	4.4	30.0	0.8	0.3	0.8
Guangxi	Wuzhou	50.1	456	15.7	7.9	1.9	28.7	0.3	0.1	0.3
Guangxi	Beihai	60.4	631	20.6	5.9	1.7	26.8	0.5	0.2	0.2
Guangxi	Fangcheng-gang	51.9	184	18.4	2.8	1.6	27.6	0.3	0.1	0.1
Guangxi	Qinzhou	134.8	283	22.4	7.3	1.6	25.9	0.4	0.1	0.2
Guangxi	Guigang	185.8	525	20.8	9.6	1.5	23.8	0.5	0.1	0.2
Guangxi	Yunlin	97.8	782	21.8	11.8	2.5	29.4	0.5	0.2	0.2
Guangxi	Baise	34.8	94	10.3	2.4	1.4	27.7	0.2	0.1	0.1
Guangxi	Hezhou	107.2	192	14.2	3.6	1.0	26.6	0.4	0.1	0.2
Guangxi	Hechi	33.1	142	7.2	2.6	1.0	24.6	0.2	0.1	0.1

(continued)

Province	City	Population (10,000)	Population density (persons/km²)	GDP (billion yuan)	Retail sales (billion yuan)	Total wage (billion yuan)	Average wage (yuan)	Cell phones (million)	Internet (million)	Buses (1,000)
Guangxi	Laibin	105.3	241	15.7	3.0	1.4	30.0	0.4	0.1	0.2
Guangxi	Chongzuo	35.8	121	5.9	1.1	0.6	25.3	0.2	<0.1	0.0
Guizhou	Liupanshui	53.0	1085	15.3	6.1	2.2	29.1	0.3	<0.1	0.4
Guizhou	Zunyi	85.3	648	23.9	11.1	2.9	29.2	0.9	0.2	0.5
Guizhou	Anshun	84.7	497	7.5	3.0	1.6	26.7	0.4	<0.1	0.3
Hainan	Sanya	55.7	291	17.3	5.1	1.6	28.4	0.3	0.1	0.4
Hebei	Xingtai	61.5	4554	18.7	6.8	4.2	31.4	0.7	0.1	1.8
Hebei	Zhangjiakou	89.7	2384	31.0	11.9	4.4	31.0	1.2	0.2	0.9
Hebei	Chengde	54.5	717	19.0	6.7	3.2	30.5	0.8	0.1	0.6
Hebei	Cangzhou	53.3	2912	32.7	6.5	2.9	26.8	0.9	0.1	1.1
Hebei	Langfang	81.0	2775	28.4	7.4	5.0	39.9	0.7	0.1	0.5
Hebei	Hengshui	31.1	1139	14.2	7.1	2.2	26.0	0.6	0.1	0.9
Heilongjiang	Qiqihar	142.0	325	34.1	2.1	6.1	26.9	1.0	0.2	1.0
Heilongjiang	Jixi	88.1	383	14.0	6.4	3.4	24.1	0.6	0.1	0.7
Heilongjiang	Hegang	67.9	149	13.4	5.2	3.2	26.6	0.5	0.1	0.4
Heilongjiang	Shuangya	50.2	285	11.0	3.3	2.2	27.6	0.4	<0.1	0.4
Heilongjiang	Yichun	81.0	41	11.5	3.4	-	-	0.4	0.1	0.2
Heilongjiang	Jiamusi	81.5	435	21.0	10.7	2.3	27.9	1.0	0.1	0.5
Heilongjiang	Qitaihe	55.3	152	18.7	4.3	-	-	0.4	0.1	0.4

Heilongjiang	Mudanjiang	79.9	324	20.1	12.3	2.6	28.6	0.4	0.1	0.7
Heilongjiang	Heiheshi	19.2	13	3.9	0.4	0.8	29.8	0.3	<0.1	0.1
Heilongjiang	Suihua	89.9	326	5.7	3.6	0.4	17.4	0.2	<0.1	0.3
Henan	Kaifeng	85.4	2359	18.9	3.6	3.3	22.3	0.6	0.1	0.6
Henan	Anyang	107.5	1977	31.2	13.5	5.0	30.1	0.8	0.3	0.7
Henan	Hebi	61.0	898	18.1	4.0	2.8	22.7	0.5	0.1	0.3
Henan	Xinxiang	101.4	2931	26.9	15.3	4.3	22.7	1.0	0.3	0.9
Henan	Jiaozuo	83.5	1970	22.2	8.4	4.4	26.8	1.1	0.1	0.7
Henan	Puyang	67.1	2582	22.1	5.2	5.3	28.4	0.4	0.1	0.4
Henan	Xuchang	41.2	4244	16.9	7.6	1.9	24.0	0.4	0.2	0.5
Henan	Luohe	139.2	1364	34.4	10.8	2.9	20.4	0.7	0.1	0.8
Henan	Sanmenxia	29.2	1475	9.9	3.9	1.8	26.4	0.3	0.2	0.2
Henan	Shangqiu	173.2	1083	20.4	7.7	2.3	17.2	0.7	0.1	0.8
Henan	Xinyang	145.8	404	23.9	10.8	2.7	20.4	0.7	0.1	0.2
Henan	Zhoukou	52.7	3563	9.4	5.8	2.2	23.0	0.4	0.1	0.2
Henan	Zhumadian	66.1	857	15.8	6.4	1.8	16.4	0.5	0.1	0.2
Hubei	Huangshi	71.5	3019	30.4	13.3	3.2	17.1	0.9	0.1	0.8
Hubei	Shiyan	52.8	442	32.7	13.6	5.5	23.0	1.0	0.1	0.7
Hubei	Ezhou	107.2	713	32.4	12.7	2.1	12.7	0.6	0.1	0.5
Hubei	Jingmen	67.9	313	21.1	8.4	1.9	25.6	0.5	0.1	0.4
Hubei	Xiaogan	96.8	1023	14.0	5.8	2.1	18.3	0.5	0.0	0.4
Hubei	Jingzhou	116.9	741	24.9	28.7	2.9	21.3	0.8	0.1	0.7
Hubei	Huanggang	36.8	1042	8.0	5.1	0.9	17.6	0.2	<0.1	0.4

(continued)

Province	City	Population (10,000)	Population density (persons/ km²)	GDP (billion yuan)	Retail sales (billion yuan)	Total wage (billion yuan)	Average wage (yuan)	Cell phones (million)	Internet (million)	Buses (1,000)
Hubei	Xianning	59.8	399	10.9	4.8	1.4	21.0	0.3	0.1	0.1
Hubei	Suizhou	64.7	489	14.5	8.1	1.1	23.2	0.9	0.1	0.5
Hunan	Hengyang	104.3	1509	31.8	15.9	5.4	32.2	0.6	0.1	0.9
Hunan	Shaoyang	67.3	1544	12.3	5.2	2.2	23.7	0.5	0.1	0.3
Hunan	Zhangjiajie	49.9	182	10.4	3.9	1.0	27.6	0.4	0.1	0.2
Hunan	Yiyang	132.7	686	23.1	7.9	2.5	23.7	0.6	0.1	0.4
Hunan	Chenzhou	66.6	297	25.6	16.3	2.9	31.9	0.6	0.1	0.7
Hunan	Yongzhou	109.6	345	18.6	5.9	2.3	26.2	0.6	0.1	0.5
Hunan	Huaihua	34.8	522	12.7	6.3	1.7	29.9	0.6	0.1	0.4
Hunan	Loudi	44.9	1053	16.7	2.6	1.9	23.7	0.5	<0.1	0.2
Inner Mongolia	Wuhai	48.1	274	31.1	6.1	3.7	35.6	0.5	0.1	0.4
Inner Mongolia	Tongliao	76.3	270	32.0	9.3	1.9	21.2	0.4	0.1	0.2
Inner Mongolia	Huolunbeier	26.9	187	13.0	5.6	1.4	31.2	0.3	0.1	0.2
Inner Mongolia	Bayanzhuoer	53.6	228	15.7	4.8	1.8	26.8	0.5	<0.1	0.1
Inner Mongolia	Wulanchabu	30.4	2038	8.9	3.2	1.6	27.4	0.3	<0.1	0.1
Jiangsu	Xuqian	159.5	281	30.9	9.7	2.1	29.4	0.8	0.1	0.4
Jiangxi	Jingdezhen	45.8	901	19.6	13.2	2.0	22.2	0.2	0.1	0.4
Jiangxi	Pingxiang	85.0	1220	26.1	8.8	2.3	23.2	1.0	0.1	0.3
Jiangxi	Yingtan	22.2	1793	6.6	3.4	0.5	24.4	0.2	<0.1	0.2

Jiangxi	Ganzhou	64.6	454	18.3	8.1	2.1	26.5	0.6	0.1	0.5
Jiangxi	Jian	53.7	349	9.1	3.3	0.7	22.4	0.2	<0.1	0.2
Jiangxi	Yichun	104.2	678	9.9	6.7	1.7	20.3	0.3	0.2	0.2
Jiangxi	Fuzhou	111.1	1001	17.1	7.6	1.4	20.0	0.7	0.1	0.2
Jiangxi	Shangrao	39.5	256	9.6	6.3	1.0	22.3	0.3	0.1	0.2
Jilin	Siping	61.0	938	17.4	7.7	1.9	22.5	0.9	0.1	0.3
Jilin	Liaoyuan	47.8	1081	20.3	6.0	1.3	22.4	0.3	<0.1	0.4
Jilin	Tonghua	44.9	590	19.4	6.5	1.8	24.2	0.4	<0.1	0.3
Jilin	Baishan	59.3	217	18.9	4.8	2.2	23.4	0.5	0.1	0.3
Jilin	Songyuan	55.3	417	35.0	7.3	4.5	35.9	1.0	0.1	0.5
Jilin	Baicheng	50.9	202	9.6	7.6	1.6	18.5	0.9	<0.1	0.2
Liaoning	Dandong	78.9	945	21.7	10.6	3.1	22.3	0.6	0.1	0.5
Liaoning	Fuxin	77.6	1583	16.1	10.2	3.1	24.4	0.8	0.1	0.4
Liaoning	Liaoyang	72.7	1167	33.3	9.8	3.9	30.2	1.0	0.2	0.4
Liaoning	Tieling	44.7	678	12.7	6.4	-	-	0.9	0.1	0.4
Liaoning	Chaoyang	59.8	526	13.6	4.5	2.2	28.2	0.5	0.1	0.2
Liaoning	Huludao	99.2	432	27.5	12.5	4.5	25.9	0.8	0.1	0.6
Ningxia	Shizuishan	45.4	200	20.3	4.0	2.0	31.4	0.5	0.1	0.6
Ningxia	Wuzhong	38.1	301	6.3	2.3	0.8	28.0	0.2	<0.1	0.3
Ningxia	Guyuan	44.1	160	3.6	1.4	0.7	31.1	0.2	<0.1	0.1
Ningxia	Zhongwei	39.2	73	7.0	1.6	0.6	26.7	0.2	<0.1	0.3
Shaanxi	Tongchuan	75.7	315	14.5	4.2	2.5	28.1	0.6	<0.1	0.2
Shaanxi	Xianyang	89.7	1702	32.2	8.9	3.5	24.4	1.0	0.1	0.5

(continued)

Province	City	Population (10,000)	Population density (persons/km²)	GDP (billion yuan)	Retail sales (billion yuan)	Total wage (billion yuan)	Average wage (yuan)	Cell phones (million)	Internet (million)	Buses (1,000)
Shaanxi	Weinan	96.8	793	14.2	5.0	2.4	25.6	0.5	<0.1	0.2
Shaanxi	Yanan	44.9	126	12.5	4.3	2.2	30.0	0.7	0.1	0.2
Shaanxi	Hanzhong	55.3	994	9.2	5.0	1.8	28.8	0.5	0.1	0.2
Shaanxi	Yulin	50.9	72	18.3	3.0	2.2	35.8	-	-	0.2
Shaanxi	Ankang	99.9	274	9.8	4.2	1.3	27.5	0.5	0.1	0.1
Shaanxi	Shangluo	54.9	205	5.3	1.8	0.9	24.2	0.2	<0.1	0.1
Shandong	Dezhou	63.4	517	30.7	14.2	2.7	25.7	0.7	0.1	0.7
Shandong	Liaocheng	105.0	717	21.0	10.5	2.5	25.3	0.9	0.1	0.5
Shandong	Binzhou	63.2	271	28.6	9.9	2.5	26.2	1.1	0.1	0.3
Shandong	Heze	149.6	327	20.6	11.3	2.5	24.0	1.1	0.1	0.3
Shanxi	Datong	154.7	744	21.4	17.3	9.9	29.0	0.7	0.2	1.0
Shanxi	Yangquan	68.8	1055	23.5	10.9	6.3	36.3	0.6	0.1	0.6
Shanxi	Changzhi	69.8	2090	22.1	14.8	3.2	24.1	0.7	0.1	0.6
Shanxi	Jincheng	34.3	2399	12.5	9.3	5.3	42.4	0.8	0.1	0.3
Shanxi	Yuncheng	65.9	542	10.5	10.6	1.7	24.0	0.4	<0.1	0.4
Shanxi	Yizhou	52.9	267	6.6	9.3	1.2	18.5	0.2	<0.1	0.1
Shanxi	Linfen	83.3	633	17.3	10.1	2.4	27.1	0.7	0.1	0.3
Shanxi	Luliang	27.5	205	4.9	9.2	1.1	25.3	0.3	<0.1	0.1
Sichuan	Panzhihua	69.2	343	32.9	10.0	5.1	32.4	0.8	0.1	0.7

Sichuan	Luzhou	145.5	682	30.2	11.1	3.6	24.6	1.0	0.1	0.7
Sichuan	Deyang	65.9	1017	22.0	6.1	3.4	38.9	0.7	0.1	0.3
Sichuan	Guangyuan	93.2	203	12.2	6.3	2.1	23.8	0.5	0.1	0.2
Sichuan	Suining	150.8	804	16.3	6.8	1.5	24.0	0.6	0.1	0.2
Sichuan	Neijiang	141.7	903	20.7	7.3	1.9	24.7	0.6	0.1	0.6
Sichuan	Leshan	115.0	457	29.7	10.4	3.5	24.0	1.0	0.1	0.2
Sichuan	Nanchong	193.4	765	24.7	12.5	2.6	22.7	1.0	0.1	0.5
Sichuan	Meishan	85.5	642	15.3	5.2	1.0	26.5	0.4	0.1	0.2
Sichuan	Yibin	80.0	708	28.4	9.0	3.4	29.5	0.7	0.1	0.4
Sichuan	Guangan	126.1	821	13.1	0.5	0.9	24.7	0.4	<0.1	0.0
Sichuan	Dazhou	44.2	972	10.2	5.3	1.8	29.8	0.4	<0.1	0.1
Sichuan	Yaan	35.2	329	6.9	2.8	1.0	25.2	0.2	<0.1	0.0
Sichuan	Bazhong	143.3	558	9.0	3.9	1.2	20.6	0.3	0.1	0.1
Sichuan	Ziyang	108.7	665	17.3	4.6	1.3	26.9	0.4	<0.1	0.1
Xizang	Lhasa	21.7		3.1	0.0	0.0	0.0	0.0	<0.1	0.1
Yunan	Qujing	69.5	447	27.2	4.9	2.2	34.9	0.7	<0.1	0.5
Yunan	Baoshan	89.1	178	9.2	3.5	1.4	20.2	0.4	0.1	0.2
Yunan	Zhaotong	81.7	365	10.2	3.6	1.6	29.0	0.4	<0.1	0.1
Yunan	Lijiang	15.3	122	4.2	1.7	0.7	26.2	0.3	<0.1	0.2
Yunan	Simao	21.8	53	4.6	1.9	0.8	26.7	0.3	<0.1	0.1
Yunan	Lincang	30.7	116	2.9	1.6	0.6	29.8	0.2	<0.1	0.1
Zhejiang	Quzhou	82.2	401	26.5	9.6	2.8	39.4	0.7	0.1	0.6
Zhejiang	Lishui	38.5	1165	14.4	7.1	2.0	43.2	0.6	0.1	0.2

Notes

NOTES TO CHAPTER 2

1. The special economic zones are Shenzhen, Zhuhai, Shantou, Xiamen, and Hainan.
2. The other 10 cities with missing data are Tieling, Yichun, Qitaihe, Foshan, Jiangmen, Meizhou, Shanwei, Yunfu, Liuzhou, and Yulin. Data are missing for these 15 cities in both the 2010 and 2011 editions of *China City Statistical Yearbook*.

NOTES TO CHAPTER 3

1. In 1996, they proliferated to 12.9 million, engaging 22.5 million persons (Ministry of Interior Trade, 1997a). The 1996 figures were the last reported official statistics for individually-owned retail establishments. After that, official statistics reported only those enterprises that meet a minimum size requirement.
2. The exceptions are (1) the applicants that already have three stores of 3,000 m^2 (or larger) in the province and 30 stores in China, and (2) those that already have 30 stores of 300 m^2 in the province and 300 stores in China.

NOTES TO CHAPTER 6

1. The State-Owned Assets Supervision and Administration Commission of the State Council was created by the state government in 2003. A local commission was formed in each province and municipality to manage the state-owned assets and properties including the state-held shares in stock companies.

NOTES TO CHAPTER 7

1. A marketing form named Winwing in Shanghai provides such services to producers. See http://www.winwing.com.cn/about.htmlis.

NOTES TO CHAPTER 8

1. The ten-story, 70,000 m^2 Westgate Mall opened to shoppers in 1998 on Nanjing Road West in Jing'an District.

2. The 34,000 m² CITIC Square opened in 2000.
3. In addition to CITIC Square on Nanjing Road West, CITIC Pacific Ltd. had developed and owns other large-scale residential and commercial properties in Shanghai, such as Royal Pavilion and New Westgate Garden.
4. SZITIC Commercial Property Co. Ltd. is a retail property subsidiary of the Chinese state-owned trust and investment firm, Shenzhen International Trust & Investment Co. Ltd. (SZITIC). See also Chapter 5.
5. For example, the Chinese partner of Join Buy City Plaza in Shanghai placed 50 percent of its holdings for sale in 2005.
6. The shopping center was completed jointly by Morgan Stanley and the Hong Kong-based Chongbang Group. Chongbang was established in 2003 with investment from both Hong Kong and Singapore.
7. Ikea Group owns 49 percent of IICG (Chen, 2011). It currently owns and operates 30 shopping centers in 14 countries, mostly in Europe.
8. These are Westgate Mall (42,000 m²), Plaza 66 (52,000 m²), CITIC Square (34,500 m²), and Join Buy City Plaza (91,000 m²).
9. These are Bailian-Shimao International Plaza (58,000 m²), New World City (120,000 m²), Raffles City (85,000 m²), Henderson Metropolitan Center, 353 Plaza, and Hongyi Plaza.
10. Beijing New Yansha Causeway Bay Company Ltd. was formed by Beijing New Yansha Holding (Group) Company Ltd.—a subsidiary of Beijing Tourism Group—and Shenzhen Causeway Bay Group.

References

Ai, Y. (2005, December 21). Six potential crises will hurt Trust Mart's operations in China. *Fortune Times*. Retrieved from http://www.linkshop.com.cn/web/Article_News.aspx?ArticleId=55750 (accessed on July 7, 2013)

Alexander, N. (1997). *International retailing*. Oxford: Blackwell Publishers Ltd.

——— & Quinn, B. (2002). International retail divestment. *International Journal of Retailing and Distribution Management, 30*(2), 112–125.

Amin, A. (2003). Spaces of corporate learning. In J. Peck & H. W. Yeung (Eds.), *Remaking the global economy* (pp. 114–129). London: Sage Publications.

An, G. (1998). Will Wangfujing fall into a deep well? *Science and Technology Think Tank, 1,* 13–14.

Applebaum, W. (1954). Marketing geography. In P. E. James & C. F. Jones (Eds.), *American geography: Inventory and prospect.* Syracuse, New York: Syracuse University Press.

Atsmon, Y., Dixit, V., & Wu, C. (2011). Tapping China's luxury-goods market. McKinsey & Company. Retrieved from http://www.mckinsey.com/insights/marketing_sales/tapping_chinas_luxury-goods_market?p=1 (accessed on April 3, 2013)

Atsmon, Y., Ducarme, D., Magni, M. & Wu, C. (2012a). *Luxury without borders: China's new class of shoppers take on the world.* McKinsey & Company. Retrieved from http://www.mckinseychina.com/2012/12/12/luxury-without-borders-chinas-new-class-of-shoppers-take-on-the-world/ (accessed on October 15, 2013)

Atsmon, Y., Magni, M., Jin, A. & Li, L. (2012b). *Annual Chinese consumer report: From mass to mainstream: keeping pace with China's rapidly changing consumers.* McKinsey & Company. Retrieved from http://www.mckinseychina.com/2012/09/25/from-mass-to-mainstream-keeping-pace-with-chinas-rapidly-changing-consumers/ (accessed on October 15, 2013)

"Auchan expands prudently in China." (2011). *Retailer Link*. Retrieved from http://www.linkshop.com.cn/web/archives/2011/178156.shtml (accessed on July 25, 2013)

"Auchan recruits tenants for its shopping center project in Ningbo." (2012). *Retailer Link*. Retrieved from http://www.linkshop.com.cn/web/archives/2012/230306.shtml (accessed on July 25, 2013)

Australian Center for Retail Studies and TNS. (2007). *Luxury brands in China* (A research report for KPMG). Retrieved from http://www.kpmg.com.cn/en/virtual_library/Consumer_markets/CM_Luxury_brand.pdf (accessed on July 25, 2013)

Azuma, N. (2012, November 30–December 2). The rise of virtually integrated specialist clothing retail multiples and its implications to retail internationalization in Asia—from the experiences of UNIQLO. Paper presented at the 10th Society of Asian Retailing and Distribution Workshop, Kobe, Japan.

Bai, Y. (2011). B&Q struggles in adapting to the China market. Retrieved from http://www.linkshop.com.cn/web/archives/2011/179027.shtml (accessed on September 28, 2011)

Baidu Baike. (2013a). About Taobao. Retrieved from http://baike.baidu.com/view/1590.htm (accessed on July 24, 2013)

———. (2013b). About Dangdang. Retrieved from http://baike.baidu.com/view/126090.htm (accessed on July 25, 2013)

Baike. (2013). About JD Commerce. Retrieved from http://www.baike.com/wiki/%E4%BA%AC%E4%B8%9C%E5%95%86%E5%9F%8E (accessed on July 25, 2013)

Bailian Group. (2006). *Bailian Group 2005 annual report.* Retrieved from http://bldmo.blemall.com/pdf/2005-4J.pdf (accessed on June 10, 2012)

———. (2011). *Bailian Group 2010 annual report.*
Retrieved   from   http://www.sse.com.cn/sseportal/cs/zhs/scfw/gg/ssgs/2011-03 -11/600631_2010_n.pdf (accessed on June 10, 2012)

"Bailian Group plans to invest in Huishang and form strategic partnership." (2008). *21st Century Economic Journal.* Retrieved from http://www.linkmall.com.cn/corp/20080608/184632.shtml (accessed on June 12, 2012)

"Bailian is to invest in Huishang Group." (2008). *World Economic Journal.* Retrieved from http://www.linkmall.com.cn/corp/20080608/184632.shtml (accessed on June 12, 2012)

Baljko, J. (2006). Ahold is opening pilot store in China. *Supermarket News.* Retrieved from http://supermarketnews.com/archive/ahold-opening-pilot-store-china (accessed on August 17, 2012)

Barboza, D. (2005, January 15). China, new land of shoppers, builds malls on gigantic scale. *New York Times.* Retrieved from http://www.nytimes.com/2005/05/25/business/worldbusiness/
25mall.html?pagewanted=all&_r=0 (accessed on July 24, 2013)

———. (2008, November 24). Report says Chinese tycoon held in stock scandal. *New York Times.* Retrieved from http://www.nytimes.com/2008/11/25/business/worldbusiness/25yuan.html?adxnnl=1&adxnnlx=1314903821-hZRns/A37s1aNGPi2LSNNQ (accessed on July 24, 2013)

———. (2009, March 13). For bribing officials, Chinese give the best. *New York Times.* Retrieved from http://www.nytimes.com/2009/03/14/world/asia/14gifts.html (accessed on July 24, 2013)

Barry. (2011, July 28). What makes a city tier in China? *The China Sourcing Blog.* Retrieved from http://www.chinasourcingblog.org/2011/07/what-makes-a-city-tier-in-chin.html (accessed on May 24, 2012)

"Beijing Aika Shopping Center undergoes transformation." (2006, May 18). *Retailer Link.* Retrieved from http://www.linkshop.com.cn/web/Article_News.aspx?ArticleId=58905 (accessed on July 10, 2013)

Beijing Almanac Compilation Committee. (1997). *Beijing almanac 1997.* Beijing: Author.

Beijing Intelligence Tapping and Management Consulting Ltd. (1997a). Frustrations of retail chain growth. *Science and Technology Think Tank, 8,* 14–17.

———. (1997b). A report on opening-up of China's retail sector. *Science and Technology Think Tank, 11,* 7–12.

Beijing New Yansha Causeway Bay Company Limited. (2006). *New Yansha mall growth and development.* Beijing: Author.

———. (2007). *New Yansha mall achievements.* Beijing: Author.

Beijing Planning Commission. (2004). General plan of Beijing. Retrieved from http://www.cityup.org/news/urbanplan/20070903/31215.shtml (accessed on July 1, 2013)

"Beijing Wu-Mart acquires Tianjin Daiei." (2005). *Economic News Daily.* Retrieved from http://finance.sina.com.cn (accessed on February 5, 2005)

Berry, B. J. L. (1961). City size distributions and economic development. *Economic Development and Cultural Change, 9*, 537–588.

———. (1972). Hierarchical diffusion: The basis of developmental filtering and spread in a system of growth centers. In N. Hansen (Ed.), *Growth Centers in Regional Economic Development* (pp. 103–138). Glencoe, IL: The Free Press.

Beyard, M., & O'Mara, W. (1999). *Shopping centre development handbook* (3rd ed.). Washington, DC: ULI-the Urban Land Institute.

"Blackstone divests in China, New World Development takes over." (2011). *Soufun.* Retrieved from http://sydc.gz.soufun.com/2011–09–27/5976838.htm (accessed on January 24, 2013)

Bloch, P. H., Bush, R. F., and Campbell, L. (1993). Consumer 'accomplices' in product counterfeiting. *Journal of Consumer Marketing, 10*(4), 27–36.

Blomley, N. (1996). 'I'd like to dress her all over': masculinity, power and retail space. In N. Wrigley & M. Lowe (Eds.), *Retailing, consumption and capital: Toward the new retail geography* (pp. 238–256). Essex: Longman Group Ltd.

Bloomberg News. (2011, July 5). Foreign retailers grab land in China. *Toronto Star*, p. B5.

Borgström, B., Hertz, S., & Nyberg, A. (2008). Entry strategy and international retail operations: Comparing effects of different entry strategies by Netto and Lidl in the Swedish grocery market. *Nordic Retail and Wholesale Conference Proceedings.* Jönköping University, Jönköping International Business School, JIBS, Centre of Logistics and Supply Chain Management.

Boush, D., Shipp, S., Loken, B., Gencturk, E., Crockett, S., Kennedy, E., . . . Strobel, J. (1987). Affect generalization to similar and dissimilar line extensions. *Psychology & Marketing, 4*(Fall), 225–241.

Bradshaw, M. J. (1996). The prospects for the post-socialist economies. In P. W. Daniels & W. F. Lever (Eds.), *The global economy in transition* (pp. 263–288). Essex , England: Addison Wesley Longman Limited.

"British supermarket giant Tesco lands in China." (2004). Retrieved from http://news.bbc.co.uk/chinese/simp/hi/newsid_3890000/ (accessed on July 14, 2004)

Burkitt, L. (2012, September 14). Home Depot learns Chinese prefer 'do-it-for-me.' *The Wall Street Journal.* Retrieved from http://online.wsj.com/article/SB100008 72396390444433504577651072911154602.html (accessed on May 24, 2013)

Burstedt, J. (2011). Retail development challenges in China: How Inter Ikea Center Group's market analysis and experiences might apply to other foreign companies. *Retail Property Insight, 18*(3), 18–25.

Burt, S., Dawson, J. & Leigh, S. (2003). Failure in international retailing: Research propositions. *International Review of Retail Distribution and Consumer Research, 13*(4), 355–373.

Cafolla, L. (2007, October). China is set to become the second biggest consumer of luxury goods by 2015. *A Plus.* Retrieved from http://app1.hkicpa.org.hk/APLUS/0710/p24_29.pdf (accessed on July 25, 2013)

"CapitaLand moves closer to China REIT." (2005, July 9). *Toronto Star.* Retrieved from http://biz.thestar.com.my/news/story.asp?file=/2005/7/9/business/11441784&sec=business (accessed on July 24, 2013)

Carrefour Corporate Website. (2012). About us. www.carrefour.com (accessed on March 31, 2012)

Caulkin, S. (2003, April 19). Ethics and profits do mix. *The Observer.* Retrieved from http://www.guardian.co.uk/business/2003/apr/20/globalisation.corporateaccountability (accessed on July 24, 2013)

Chandrasekhar, R. (2006). *Best Buy Inc.—dual branding in China* (research report). London, Ontario: The University of Western Ontario, Richard Ivey School of Business.

Chang, S. (2011, February 28). Media Markt opens its second retail store in China. *Made in China*. Retrieved from http://micgadget.com/11483/media-markt-opened-its-second-retail-store-in-china/ (accessed on June 29, 2013)

Che, Y. (2002, October 9). President Jiang Zemin receives Wal-Mart CEO. *People's Daily* (overseas edition), p. 1.

Chen, B., Zou, H., & Liu, B. (2005). Chongqing General Trading Groups becomes the largest shareholder of C-Best. *Chongqing Evening News*. Retrieved from http://www.linkshop.com.cn/web/Article_News.aspx?ArticleId=52830 (accessed on July 24, 2013)

Chen, H. (2006). The myths of Carrefour and Wal-Mart withdraw from South Korea. *Retailer Link*. Retrieved from http://www.linkshop.com.cn/web/Article1.aspx?ArticleId=59951&ClassID=21/ (accessed June, 30 2006)

Chen, Q. (2011, September 8). Developer plans shopping center project in China. *China Daily, p.2.*

Cheng, S. (2004, November 29). Characteristics of shopping centre development in China. *Global Finance and Economic Observer.*

Chevalier, M. & Lu, P. (2010). *Luxury China: Market opportunities and potential.* Singapore: John Wiley & Sons (Asia) PTE. Ltd.

China Chain Store Association. (2005). *China chain store almanac 2005.* Beijing: China Commerce Publishing House.

———. (2006). *China chain store almanac 2006.* Beijing: China Commerce Publishing House.

———. (2007). *China chain store almanac 2007.* Beijing: China Commerce Publishing House.

———. (2010). *China chain store almanac 2010.* Beijing: China Commerce Publishing House.

———. (2011). *China chain store almanac 2011.* Beijing: China Commerce Publishing House.

"China further opens its circulation sector." (1999, August 26). *People's Daily* (overseas edition), p. 2.

China Internet Network Information Center. (2011). *The 28th survey report on internet development in China*. Retrieved from http://research.cnnic.cn/html/1295343214d2557.html (accessed on May 24, 2012)

"China still poses retail challenge for U.S.-based Best Buy." (2012). *China Retail News*. Retrieved from http://www.chinaretailnews.com/2012/07/02/5591-china-still-poses-retail-challenge-for-u-s-based-best-buy/ (accessed on July 24, 2013)

"China's Gome still haunted by recent scandal." (2010, August 5). *Global Times*. Retrieved from http://business.globaltimes.cn/industries/2010–08/560258.html (accessed on October 11, 2010)

"China's largest shopping mall to be completed in Beijing." (2004, April 28). *Ming Pao*, p. 25.

"China's luxury consumers younger than world average." (2011, June 3). *People's Daily*. Retrieved from http://english.peopledaily.com.cn/90001/90778/90862/7399847.html (accessed on July 24, 2013)

Chinese Academy of Social Sciences. (2012a). *Annual report on urban development of China No.5.* Beijing: Social Sciences Academic Press (China).

———. (2012b). *The blue book of China's social development.* Beijing: Author.

"Chinese creativity: Who are the emerging designers?" (2011, March 16). *Jing Daily*. Retrieved from http://www.jingdaily.com/chinese-creativity-who-are-the-emerging-designers/8099/ (accessed on July 24, 2013)

"Chinese electronics store opens outlet on roof of the world". (2013). *China Retail News*. Retrieved from http://www.chinaretailnews.com/2013/05/21/6568-chinese-electronics-store-opens-outlet-on-roof-of-the-world/ (accessed on June 3, 2013)

"Chinese luxury goods consumption reached US$10.7 Billion." (2011). *China Retail News*. Retrieved from http://www.chinaretailnews.com/2011/06/14/5015-chinese-luxury-goods-consumption-reached-usd10–7-billion/ (accessed on July 24, 2013)

"Chinese shoppers spent 400% more on luxury goods overseas than at home." (2011, June 7). *Jing Daily*. Retrieved from http://www.jingdaily.com/report-chinese-shoppers-spent-400-more-on-luxury-goods-overseas-than-at-home/9821/ (accessed on July 24, 2013)

Chong, X. (2012). Ito Yokado establishes solely owned company in China, with headquarters office in Beijing. Retrieved from http://www.linkshop.com.cn/web/archives/2012/214946.shtml (accessed on July 5, 2013)

Christopherson, S. (1996). The production of consumption: Retail restructuring and labour demand in the USA. In N. Wrigley & M. Lowe (Eds.), *Retailing, consumption and capital: Towards the new retail geography* (pp. 159–177). Essex, England: Longman Group Limited.

Clarke, D. (1996). The limits to retail capital. In N. Wrigley & M. Lowe (Eds.), *Retailing, consumption and capital: Toward the new retail geography* (pp. 284–301). Essex, England: Longman Group Limited.

Coe, N. (2004). The internationalization/globalization of retailing: Towards an economic-geographical research agenda. *Environment and Planning A, 36*(9), 1571–1594.

—— & Wrigley, N. (2007). Host economy impacts of transnational retail: The research agenda. *Journal of Economic Geography, 7*, 341–71.

Cole, M. (2009). Defining China's second- and third-tier cities: An attempt at setting standards for what qualifies as a second- or third- tier city in China. *Rightsite Asia*. Retrieved from http://rightsite.asia/en/article/defining-chinas-second-and-third-tier-cities (accessed on May 24, 2012)

Competition Bureau of Canada. (2004). *Merger enforcement guidelines*. Ottawa: Author.

"Consumed by fashion: Sweden's H&M tells the story of China's rising middle class aspirations." (2012, March 1). *China Economics Review*. Retrieved from https://my.jwt.com/public/jwt_net.nsf/documents/8A826AA6579034C9852579B40050FE87?OpenDocument (accessed on July 24, 2013)

Cordell, V. V., Wongtada, N. & Kieschnick Jr., R. L. (1996). Counterfeit purchase intentions: Role of lawfulness attitudes and product traits as determinants. *Journal of Business Research, 35* (1), 41–53.

Cova, B. (1997). Community and consumption towards a definition of the "linking value" of product or services. *European Journal of Marketing, 31*(3–4), 297–316.

Crawford, F. (2001). Business without borders. *Chain Store Age, 12*, 86–96.

Currah, A. & Wrigley, N. (2004). Networks of organizational learning and adaptation in retail TNCs. *Global Networks, 4*(1), 1–23.

Daniel, C. & Hernandez, T. (2012). *Canada's leading retailers: Latest trends and strategies* (11th ed., Research Report 2012–11). Toronto: Ryerson University, Center for the Study of Commercial Activity.

Dauer, U. (2013, January 16). Europe's Metro to exit retail market in China. *Wall Street Journal* (Asia Business section), p. B5.

Davis, R. L. (1976). *Marketing geography: With special reference to retailing*. London and New York: Methuen.

Dawson, J. A. (1980). Retail activity and public policy. In J. A. Dawson (Ed.), *Retail geography* (pp. 193–235). London: Croom Helm.

——. (1994). Internationalization of retailing operations. *Journal of Marketing Management, 10*, 267–282.

——. (2003). Introduction. In J. Dawson, M. Mukoyama, S. C. Choi & R. Larke (Eds.), *The internationalization of retailing in Asia* (pp. 1–5). London and New York: RoutledgeCurzon.

————. (2008). Scoping and conceptualizing retailer internationalization. *Journal of Economic Geography*, 8(1), 79–103.

DeSwart, L. (2006, December). Explosive growth prompts China to turn to ICSC for shopping center and retail expertise. *Managing-Marketing-Leasing Today*. Retrieved from http://blog.sina.com.cn/s/blog_7b76d3030100whtr.html (accessed on June 13, 2012)

Dicken, P. (2003). *Global shift: Reshaping the global economic map in the 21st century* (4th ed.). London: Sage.

Donadio, R. (2010, September 14). Made in Italy . . . but by the Chinese. *Toronto Star*, p. A3.

Doucet, M. (2001). *The Department store shuffle: Rationalization and change to the greater Toronto area* (Research Report 2001–5). Toronto: Center for the Study of Commercial Activity, Ryerson University.

Douglas, S. (2001). Executive insights; integrating branding strategy across markets: Building international brand architecture. *Journal of International Marketing*, 9(2), 97–115.

Du, C. (2004). Makro looks forward to the arrival of Spring. *The IT Manager World*. Retrieved from http://www.ceocio.com.cn/e/action/ShowInfo. php?classid=148&id=121924 (accessed on July 22, 2013)

Ducatel, K. & Blomley, N. (1990). Re-thinking retail capital. *International Journal of Urban and Regional Research*, 14, 207–227.

Editorial Board of *Science and Technology Thank Tank*. (1997). An overview of regulations on foreign investment in retailing in China. *Science and Technology Think Tank, 11*, 4–6.

Elliott, R. & Wattanasuwan, K. (1998). Brands as symbolic resources for the construction of identity. *International Journal of Advertising*, 17(2), 131–144.

"Factory in Zhongshan City makes luxury handbags for Prada." (2011, May 30). *Ming Pao*. Retrieved from http://finance.sina.com.hk/news/40/2/1/3840341/1. html (accessed on May 24, 2012)

Finkelstein, A. (2012). Taubman Asia to invest in 1 million-sf shopping center in China. *World Property Channel*. Retrieved from http://www.worldpropertychannel. com/asia-pacific-commercial-news/taubman-asia-beijing-wangfujing-department-store-group-taubman-tcbl-xian-saigao-city-plaza-new-chinese-shopping-malls-shaanxi-fuli-real-estate-development-co-ltd-6032.php (accessed on July 24, 2013)

Five Star. (2012). Property standards for new stores. Retrieved from http://www. five-star.cn/chainDep/merchants_standard.jsp (accessed on May 25, 2012)

Flannery, R. (2011, April 21). Shopping malls become China real estate hot spot, as economy shifts. *Forbes*. Retrieved from http://www.forbes.com/sites/russellflannery/2011/04/21/shopping-malls-become-china-real-estate-hot-spot-as-economy-shifts/ (accessed on July 24, 2013)

Fong, M. (2006, February 20). Zara joins a fashion parade as China opens to retailers: Spanish chain is set for Shanghai start. *The Wall Street Journal*. Retrieved from (http://online.wsj.com/article/SB114038784361278113.html (accessed on May 24, 2013)

Foord, J., Bowlby, S. & Tillsley, C. (1996). The changing place of retailer-supplier relations in British retailing. In N. Wrigley and M. Lowe (Eds.), *Retailing, consumption and capital: Towards the new retail geography* (pp. 68–89). Essex, England: Longman Group Limited.

Frost Brown Todd ALP. (2007). What trends are shaping shopping center developments? Retrieved from http://www.frostbrowntodd.com/resources-174.html (accessed on July 24, 2013)

Fu, J. (2007). B&Q is sued by a group of suppliers for unfair contracts and arrears. *Retailer Link*. Retrieved from http://www.linkshop.com.cn/web/archives/2007/74085.shtml (accessed on July 24, 2013)

Gamble, J. (2011). *Multinational retailers and consumers in China: Transferring organizational practices from the United Kingdom and Japan*. Houndmills, England: Palgrave Macmillan.

Giacalone, J. (2006). The market for luxury goods: the case of the Comite Colbert. *Southern Business Review, 32*(1), 33–40.

Glaeser, E. L., Kolko, J. & Saiz, A. (2000). *Consumer City* (Working Paper 7790). Cambridge, Massachusetts: National Bureau of Economic Research.

"Globalization's winners and losers: Lessons from retailers J. C. Penney, Home Depot, Carrefour, Ikea and others." (2006). *Strategic Direction, 22*(9), 27–29.

Goldkorn, J. (2010, May 21). Commerce official Guo Jingyi convicted: Fallout from Huang Guangyu. *Danwei*. Retrieved from http://www.danwei.org/corruption/guo_jingyi_convicted.php (accessed on July 2, 2013)

Goldman, A. (2001). The transfer of retail formats into developing economies: The example of China. *Journal of Retailing, 77*, 221–242.

"Gome and Suning are ranked among the top 30 EEO retailers." (2011). *Retailer Link*. Retrieved from http://www.linkshop.com.cn/club/archives/2011/411919.shtml (accessed on July 24, 2013)

Gong, H. (2002). Growth of tertiary sector in China's large cities. *Asian Geographer, 21*(1), 85–100.

Gong, X. (2004, December 16). Asia Pacific Plaza revamps its business plan once again. *Youth Daily*.

Government of Beijing, (1999). *A preliminary analysis of the current situation of foreign-invested commercial enterprises in Beijing*. Beijing: Author.

"Government pushing support of local brands to compete with international giants." (2011, April 19). *Jing Daily*. Retrieved from http://www.jingdaily.com/how-far-off-are-local-chinese-luxury-brands/8917/ (accessed on July 24, 2013)

Green, C. & Ruhleder, K. (1995). Globalization, borderless worlds and the Tower of Babel. *Journal of Organizational Change Management, 8*(4), 55–68.

Gregory, R. R. & Stuart, R. C. (1994). *Soviet and post-Soviet economic structure* (5th ed.). New York: Harper Collins.

Griffith, D. & Amrhein, C. G. (1997). *Multivariate statistical analysis for geographers*. Upper Saddle River, New Jersey: Prentice Hall.

Gu, B. (2006, August 3). The submarine emerges from under water: RT-Mart is to make another Wal-Mart in China. *Oriental Entrepreneur*.

Gu, G. (1998). The white book on retail chain development in China. *Science and Technology Think Tank, 3*, 4–11.

———. (2010). Three significant trends in retail development in China. *Retailer Link*. Retrieved from http://www.linkshop.com.cm/web/archives/2010/104712.shtml (accessed on March 21, 2012)

Guo, C. Y. (2006). Current practice of public hearing of large retail facility project lacks public trust. *China Commerce Daily*. Retrieved from http://www.linkshop.com.cn/web/Article_News.aspx?ArticleId=58935 (accessed July 24, 2013)

"Guo Jingyi receives death sentence with a two-year reprieve for accepting bribe from Gome." (2010). Retrieved from http://economy.enorth.com.cn/system/2010/05/21/004704855.shtml (accessed on July 24, 2013)

"H&M: Democratic style keep price flat." (2012, October 1). *People's Daily*. Retrieved from http://www.chinadaily.com.cn/bizchina/2012–10/01/content_15794506.htm (accessed on July 24, 2013)

Haggett, P. (1965). *Location analysis of human geography*. New York: St. Martins Press.

"Hainan now the world's fourth duty free zone." (2011, May 10). *e-Travel Blackboard*. Retrieved from http://www.etravelblackboard.com/article/118395/hainan-now-the-worlds-fourth-duty-free-zone (accessed on July 24, 2013)

Hansegard, J. & Burkitt, L. (2011, December 5). Feeling success in China, H&M targets smaller cities. *The Wall Street Journal*. Retrieved from http://online. wsj.com/article/SB10001424052970204826704577074052812729344.html (accessed on May 24, 2013)

Harris, C. D. (1943). A functional classification of cities in the United States. *Geographical Review*, 33(1), 86–99.

Hartshorne, A. T. (1992). *Interpreting the city: An urban geography* (2nd ed.). New York: John Wiley & Sons, Inc.

He, R. (1998). General manager of Asia Group resigns. *Science and Technology Think Tank*, 1, 10.

Heredia, B. (1997). Prosper or perish? Development in the age of global capital. *Current History*, 11, 383–388.

Hernandez, T. & Simmons, J. 2006. Evolving retail landscapes: Power retail in Canada. *The Canadian Geographer*, 50(4), 465–486.

"Home Depot is reported to enter China via acquisition of B&Q." (2005). *Retailer Link*. Retrieved from http://www.linkshop.com.cn/web/Article_News. aspx?ArticleId=47191 (accessed on July 25, 2013)

Hong, Y. (2005, August 2). Beijing Aika Shopping Center opens for business. *Beijing Evening News*. Retrieved from http://www.linkshop.com.cn/web/Article_ News.aspx?ArticleId=52493 (accessed on July 10, 2013)

"How much do you know about the trade-in program?" (2010, April 23). *South Daily*. Retrieved from http://news.xinhuanet.com/jiadian/2010–04/23/ content_13409718.htm (accessed on July 10, 2013)

Hu, B. (2008). Dashang sues Jinan Commission of State-Owned Assets Supervision and Administration for transferring ownership of Jinan People's Department Store to a different partner. Retrieved from http://www.linkshop.com.cn/web/ archives/2008/99738.shtml (accessed on June 14, 2012)

Hughes, A. (1996). Forging new cultures of food retailer-manufacturer relations? In N. Wrigley & M. Lowe (Eds.), *Retailing, consumption and capital: Towards the new retail geography* (pp. 90–115). Essex, England: Longman Group Limited.

Hughes, J. & Seneca, J. (1997, February 3). Two business revolutions at work. *Business News New Jersey*, p. 9.

"Ikea is to expand its China mall development plan." (2012). *Retailer Link*. Retrieved from http://www.linkshop.com.cn/web/archives/2012/235937.shtml (accessed on July 24, 2013)

International Council of Shopping Centers. (2011). *Economic impact of shopping centers*. New York.

"International REITs purchase 30 shopping centres in China." (2005). *Retailer Link*. Retrieved from http://www.linkshop.com.cn/web/Article_News.aspx? ArticleId=52225 (accessed on July 24, 2013)

"Japanese retailer plans to open three new Aeon Malls in China." (2012). *Retailer Link*. Retrieved from http://www.linkshop.com.cn/web/archives/2012/227011. shtml (accessed on July 12, 2013)

"Japan's Daiei to sell 39 outlets to cut debts." (2006). Reuters. Retrieved from http:// today.reuters.com/news/articleinvesting.aspx?type=bondsNews&storyID=2006– 09–02T024824Z_01_T15725_RTRIDST_0_RETAIL-JAPAN-DAIEI.XML (accessed September 1, 2006)

"Japan's Isetan, Misukoshi to merge in Spring [of 2008]." (2007, August 17). *International Business Times*. Retrieved from http://www.ibtimes.com/japans-isetan-mitsukoshi-merge-spring-paper-199363 (accessed on July 5, 2013)

"Japan's Yamada Denki opens third store in China." (2012, March 26). *China Retail News*. Retrieved from http://www.chinaretailnews.com/2012/03/26/5477-japans-yamada-denki-opens-third-store-in-china/ (accessed on July 24, 2013)

Jefferson, M. (1939). The law of the primate city. *Geographic Review*, 29, 226–232.

Jennings, R. (2006, February 24). Mall culture hits China. *Asia Times*. Retrieved from http://www.atimes.com/atimes/China_Business/HB24Cb01.html (accessed on July 10, 2013)

Jiang, Z. (2005). Summit Mall opens with two thirds units not ready for business. *Economic News Daily*. Retrieved from http://www.linkshop.com.cn/web/Article_News.aspx?ArticleId=55684 (accessed on July 24, 2013)

Jin, Y. (1998). Why so many department stores in large urban centres fail? *Science and Technology Think Tank, 5*, 9–13.

Jones, K. & Doucet, M. (1999). *The impact of big-box development on Toronto's retail structure* (Research Report 1). Toronto: Ryerson University, Center for the Study of Commercial Activity.

Jones, K. & Simmons, J. (1993). *Location, location, location: Analyzing the retail environment*. Toronto: Nelson Canada.

Khanna, T. & Palepu, K. G. (2010). *Winning in emerging markets: A road map for strategy and execution*. Cambridge, MA: Harvard Business Press.

Kim, Y. (2004). Who will be winners and losers? Comparative analysis between regional malls and big-box retailers. *Journal of Shopping Centre Research, 11*(1), 9–32.

Kingsbury, K. (2007, May 3). H&M sets up shop in China. *Time Magazine*. Retrieved from http://www.time.com/time/magazine/article/0,9171,1617522,00.html (accessed on May 24, 2013)

Kmitta, J. & Ball, M. (2001). The graying of North America's malls. *Business Geographic, 4*, 16–19.

Knox, P. (1991). The restless urban landscape: Economic and sociocultural change and the transformation of metropolitan Washington, D.C. *Annals of the Association of American Geographers, 81*, 181–209.

——, Agnew, J. & McCarthy, L. (2003). *The geography of the world economy* (4th ed.). New York: Arnold.

Koh, M. (2013, February 4). Parkson goes big in China with Qingdao mall. *The Edge*. Retrieved from http://www.theedgemalaysia.com/property/228773-parkson-goes-big-in-china-with-qingdao-mall.html (accessed on May 27, 2013.)

Koopman, J. C. (2000). Successful global retailers a rare breed. *Canadian Manager*, Spring Issue, 22–28.

Kopun, S. (2012, March 23). Consumers get upper hand in mobile era. *The Toronto Star*, p. B1.

Kowinski, W. S. (1985). *The malling of America: An inside look at the great consumer paradise*. New York: William Morrow and Company, Inc.

Kuo, L. (2013, April 17). Why China's luxury shoppers are spurning Louis Vuitton for Burberry. *Quartz*. Retrieved from http://qz.com/75441/chinas-luxury-shoppers-are-spurning-lv-for-burberry/ (accessed on July 24, 2013)

Lai, K. & Zaichkowsky, J. L. (1999). Brand imitation: Do the Chinese have different views? *Asia Pacific Journal of Management, 16*(2), 179–192.

Lang, L. (2013). Yamada suspends store opening plan in China. *21st Century Economic Journal*. Retrieved from http://www.linkshop.com.cn/web/archives/2012/233127.shtml (accessed on July 24, 2013)

Lang, Z. (2010). Media Markt opens its first store in Shanghai, challenging Gome and Suning. *Economic Daily*. Retrieved from http://www.linkshop.com.cn/club/dispbbs.aspx?rootid=391883&id=269034 (accessed on July 24, 2012)

Le, Y. (2013, April 18). Reshuffling of the top 100 retail chains: Wal-Mart surpasses Carrefour. *First Financial Post*. Retrieved from http://shipin.people.com.cn/n/2013/0418/c85914–21183827.html (accessed on July 19, 2013)

—— and Yan, Q. (2012, October 8). Friendship Group plans to increase its shopping center inventories to 24 during the 12th Five-Year Period. *First Financial Post*. Retrieved from http://finance.ifeng.com/news/corporate/20121008/7112225.shtml (accessed on Jan 10, 2013)

Leblanc, J. (2012, April 28). Buying power grows in China. *Toronto Star*, p. W21.

Lever, W. F. & Daniels, P. W. (1996). Introduction. In P. W. Daniels & W. F. Lever (Eds.), *The global economy in transition* (pp. 1–10). Essex, *England: Addison Wesley Longman Limited*.

Levitt, T. (1999). The globalization of markets. In R. Z. Aliber & R. W. Click (Eds.). *Readings in international business: a decision approach* (pp. 249–265). Cambridge, MA: Massachusetts Institute of Technology.

Li, F. (1997a). China's retailing industry faces a revolutionary storm. *Science and Technology Think Tank, 8*, 1.

———. (1997b). What happened to department stores in China? *Science and Technology Think Tank, 9*, 2–9.

———. (1997c). What does Red Apple tell us? *Science and Technology Think Tank, 8*, 29–33.

———. (1998). A wake-up call for certain department stores in Beijing. *Science and Technology Think Tank, 2*, 7–9.

Li, G. (2013). Wu-Mart acquires 36 Lotus stores in China. *Retailer Link*. Retrieved from http://www.linkshop.com.cn/web/archives/2013/267962.shtml (accessed on October 19, 2003).

Li, V. (2010). Has Bain Capital won Gome? What does Gome's shareholder dispute signify for the future of private businesses in China? Retrieved from http://www.diazreus.com/news-articles-bain-capital-won-gome.html (accessed on July 24, 2013)

Li, W. (2006a, April 11). Carrefour adjusts its China business strategy, Champion Supermarket changes hands. *First Financial Post*. Retrieved from http://finance.qq.com/a/20060411/000368.htm/ (accessed on July 24, 2013)

———. (2006b, October 5). Metro modifies its growth pattern and plans to open a second store in Beijing by leasing property. *New Capital Times*. Retrieved from http://www.linkshop.com.cn/web/Article_News.aspx?ArticleId=63381 (accessed July 24, 2013)

Li, Y. (2004, July 14). Shopping mall: The new retail giant in China. *People's Daily* (overseas edition), p. 2.

Li. Y. (2012a, September 14). Chinese traveler was caught with 247 items of luxury goods at Shanghai Pudong Airport. *Canadian Chinese Times*, p. B5.

———. (2012b, January 12). The flourishing market of pre-paid purchase cards becomes a grey zone for tax evasion and money laundering. *Times Weekly*. Retrieved from http://biz.cn.yahoo.com/ypen/20120112/811710.html (accessed on July 24, 2013)

———. (2013, July 8). More than 60 percent of the Top 100 retail chains have embraced in e-commerce. *Economic Daily*. Retrieved from http://www.chinadaily.com.cn/qiye/2013–07/08/content_16746780.htm (accessed on July 24, 2013)

Li, Z. (2010, January 4). When will China create luxury? *Beijing Today*. Retrieved from http://www.beijingtoday.com.cn/tag/world-luxury-association (accessed on July 24, 2013)

Liang, J. (2012, June 27). Sixty million Chinese benefit from the latest personal income tax reduction. *People's Daily* (overseas edition), p. 2.

Lin, G. (2004). Toward a post-socialist city? Economic tertiarization and urban reformation in the Guangzhou metropolis, China. *Eurasian Geography and Economics, 45*(1), 18–44.

Liu, C. (2005, September 23). Macquarie and Morgan Stanley to acquire 30 commercial properties from Wanda Group. *Morning News*. Retrieved from http://news.winshang.com/news-23626.html (accessed on July 24, 2013)

Liu, C. (2013, June 3). Isetan store closes in Shenyang. *China Daily*. Retrieved from http://www.chinadaily.com.cn/china/2013–06/03/content_16561738.htm (accessed on July 24, 2013)

Liu, X. (2006). The top 500 companies in China: A brief review of Tesco's development in China. *Shanghai Info Service Platform*. Retrieved from http://www.istis.sh.cn/list/list.aspx?id=4128 (accessed on July 24, 2013)

Lo, L. & Wang, L. (2006). Consuming Wal-Mart: A case study in Shenzhen. In S. D. Brunn (Ed.), *Wal-Mart world*. New York: Routledge, Taylor & Francis Group, 315–330.

"Local governments are prohibited from approving foreign invested retail enterprises." (1997, August 11). *People's Daily*, p. 2.

Lowe, M. & Wrigley, N. 1996. Towards the new retail geography. In N. Wrigley & M. Lowe (Eds.), *Retailing, consumption and capital: Toward the new retail geography* (pp. 3–30). Essex, England: Longman Group Limited.

"Lower tax on luxury goods should be the trend, Ministry of Commerce officials say." (2011, July 2). *Retailer Link*. Retrieved from http://www.linkshop.com.cn/web/archives/2011/167443.shtml (accessed July 24, 2013)

Lu, G. (2000). Speech at the forum on retail chain development. *Supplementary papers presented at the second forum on chain store development in China.* Beijing: China Chain Store Association.

Lu, P. (2012, February 8). Minimum wage in urban areas continues to improve. *People's Daily* (overseas edition), p.1.

Lu, V. (2011, July 29). High-tech battle in counterfeiting war. *Toronto Star*, p. B1.

Luo, H., Wang, Y. & Wu, J. (2010, August 24). Merger of C-Best and New Century is approved by Chongqing Government. *Chongqing Evening News*. Retrieved from http://www.linkshop.com.cn/web/archives/2010/141085.shtml (accessed on July 24, 2013)

"Luxury brands step up online video marketing efforts with Youku." (2011, June 20). *China Screen News*. Retrieved from http://china-screen-news.com/2011/06/luxury-brands-step-up-online-video-marketing-efforts-with-youku/ (accessed on July 24, 2013)

"Luxury goods and the China price." (2011, January 12). *IP Finance*. Retrieved from http://ipfinance.blogspot.com/2011/01/luxury-goods-and-china-price.html (accessed on July 24, 2013)

Ma, L. (2002). Urban transformation in China, 1949–2000: A review and research agenda. *Environment and Planning A, 33*(9), 1545–1569.

Ma, X. (2004, November 3). Lee Scott: Wal-Mart will not operate wholly-owned stores in China. *Beijing Morning News*, p.2.

Ma, Y. (2006). Expansion trajectories of foreign retailers in China. *Retailer Link*. Retrieved from http://www.linkshop.cn/web/Article_News.aspx?ArticleId=56886 (accessed on July 24, 2013)

MacDonald, C. (2011). Ethnics of profit: Excessive profits, profits unjustly gained, and the profit motive. *The Business Ethnics Blog*. Retrieved from http://businessethicsblog.com/2011/03/29/ethics-of-profit-part-3-the-profit-motive/ (accessed on July 24, 2013)

Malaysia Industrial Development Authority. (2011). *Malaysia business-FAQ's*. Retrieved from http://home.swipnet.se/~w-10652/Malaysia_business_FAQ_1.html#Regulatory (accessed on July 24, 2013)

Marsden, T. & Wrigley, N. (1996). Retailing, the food system and the regulatory state. In N. Wrigley & M. Lowe (Eds.), *Retailing, consumption and capital: Towards the new retail geography* (pp. 33–47). Essex, England: Longman Group Limited.

Master, F. & Ciancio, A. (2012, September 25). Prada sees profit jump, dismisses "hysteria' over luxury slowdown. *Toronto Star*, p. B6.

Mata, J. (1991). Sunk costs and entry by small and large plants. In P. A. Geroski & J. Schwalback (Eds.), *Entry and market contestability: An international comparison*. Oxford: Blackwell.

Mattson-Teig, B. (2012, September 20). ICSC World Summit reveals opportunities and challenges in today's global market. *National Real Estate Investor*. Retrieved from http://retailtrafficmag.com/development/trends/icsc_world_summit_recap_09202012/ (accessed on July 24, 2013)

McMillan, A. F. (2007, April 5). Looking beyond Beijing. *New York Times*. Retrieved from http://www.nytimes.com/2007/04/05/realestate/05iht-web-0404resecond.5161520.html?_r=1 (accessed on May 24, 2012)

Ministry of Commerce. (2004a). Regulations on foreign-invested enterprises in commercial sectors. In *China chain store almanac 2003–2004* (pp. 495–499). Beijing: Author.

———. (2004b). *Guidelines for development of municipal plans for commercial activity development*. Beijing: Author.

———. (2004c). *Standard definitions of retail formats and facility types*. Beijing: Author.

———. (2004d). National strategies for reform and future development of China's distribution system. In *China chain store almanac 2005* (pp. 450–455). Beijing: Author.

———. (2005a). *Further notice on the importance of developing municipal plans for commercial activity development*. Beijing: Author.

———. (2005b). Announcement of experiment with development of chain stores in rural China (Document No. 45). *China chain store almanac 2005* (pp. 466–468). Beijing: Author..

———. (2005c). *Regulations on promotion of consumer goods by retailers*. Beijing: Author.

———. (2006a). *National circular about the urgency of completing municipal plans for commercial activity development*. Beijing: Author.

———. (2006b). *Regulations on foreign merger and acquisition of enterprises in China*. Beijing: Author.

———. (2007). The 11th Five-Year Plan for domestic trade development. In *China chain store almanac 2007*. Beijing: Author.

——— & China Development Bank. (2005). *Protocol of collaboration in financing domestic retail enterprises*. Beijing: Author.

——— & China Development Bank. (2007). *Expansion of financial support for development of domestic retail enterprises*. Beijing: Author.

"Ministry of Commerce demands Best Buy to rectify its erroneous business deeds." (2008). *Retailer Link*. Retrieved from http://www.linkshop.com.cn/web/archives/2008/88073.shtml (accessed on August 2, 2008)

Ministry of Commerce, Ministry of Public Security, State Bureau of Taxation, & State Bureau of Industry and Commerce Administration. (2005). Administrative measures to rectify unfair treatment of suppliers by retailers. In *China chain store almanac 2006* (pp. 484–487). Beijing: Author.

Ministry of Commerce, State Commission of Economic Development and Reform, Ministry of Public Security, State Bureau of Taxation, & State Bureau of Industry and Commerce Administration. (2006). Regulations on fair trade between retailer and suppliers. In *China chain store almanac 2007* (pp. 473–475). Beijing: Author.

Ministry of Commerce, State Commission of Economic Development and Reform, Ministry of Public Security, State Bureau of Taxation, & State Bureau of Industry and Commerce Administration. (2007). Regulations on merchandise promotion by retailers. In *China chain store almanac 2007* (pp. 471–472). Beijing: Author.

Ministry of Finance & Ministry of Commerce. (2008). *A circular about promotion of consumer electronics in rural areas*. Retrieved from http://jdxx.zhs.mofcom.gov.cn/admin/news.do?method=view&id=8436120 (accessed on July 10, 2013)

———. (2009). *The consumer electronics trade-in program*. Retrieved from http://www.gov.cn/zwgk/2009–07/02/content_1355598.htm (accessed on July 10, 2013)

Ministry of Interior Trade. (1997a). *Almanac of China's domestic trade 1997*. Beijing: Author.

———. (1997b). National standards for operation and management of commercial chains. *Science and Technology Think Tank*, 10, 4.

Mitchell, A. (1993). New marketing vision [December/January issue]. *Marketing Business*, 4, 12–17.

Moore, A. (2009, October 20). Professor Freeman discusses ethics and profits. *Australia Broadcasting Corporation*. Retrieved from http://www.abc.net.au/lateline/business/items/200910/s2719525.htm (accessed on July 24, 2013)

"Morgan Stanley is in negotiation to purchase Air Modern Mall for 20 million yuan." (2006, April 21). *East Morning News*. Retrieved from http://biz.zjol.com.cn/05biz/system/2006/04/20/006580981.shtml (accessed on July 24, 2013)

Moss, N. & Chan, R. (2012). Shopping center development—the most active global cities [June issue]. *CBRE Global Viewpoint*, pp. 1–5.

Nakata, C. & Sivakumar, K. (1997). Emerging market conditions and their impact on first mover advantages: An integrative review. *International Marketing Review* 14(6), 461–485.

National Bureau of Statistics of China. (1997). *China statistics yearbook*. Beijing: China Statistical Publishing House.

———. (2011a). *China statistical yearbook*. Beijing: China Statistical Publishing House.

———. (2011b). *China city statistical yearbook*. Beijing: China Statistical Publishing House.

———. (2013). Domestic economy grows steadily in 2012. Retrieved from http://www.stats.gov.cn/tjfx/jdfx/t20130118_402867146.htm (accessed on May 2, 2013)

Nelson, H. J. (1955). A service classification of American cities. *Economic Geography*, 31(3), 189–210.

"New South China Mall." (2012). Retrieved from http://en.wikipedia.org/wiki/New_South_China_Mall (accessed on December 5, 2012).

New World Department Store China Limited. (2013). *2012 annual report*. Retrieved from http://www.nwds.com.hk/html/eng/investor/report.aspx (accessed on May 27, 2013)

Norusis, M. (2011). *IBM SPSS statistics 19 statistical procedures companion*. Upper Saddle River, New Jersey: Addison Wesley.

"Number of credit cards and debit cards issued in China has reached 3.69 billion." (2013, May 25). *People's Daily* (overseas edition), p. 1.

Office of Commercial Chains Administration, MIT. (1997). A report on retail chain development in China. *Science and Technology Think Tank*, 8, 5–13.

———. (1998). Salient problems of retail chain development and policy recommendations. *Science and Technology Think Tank*, 5, 4–6.

Oliver, C. (2012, April 23). China tops world in shopping mall construction. *The Wall Street Journal*. Retrieved from http://www.marketwatch.com/story/china-tops-world-in-shopping-mall-construction-2012–04–23 (accessed on July 13, 2012)

Parkson Retail Group Limited. (2005). *Parkson prospectus—Hong Kong public offering and international placing*. Retrieved from http://www.parksongroup.com.cn/upload/200701/116945291380658800.pdf (accessed on May 27, 2013).

Passariello, C. (2011, June 24). Prada is making fashion in China. *The Wall Street Journal*. Retrieved from http://online.wsj.com/article/SB10001424052702304231204576403680967866692.html (accessed on July 24, 2013)

Pearson Education. (n.d.). Emerging markets defined. Retrieved from http://www. pearsoned.co.uk/bookshop/article.asp?item=361 (accessed on July 24, 2013)

Petcu, O. (2011). The need for a code of ethics in luxury [retailing]. *CPP-Luxury. Com: Business of luxury.* Retrieved from http://www.cpp-luxury.com/en/the-need-for-a-code-of-ethics-in-luxury_1531.html (accessed on July 24, 2013)

Pham, D. (2012, May 16). Smartphones have large impact on U.S. searching and shopping behavior. *Google Mobile Ads Blog.* Retrieved from http:// googlemobileads.blogspot.ca/2012/05/smartphones-have-large-impact-on-us. html (accessed on May 24, 2012)

Pitman, S. (2006, March 7). Luxury goods makers declare war on China counterfeits. *Cosmetics Design Europe.* Retrieved from http://www.cosmeticsdesign-europe. com/Market-Trends/Luxury-goods-makers-declare-war-on-China-counterfeits (accessed on May 24, 2012)

"Prada contracts production to Dongguan of China." (2011). Retrieved from http://fashion.163.com/11/0530/17/75ANHIDU00264J94_2.html (accessed on July 24, 2013)

Qin, H. (2011). Map of China for luxury goods. Retrieved from http://larrywellsreview.com/map-of-china-for-luxury-goods/ (accessed on July 24, 2013)

Rapoza, K. (2012). Guess where over half of the world's new malls are being built? *Forbes.* Retrieved from http://www.forbes.com/sites/kenrapoza/2012/06/20/ half-of-worlds-new-shopping-malls-in-china/ (accessed on July 24, 2013)

"Reading China with statistics: automobile expands the activity space of the Chinese consumers." (2012, August 14). *People's Daily* (overseas edition), p. 2.

"Revisiting Best Buy's acquisition of Five Star at the first anniversary." (2008). *Retailer Link.* Retrieved from http://blog.linkshop.com.cn.cjzf/archives/2008/ 100076.html (accessed on October 12, 2010)

Rugman, A. H. & Gestrin, M. (1997). New rules for multinational investment. *The International Executive, 39*(1), 21–33.

"Sales of multi-purpose, pre-paid purchase cards reach 96.5 billion yuan in 2010 in China." (2011). *iResearch.* Retrieved from http://www.iresearch.com.cn/ Report/View.aspx?Newsid=151488. (accessed on July 24, 2013)

Sanchanta, M. (2010, December 18). Uniqlo makes global push: Japanese clothing giant Fast Retailing to open stores in India and Brazil, expand presence in China. *The Wall Street Journal.* Retrieved from http://online.wsj.com/article/SB 10001424052748704368004576028453572446140.html (accessed on May 24, 2013.)

Sarma, N. N. (2007, April 8–10). Ethics in retailing—perceptions of management and sales personnel. Paper presented at International Conference on Marketing & Society [conference location is not available]. Published by Indian Institute of Management Kozhikode. Retrieved from http://dspace.iimk.ac.in/ bitstream/2259/388/1/61–68.pdf (accessed on July 24, 2013)

Saunders, J. and Guogun, F. (1996). Dual branding: How corporate names add value. *Marketing Intelligence & Planning, 14*(7), 29–34.

Schulz, D. P. (2013, July). Top 100 retailers: Digital commerce generates headlines, but bricks-and-mortar remain the foundation of the nation's retail power players. *Stores Magazine.* Retrieved from http://www.stores.org/STORES%20 Magazine%20July%202013/top-100-retailers (accessed on July 24, 2013)

"Setbacks of Best Buy in China." (2010). *Retailer Link.* Retrieved from http://www. linkshop.com/cn/club/dispbbs.aspx?doardid=10&rootid=384838 (accessed on October 17, 2010)

Shanghai Commerce Information Center & FMCG Research Center. (2006). *2006 survey of merchandise suppliers for retailer satisfaction.* Shanghai: Author.

Shanghai Commission of Commerce & Shanghai Commission of Economic Development and Planning. (2001). *Procedures for public hearing of hypermarket development proposals.* Shanghai: Author.

Shanghai Economic Commission. (2005). *Shanghai commercial development report*. Shanghai: Shanghai Science and Technology Publishing House.

"Shanghai Lawson begins to make a profit." (2004, December 19). *East Morning News*. Retrieved from http://www.linkshop.com.cn/web/archives/2004/45869.shtml (accessed on July 11, 2012)

Shanghai Shopping Center Association. (2010). *2009 Shanghai shopping center development report*. Shanghai: Author.

———. (2011). *2010 Shanghai shopping center development report*. Shanghai: Author.

"Shanghai strives to become an international city of commerce". (1994, January 12). *People's Daily* (overseas edition), p. 1.

Shao, H. (2011, August 19). Rent increases prompt retailers to invest in commercial properties. *Economic Herald*. Retrieved from http://www.linkshop.com.cn/web/archives/2011/173653.shtml (accessed on July 24, 2013)

Shen, X. (2011, February 18). Luxury a magnet for China sales. *HK Trade Development Council Research*. Retrieved from http://www.hktdc.com/info/mi/a/imn/en/1X07BP3U/1/International-Market-News/Luxury-a-magnet-for-China-sales.htm (accessed on July 24, 2013)

Shi, L. & Shang, Q. S. (2010). Best Buy poised to expand in China. *Retailer Link*. Retrieved from http://www.linkshop.com.cn/web/archieves/2010/137400.shtml (accessed on October 17, 2010)

Shi, X., Huang, T. & Chen, L. (2005, April 23). Pricemart's irregular expansion causes suspicion of economic crime. *Outlook Weekly*. Retrieved from http://www.linkshop.com.cn/web/Article_News.aspx?ArticleId=49367 (accessed on July 24, 2013)

Siebers, L. Q. (2011). *Retail internationalization in China: Expansion of foreign retailers*. Houndmills, England: Palgrave Macmillan.

Simmons, J. & Graff, T. (1998). *Wal-Mart comes to Canada* (Research Report 1998-9). Toronto: Ryerson Polytechnic University, Centre for the Study of Commercial Activity.

Simmons, J. & Kamikihara, S. (1999). *Internationalization of commercial activities in Canada* (Research Report 1999-7). Toronto: Ryerson Polytechnic University, Centre for the Study of Commercial Activity.

———. (2003). *Commercial activity in Canada* (Research Report 2003-4). Toronto: Ryerson University, Centre for the Study of Commercial Activity.

Simon Property Group. (2012). About us. Retrieved from http://www.simon.com/about_simon/index.aspx (accessed on July 15, 2013)

"Simon Property Group and Bailian Group agree to jointly develop a premium outlet center in China." (2012). Retrieved from http://investors.simon.com/phoenix.zhtml?c=113968&p=irol-newsArticle&ID=1668018&highlight= (accessed on July 24, 2013)

"Simon, SZITIC CP and MSREF join forces to develop retail in China." (2006). Retrieved from http://phx.corporate-ir.net/phoenix.zhtml?c=113968&p=irol-newsArticle&ID=734201&highlight= (accessed on July 24, 2013)

Staff Reporter. (2012, May 5). Uniqlo plans outlet mall revolution for China market. *Want China Times*. Retrieved from http://www.wantchinatimes.com/news-subclass-cnt.aspx?id=20120525000037&cid=1102 (accessed on May 24, 2013)

State Commission of Development and Reforms. (2009). Letter of advice regarding unified electricity and water prices for industrial users and the commercial sector. In *China chain store almanac 2010* (p. 560). Beijing: China Commerce Publishing House.

State Council. (2005a). Ordinance of prohibiting multi-level marketing in China. *China chain store almanac 2006* (pp. 445-448). Beijing: China Commerce Publishing House.

———. (2005b). Regulations on direct marking in China. *China chain store almanac 2006* (pp. 438–444). Beijing: China Commerce Publishing House.

State Economic and Trade Commission & Ministry of Foreign Trade. (1999). Interim stipulations about foreign-invested commercial enterprises. *Essays on Commerce Economy, 5*, 38–40.

"Statistics of high education applications and enrolment." (2012, May 26). *People's Daily* (overseas edition), p. 8.

Sternquist, B. (2007). *International retailing* (2nd ed.). New York: Fairchild Publications.

Su, R. (1998). The era of low profit margin has arrived for China's retail industry. *Science and Technology Think Tank, 2*, 11.

Su, Z. (1998). A preliminary analysis of the constraints to development of department store chains. *China Business and Trade, 6*, 39–40.

Sui, C. (2011, April 15). Taiwan passes luxury tax to cool property market. *BBC News*. Retrieved from http://www.bbc.co.uk/news/world-asia-pacific-13091236 (accessed on October 15, 2013)

Sun, J. (1993). A discussion on the project of "A Hundred Large retail Stores in Beijing." *Beijing City Planning and Construction Review, 2*, 46–50.

Sun, W. (2005). Annual review of consumer electronics retailing. In *China chain store almanac 2005* (pp. 71–80). Beijing: China Commerce Publishing House.

———. (2006). Annual review of consumer electronics retailing. In *China chain store almanac 2006* (pp. 65–74). Beijing: China Commerce Publishing House.

———. (2007). Annual review of consumer electronics retailing. In *China chain store almanac 2007* (pp. 78–85). Beijing: China Commerce Publishing House.

Sun, Y. (1997). *Retail opportunities in the People's Republic of China*. Toronto: Ryerson Polytechnic University, Centre for the Study of Commercial Activity.

———. (2002). *Beijing: The retail response to the economic reform*. Toronto: Ryerson University, Centre for the Study of Commercial Activity.

Tacconelli, W. & Wrigley, N. (2009). Organizational challenges and strategic responses of retail TNCs in post-WTO-entry China. *Economic Geography, 85*(1), 49–73.

Teah, M. & Phau, I. (2010, July 2–5). A conceptual investigation into brand mimicry in the luxury brand industry. Paper presented at the 17th International Conference on Recent Advances in Retailing and Services Science, Istanbul, Turkey.

"Tesco is to build a second Lifespace Mall in Xiamen." (2012). *Retailer Link*. Retrieved from http://www.linkshop.com.cn/web/archives/2012/230267.shtml (accessed on July 24, 2013)

The Associated Press. (2012, October 16). 10% growth seen in 2012 for luxury goods market. *Toronto Star*, p. B10.

"The future of the world's largest mall is uncertain." (2005). *Retailer Link*. Retrieved from http://www.linkshop.com.cn/web/Article_News.aspx?ArticleId=51290 (accessed on July 24, 2013)

"The journey of luxury goods and price inflation." (2011). *People Net*. Retrieved from http://mnc.people.com.cn/GB/15245056.html (accessed on July 24, 2013.)

"The not-so-great mall of China: Welcome to the world's largest (and loneliest) shopping centre." (2009). Retrieved from http://www.dailymail.co.uk/news/article-1223747/Ghost-mall-The-worlds-largest-loneliest-shopping-centre.html (accessed on December 6, 2012)

"The opening of CEPA Mall is greeted by sparse shoppers." (2005, January 27). *East Morning News*. Retrieved from http://www.linkshop.com.cn/web/Article_News.aspx?ArticleId=47256 (accessed on July 11, 2013)

"The reasons behind the merger of Lianhua and Hualian." (2009, July 5). *China Management Daily*. Retrieved from http://www.linkshop.com.cn/web/archives/2009/115583.shtml (accessed on June 12, 2012)

"The red capitalist Rong Yiren passed away." (2005, November 5). *Chinese Canadian Post*, p. 4.

"Top management at C-Best reshuffles." (2011, September 16). *Stock News Daily*. Retrieved from http://www.linkshop.com.cn/web/archives/2011/177650.shtml (accessed on July 24, 2014)

"Traditional mall now a hard sell." (2004, September 21). *Toronto Star*, p. D2.

United Nations Development Programme. (1999). *Human development report 1999*. New York: Oxford University Press.

Urban Land Institute. (1985). *Shopping center development handbook* (2nd ed.). Washington D.C.: Author.

Vida, R. & Fairhurst, A. (1998). International expansion of retail firms: A theoretical approach for future investigations. *Journal of Retailing and Consumer services*, 5(3), 143–151.

Waller, R. (2010). Tesco China property strategies. Retrieved from http://www.tescoplc.com/files/pdf/Events/china_property_strategy.pdf (accessed on July 24, 2013)

"Wal-Mart aims to control Trust-Mart by 2010." (2007). Retrieved from http://www.linkshop.com.cn/web/archives/2007/69237.shtml (accessed on March 16, 2007).

Wal-Mart China. (2004).Wal-Mart China awarded Outstanding Social Welfare Contribution. http://www.wal-martchina.com/english/news/20040601.htm.

———. (2007). About Wal-Mart. Retrieved from http://www.wal-martchina.com (accessed on October 17, 2010)

———. (2012). Wal-Mart store distribution. Retrieved from www.walmartstore.com (accessed on March 31, 2012)

"Wal-Mart to double outlets in China." (2005, July 25). *China Daily*. Retrieved from http://www.chinadaily.com.cn/english/doc/2005–07/25/content_463079.htm (accessed on July 24, 2013)

"Wal-Mart's Asia HQ Office will have a new home in Shenzhen." (2004, October 27). *Shenzhen Economic Daily*. Retrieved from http://www.linkshop.com.cn/web/Article_News.aspx?ArticleId=47682&ClassID=90 (accessed on July 11, 2013)

Wan, D. W. (1999). Fifty years of commerce development in the new China. In *Almanac of China's domestic trade, 1999 (A special issue to mark the occasion of the 50th anniversary of the People's Republic of China)* (pp. 3–33). Beijing: China Domestic Trade Publishing House.

Wanda Group. (2012). Timelines of Wanda development. Retrieved from http://www.wanda.cn/about/history/ (accessed on July 13, 2012)

Wang, C. (2012, September 28). Democratic style keeps price flat. *China Daily*. Retrieved from http://europe.chinadaily.com.cn/epaper/2012–09/28/content_15790138.htm (accessed on July 24, 2013.)

Wang, E. (2011). Understanding the 'retail revolution' in urban China: A survey of retail formats in Beijing. *The Service Industries Journal*, 31(2), 169–194.

——— & Chan, W. C. (2007). Store wars: Changing retail ownership in Beijing. *Eurasian Geography and Economics*, 48(5), 573–602.

"Wang Jianlin discloses Wanda's business secrets." (2012). *Retailer Link*. Retrieved from http://www.linkshop.com.cn/web/archives/2012/227151.shtml (accessed on July 24)

Wang, L. (2006). What should be the limit of government intervention in creation of business enterprises? *Retailer Link*. Retrieved from http://www.linkshop.com.cn/web/Article_News.aspx?ArticleId=61854 (accessed on June 11, 2012)

Wang, Q. (2011). Media Markt takes advantage of Best Buy's misfortune, and woos its customers. *First Financial Post*. Retrieved from http://www.linkshop.com.cn/web/archives/2011/155353.shtml (accessed on October 15, 2013)

Wang, S. (2003). Internationalization of retailing in China. In J. Dawnson, M. Mukoyama, S. C. Choi & R. Larke (Eds.), *Internationalization of retailing in Asia* (pp. 114–135). London, U.K.: Routledge-Curzon.

———— & Guo, C. (2007). A tale of two cities: Restructuring of retail capital and production of new consumption spaces in Beijing and Shanghai. In F. Wu (Ed.), *China's emerging cities: The making of new urbanism* (pp. 256–283). London and New York: Routledge, Taylor & Francis Group.

———— & Jones, K. (2001). China's retail sector in transition. *Asian Geographer, 1–2*, 25–51.

———— & Jones, K. (2002). Retail structure of Beijing. *Environment and Planning A, 10*, 1785–1808.

———— & Smith, P. J. (1997). In quest of forgiving environments: Residential planning and pedestrian safety in Edmonton, Canada. *Planning Perspectives: An International Journal of History, Planning and the Environment, 2*, 225–250.

———— & Zhang, Y. (2005). The new retail economy of Shanghai. *Growth and Change, 36*(1), 41–73.

———— & Zhang, Y. (2006). Penetrating the Great Wall and conquering the Middle Kingdom: Wal-Mart in China. In S. Brunn (Ed.), *Wal-Mart world: The world's biggest corporation in the global economy* (pp. 293–314). New York: Routledge.

————, Zhang, Y. & Wang, Y. (2006). Opportunities and challenges of shopping center development in China: A case study of Shanghai. *Journal of shopping center research, 13*(1), 19–55.

Wang, T. (2011, June 3). Taiwan imposes luxury tax, a test of the governing ability of the Ma government. *Norstar Times*, p. B4.

Wang, Y. (1997). How to make good profits for department stores? *Science and Technology Think Tank, 11*, 25.

Wassener, B. (2011, June 26). Luxury brands follow the money to Asia. *New York Times*. Retrieved from http://www.nytimes.com/2011/06/25/business/global/25iht-luxury25.html?pagewanted=all (accessed on July 24, 2013)

Welch, D. (2012, March 25). Amazon's success bad news for Wal-Mart: Pressure is on for giant retailers to fix its lagging e-commerce operation. *Toronto Star*, p. A13.

"What is an emerging market economy?" (2009). *Investopedia*. Retrieved from http://www.investopedia.com/articles/03/073003.asp#axzz2Ccxu3TpT (accessed on October 24, 2012)

"Will wholesale of high-grade goods be profitable?" (1999, January 28). *China Consumers*, p. 3.

Wilson, J. & Waldmeir, P. (2013, January 10). Media Markt set to quit China. *Financial Times*. Retrieved from http://www.ft.com/intl/cms/s/0/f8aed1c8–5b24–11e2–8d06–00144feab49a.html#axzz2Zsq6CnXI (accessed on July 24, 2013)

Woetzel, J., Li, X. L. & Cheng, W. (2012). *What's next for China?* McKinsey & Company. Retrieved from http://www.mckinseychina.com/wp-content/uploads/2012/11/Whats-next-for-China-Jan-22-v2.pdf (accessed on July 8, 2013)

Wrigley, N. (1992). Antitrust regulations and the restructuring of grocery retailing in Britain and the USA. *Environment and Planning A, 24*, 727–749.

————. (2000). The globalization of retail capital: Themes for economic geography. In G. Clark, M. Gertler, and M. Feldman (Eds.), *The Oxford handbook of economic geography* (pp. 292–313). London: Oxford University Press.

———— & Currah, A. (2003). The stresses of retail internationalization: Lessons from Royal Ahold's experience in Latin America. *The International Review of Retail Distribution and Consumer Research, 13*(3), 221–243.

———— & Currah, A. (2006). Globalizing retail and the 'new e-conomy': The organizational challenge of e-commerce for the retail TNCs. *Geoforum, 37*, 340–351.

———— & Lowe, M. 1996. *Retailing, consumption and capital: Towards the new retail geography.* Essex, England: Longman Group Ltd.

Xiao, Y. (2013). Premier Wen Jiabao announces to raise pension for retirees by another 10 percent. *China News.* Retrieved from http://www.chinanews.com/gn/2013/03–05/4615885.shtml (accessed on July 1, 2013)

Xu, C. & Duan, Z. (2011). Wushang's restructuring is challenged by major shareholder Yintai. *China Management Daily.* Retrieved from http://www.linkshop.com.cn/web/archives/2011/180916.shtml (accessed on June 15, 2012)

Xu, Y. (1998). Why is it so difficult to reform state-owned retail enterprises? *Science and Technology Think Tank, 5*, 26–28.

Yamada Denki. (2013). Corporate Information. Retrieved from http://www.yamada-denki.jp/company_e/ (accessed on July 24, 2013.)

"Yamada Denki: China bound." (2010, March 9). *Japan Consuming.* Retrieved from http://www.japanconsuming.com/?p=2321 (accessed on September 2, 2011)

"Yamada Denki to open new store in China." (2011). *China Retail News.* Retrieved from http://www.chinaretailnews.com/2010/03/08/3412-yamada-denki-to-open-new-store-in-china/ (accessed on September 2, 2011)

Yan, J. & Zhang, Z. (2008). Bailian reiterates its national strategy and speeds up expansion. Retrieved from http://www.linkshop.com.cn/web/archives/2008/98688.shtml (accessed on June 11, 2012)

Yan, P. (2011). Louis Vuitton sues several businesses in Dalian for selling counterfeits. *Xinhua News.* Retrieved from http://news.xinhuanet.com/legal/2011–09/23/c_122077405_3.htm (accessed on July 24, 2013.)

Yang, F. (2004). Services and metropolitan development in China: The case of Guangzhou. *Progress in Planning, 61*(3), 181–209.

Yang, J. (2005, August 24). Beijing Aika rushed to open without tenants. *Beijing Commerce Times.* Retrieved from http://www.linkshop.com.cn/web/Article_News.aspx?ArticleId=52582 (accessed on July 10, 2013)

————. (2012). Dispute over Wushang ownership subsides, but the relationship between major shareholders in the strategic alliance becomes loose. *First Financial Post.* Retrieved from http://www.linkshop.com.cn/web/archives/2012/204697.shtml (accessed on June 15, 2012)

Yankelovich, D. (2006). *Profit with honor: The new stage of market capitalism.* New Haven, Connecticut: Yale University Press.

YCharts. (2013). *U.S. retail sales.* Retrieved from http://ycharts.com/indicators/retail_sales (accessed on May 2, 2013)

Yeates, M. (1998). *The North American city* (5th ed.). New York: Longman.

————. (1999). Commentary: Internationalization and regulation. In K. Jones (Ed.), *The internationalization of retailing in Europe* (Research Report 5, pp. 51–54). Toronto: Ryerson Polytechnic University, Centre for the Study of Commercial Activity.

Yoka.com. (2011). Yoka Hand Bags. Retrieve from http://brand.yoka.com/bag/louisvuitton (access on August 17, 2011)

Zaichkowsky, J. L. & Simpson, R. N. (1996). The effect of experience with a brand imitator on the original brand. *Marketing Letters, 7*(1), 31–39.

Zeldin, W. (2011). Taiwan: Luxury tax proposed by Ministry of Finance. *Law Library of Congress.* Retrieved from http://www.loc.gov/lawweb/servlet/lloc_news?disp3_l205402554_text (accessed on July 24, 2013)

Zhan, C. & Pan, Z. (2009). Canadian Ivanhoe Cambridge acquires controlling interest of Bailian Changsha Oriental Plaza. *Retailer Link.* Retrieved from http://www.linkshop.com.cn/web/archives/2009/117480.shtml (accessed on July 23, 2013)

Zhang, Y. (2012, January 1). Government subsidized "trade-in" program stimulates sales of consumer electronics in China. *People's Daily* (overseas edition), p. 4.

Zhao, Y. J. (2010). Best Buy expands beyond Shanghai. *Retailer Link*. Retrieved from http://www.linkshop.com/web/archives/2010/137427.shtml (accessed on July 23, 2013)

Zhao, Z. (2012a, February 9). The Chinese way of gift-giving. *People's Daily* (overseas edition), p. 5.

———. (2012b, November 23). China and U.S. join forces to break up rings of counterfeiting production. *People's Daily* (overseas edition), p. 4.

Zhen, D., Wei, Y., Zhang, Y. & Qi, Y. (2005). End-of-2005 review: Be aware of foreign retailers quietly transforming China's retail sector. *Supermarket Weekly*. Retrieved from http://www.linkshop.com.cn/web/Article_News.aspx?ArticleId=55824 (accessed on July 23, 2013)

Zhen, Y. (2007). *Globalization and the Chinese retailing revolution: Competing in the world's largest emerging market*. Oxford, England: Chandos Publishing.

Zheng, P. S. (2012, May 8). Top 100 retail chains are announced; Bailian climbs to No. 1. *Economic News Daily*. Retrieved from http://msn.finance.sina.com.cn/gdxw/20120508/0242886707.html (accessed on July 1, 2013)

Zheng, W. (1998). All-out expansion of Wangfujing Department Store. *Science and Technology Think Tank, 1*, 11–12.

"Zhongbai Group builds large shopping center in Wuhan," (2012). *Retailer Link*. Retrieved from http://www.linkshop.com.cn/web/archives/2012/224106.shtml (accessed on January 24, 2013)

Zhou, X. (2012a, March 19). State government raises basic personal amount to reduce income tax. *People's Daily* (oversea edition), p. 2.

———. (2012b, August 11). How come China is now one of the largest luxury goods consumption country in the world? *People's Daily* (overseas edition), p. 2.

———. (2012c, August 14). Why are international luxury brands more expensive in China? *People's Daily* (overseas edition), p. 2.

Zhou, Y. (2006, August 20). Wal-Mart accelerates acquisition of land and property in China for speedy expansion. *21st Century Economic News*. Retrieved from http://www.linkshop.com.cn/web/Article_News.aspx?ArticleId=61652 (accessed on June 6, 2012)

———. (2007).The failed business deal of a model company: The challenges of Bailian Group. *Retailer Link*. Retrieved from http://www.linkshop.com.cn/web/Article_News.aspx?ArticleId=67480 (accessed June 11, 2012)

Zhu, J. & Lu, Y. (2012, February 17). Business data must now be reported to State statistical authority directly, to prevent "interference." *People's Daily* (overseas edition), p. 2.

Zhu, X., Chen, G. & Wang, Z. (2012). Selling of pre-paid purchase cards has reached several hundred million yuan in Yangzhou, and is still increasing. *Yangzhou Evening News*. Retrieved from http://js.people.com.cn/html/2012/01/06/65897.html (accessed on July 23, 2013)

Zhuang, J. (2012). B&Q's "T-program" is failing in China. *Retailer Link*. Retrieved from http://www.linkshop.com.cn/web/archives/2012/215828.shtml (retrieved on July 6, 2012)

Index

Printed in the United States
by Baker & Taylor Publisher Services